Bible Believers

KEVIN
BARDON

Bible Believers

Fundamentalists
in the Modern World

Nancy Tatom Ammerman

Rutgers University Press

New Brunswick, New Jersey

LIBRARY OF CONGRESS CATALOGING-IN-PUBLICATION DATA

Ammerman, Nancy Tatom, 1950–
Bible believers.

Bibliography: p.
Includes index.
1. Fundamentalist churches—United States—Case studies.
2. United States—Church history—20th century. I. Title.

BX7800.F864A45 1987   306'.6   86-29668
ISBN 0-8135-1230-1   ISBN 0-8135-1231-X (pbk.)
British Cataloging-in-Publication information available

Fourth printing, 1997

Contents

Preface

WRITING a book on Fundamentalism was not the first thing I planned to do when I started my career as a sociologist. I wanted to stretch my experience, to study topics of which I had little personal knowledge, like racism or corporate management or mental illness. Religion seemed a little too close to home, a little too old hat. After growing up as a preacher's kid (which places me in a long tradition of clergy offspring in sociology) and going to a sectarian college, the last thing I wanted to do was study religion.

Then, for a long list of mundane reasons, I ended up studying for a doctoral examination in sociology of religion and discovered how little sociologists knew then about Fundamentalism. I became fascinated with the possibility that because of my background I might be able to gather data that would add significantly to what my colleagues knew about an important religious phenomenon. And in those days—the late 1970s—people were finally beginning to discover that Fundamentalism was an important religious phenomenon. Thus, this project was born.

As I began my research, my professors at Yale provided encouragement and guidance for which I am grateful. Kai Erikson was a remarkable dissertation director whose special sociological eye helped this project take shape and make sense. Through every step of the research and initial writing, he was the kind of friendly critic every writer needs. Barbara Hargrove also contributed her rich knowledge of the sociology of religion; Hillel Levine helped with early strategy; and Peter Berger read and critiqued the final dissertation.

Some of the ideas that now appear in Chapter 1 were published in 1982 in "Operationalizing Evangelicalism: An amendment" (*Sociological Analysis* 43:170–171). Other ideas in that chapter and in Chapter 5 were first developed in "Dilemmas in establishing a research identity" in *The New England Sociologist* (4:21–27). And ideas in

Chapters 4 and 11 have been published in "Fundamentalism: Bastion of traditionalism in the modern world," a chapter in *Religion and the Sociology of Knowledge*, edited by Barbara Hargrove (New York: Edwin Mellen, 1984).

As this project has evolved from dissertation into book, many of my colleagues at Emory University have contributed immeasurably. Steve Tipton, Rod Hunter, and Frank Lechner each read crucial portions of the manuscript and helped to sharpen its focus. The process of teaching about Fundamentalism has also had an important impact. I am indebted to the students who have listened and asked questions and contributed their own insights. I am especially grateful to Laurel Kearns, Terry Ward, and Art Farnsley, each of whom has studied Fundamentalism with me and has thereby enriched my understanding as well. My secretary at Emory, Joann Stone, has helped with a hundred details, aided in the last stages by Mary Lou McCrary. Karen Root helped with important library research, and Ellen Powell deserves enormous thanks for transferring my original typed dissertation onto a word-processing system. Without that, this book might have been another five years in the making!

I also wish to thank the Charlotte W. Newcombe Fellowship Foundation for dissertation support during 1982–1983 and the Southern Baptist Home Mission Board for a small grant that helped in the early stages of the research.

I now know why authors thank their editors. Marlie Wasserman has stuck with me through three years of reviews and revisions. My thanks go also to a reviewer who took the job seriously, saw what the book could be, and offered careful, detailed comments that helped me to craft a better product. That anonymous person was a valued partner in this process.

Beyond these scholarly debts, I must offer public thanks to my family. My husband, Jackie, has brewed coffee, proofed pages, and talked about Fundamentalism more than anyone should ever have to do. Our daughter, Abbey, has lived with this book since her conception. And since the days of her first picture books, we have always read the title and author page first—authors, after all, are important people. I hope she will continue to think so.

Finally, I must thank the people of Southside, who welcomed me and allowed me to become a part of their fellowship. They gave me not only an intimate look at their faith but a deeper understanding of my own. For their acceptance and trust, I am grateful.

None of these people, of course, is responsible for what appears on these pages. I must bear that responsibility alone. I can hope only that what follows will contribute to understanding a group of people who have created a way to deal with a world that they find otherwise insensible.

Bible Believers

CHAPTER ONE

Introduction: Studying Fundamentalism

The Bible is absolutely infallible, without error in all matters
pertaining to faith and practice, as well as in areas such as
geography, science, history, etc. The disintegration of our social
order can be easily explained. Men and women are disobeying the
clear instructions God gave in His Word.
—Falwell 1980:63

SUCH A STATEMENT sounds jarring to many modern ears.
How could anything, even the Bible, be "absolutely infallible"? And even if the Bible is taken seriously, surely one
would expect its ancient writers to have made some mistakes in history, science, and geography. Some modern thinkers may admit to a
certain amount of "social disintegration," but few would say that it
has a single cause or that the Bible contains "clear instructions" in
the first place. In dozens of ways, the Fundamentalist view of the
world contained in Jerry Falwell's statement is alien to the view held
by most Americans, most especially to those who consider themselves the guardians of knowledge.[1]

The emergence of Fundamentalism in the 1970s, seemingly
from nowhere, caught Americans by surprise. First we were faced
with a president who claimed to be a born-again Christian. For four
years the country watched Jimmy Carter to see just what an Evangelical looked like. Although we may have been surprised at his piety,
his ideas about the relationship between church and state and his
brand of Democratic politics were almost indistinguishable from
what had gone before. Next, in 1980, a large bloc of religious people,
claiming the label *Fundamentalist*, opposed Carter, and we were
faced with an even more serious challenge to our assumptions about
what Evangelicals and Fundamentalists were, where they were located, and what might be expected from them.

Scholars were caught by surprise partly because sociological
thinking about religion had been dominated by the myth of seculari-

zation.[2] In Marsden's words, "Theory and wish converged to suggest that traditionalist Protestantism would wither in the bright sun of modern culture" (1983:150). The picture of religion painted by many sociologists was one of a shrunken, emasculated apparition at the periphery of modern society. The institutional differentiation of the modern world had created not only the separation of church and state but also the separation of church from everything else of consequence. Where religion survived at all (mostly in America, in contrast to Europe), it existed as a watered-down glorification of the "American way of life."[3] According to this view, religious ways of knowing had been supplanted by scientific and rational ways of knowing. Religious institutions had been replaced by civic clubs, schools, and other voluntary associations. Individuals who maintained ties to religious institutions did so only as one of the many roles they played, one of the many hats they wore as modern, secularized people.

Such a "differentiated" religious identity clearly exists in modern society. For many, membership in a congregation is one among many memberships that establish them as proper citizens of the community. We find social scientific evidence of a differentiated religious identity in Allport's distinctions between extrinsic and intrinsic religiosity (for example, Allport and Ross 1967). Such an identity is suggested also by consistent findings indicating that religious beliefs have much less influence on everyday behavior than do social class and education.[4] And it is suggested by the profound way in which many Americans have become uncomfortable with any overlap between religion and politics or education or economic activity. For many, the church should "know its place" and stay in it. Preachers should not "meddle" in politics or business or even in decisions about whether couples stay married.

The relegation of religion to an insignificant and/or private segment of life is a dominant theme in both sociological circles and popular accounts. But that is not the only form of religion postulated by those who see modernity as essentially secular. Theorists who find such a neutering of religion objectionable (either personally or theoretically or both) have suggested an alternative religious response to modernity. Seeing religion not at the periphery but at the core of identity, they postulate an "individualized" world view as *the* modern religious alternative.[5] Because all institutions and cultures have become relativized, according to these theorists, the only common denominator is the individual. Religion is found in the individual's attempts to construct coherence. In this individualized version of the modern religious identity, people confront eternal questions of the human condition, formulating personal answers by which to live. We do this work in a social and cultural context, but there is no presumption that the individual's answers will be embodied in social institutions.

There is evidence for this kind of individualized religious identity as well. Its extreme form is described by Bellah and associates (1985). One of their subjects had named her faith after herself; when asked her religious identity, she replied, "Sheilaism." Although not everyone may be so explicit in claiming an individualized religion, a whole generation, coming of age in the 1960s, learned to distrust institutionalized religion but not necessarily to discard all religious impulses.[6] They learned to seek individual answers to life's questions and to expect others to seek answers relevant to their own lives. In a pluralistic modern world, such interiorized religions clearly exist along with an isolated, institutionally segmented religion.

Yet neither the "differentiated" nor the "individualized" version of modern religion encompasses the phenomenon of Fundamentalism.[7] Fundamentalists see their religion neither as irrelevant to other institutional involvements nor as residing in their own individual solutions to life's problems. Religion for them is grounded in an institution (the church) and in a document (the Holy Bible), both of which make the unlikely claim to ultimate truth. That truth, it is claimed, applies to all individuals and has preeminence over the claims of all other institutions. Fundamentalists simply do not accept either the cultural pluralism or the institutional differentiation that have come to be assumed in the modern world.[8]

Who Are Fundamentalists?

The Fundamentalists who have emerged in the public arena—and who are the subject of this book—are a group with a distinct way of living and believing that sets them apart from both the modern secularized world and other Christians. In fact, one of their most distinctive characteristics is their insistence on being different. "Separation from the world," a key tenet of Fundamentalism, results in individual lifestyles that are as distinctive from those of other Christians as they are from those of the rest of the world. A personal morality that forbids drinking, dancing, and divorce is but the most visible characteristic of a group that lives by very particular rules.

At the institutional level, separation from the world results in a refusal to cooperate—even in the best of causes—with others (including many Evangelicals) whose lives and beliefs do not meet Fundamentalist standards.[9] For this reason, the typical Fundamental church is independent; it belongs to no formally organized denomination but instead cooperates with a variety of independent mission boards, publishing houses, and the like.[10] Although some of these agencies are large and comprehensive enough to be quasi-denominations, each local church chooses which publications it will use, which youth program it will adopt, which missionaries to support, and which pastor to hire. The rare Fundamental church that exists within a main-line denomination is often a maverick kept uneasily within the larger organization's corral. *Compromise* and *accommodation* are among the most dreaded words in the Fundamentalist vocabulary.

Their insistence on separatism most clearly distinguishes Fundamentalists from their closest relatives, the Evangelicals. To be accurate, both are children of the revivalist tradition in conservative Protestantism. Fundamentalists share with their Evangelical brothers and sisters a conservative theology that affirms the divinity of Jesus, the reality of his resurrection and miracles, and the sure destiny of human beings in either heaven or hell. They believe that salvation is the result of a personal faith in Jesus that starts with an experience of being born again.[11]

Fundamentalists can be distinguished from other Evangelicals, however, in a variety of ways. As a starting point, identifiable organizations adopt each label and do not want to be confused with one another. Fuller Theological Seminary, for instance, is "Evangelical," while Bob Jones University is "Fundamentalist." Likewise, Billy Graham is an "Evangelical," while Falwell is a "Fundamentalist." The leaders in each camp (who are, of course, most aware of the differences) usually choose for themselves one designation and not the other.

Self-identification, however, is not entirely reliable;[12] there is a good deal of contention over labels, especially in the gray areas in the middle where the two groups genuinely overlap. Here outside criteria must be imposed to make the distinctions clear.[13] In each case, the differences surround the degree to which believers are willing to get along with the rest of the world: Evangelicals take a generally more accommodating stance on nearly everything.

The first of the doctrinal distinctions between Fundamentalists and Evangelicals is a difference in dogmatism about the literal nature of scripture. Fundamentalists are considerably more sure that every word of scripture (often as found in the King James Version) is to be taken at face value. Evangelicals are more comfortable with the ambiguities of translation and interpretation that arise when scripture is subjected to critical analysis. Fundamentalist readers of scripture are confident that they can turn to their King James Bibles to find prescriptions for living; Evangelicals are not so sure it is that simple.

The second criterion for distinguishing Fundamentalists from other Evangelicals is also a matter of degree. Fundamentalists are more likely to insist on dispensational premillennialism as the only correct belief about Christ's Second Coming. In fact, Fundamentalists are likely to see that belief as a key test of whether a person "really believes the Bible." They believe the Bible teaches that Christ will soon return to "rapture" true believers away from this world. In the time that follows, the earth will undergo a terrible "Tribulation" and the establishment of the reign of anti-Christ. Finally, the Lord's army will defeat Satan at Armageddon, and the millennium will begin. Because believers are convinced that this sequence of events will begin soon, they are concerned with the fulfillment of prophecy, reading all the words of scripture with an eye toward their hidden, "prophetic" meaning. They are helped in this task by the footnotes found in the Scofield (or more recently Ryrie) Reference Bible, which provides a common source of knowledge for Fundamentalists around the country. Although other Evangelicals may believe that Jesus will return and even that he will return before the millennium, Fundamentalists make these beliefs central to the way they understand the Bible and the way they preach the gospel.

"Ideal-typical" Fundamentalists, then, believe that Christians will soon be raptured out of this world into heaven. They also believe that this and every other fact about the world can be found in the Bible. Although they share many conservative, evangelical beliefs with other Protestants, they belong to an independent church and try to live up to strict moral standards so that everyone will notice they are different. These characteristics—separation from the world, dispensational premillennialism, and biblical literalism—provide the working definition of Fundamentalism with which we will begin.

Where Are Fundamentalists?

Realizing that Fundamentalism is a phenomenon not previously recognized or anticipated, researchers have begun to try to unravel its mysteries. Most especially, social scientists have begun to wonder (and worry about) just how big Fundamentalism's base of support is. One of the first major attempts to answer that question was the Gallup organization's 1980 effort to find Evangelicals in the United States and to document their impact on politics (Gallup 1981: 184–189). Gallup discovered that 40 percent of the American public claimed to believe that the Bible is the "actual word of God and is to be taken literally, word for word." Those who took the Bible literally, who also claimed to be born again, and who encouraged others to be saved were classified as Evangelicals; Gallup estimated that 19 percent of American adults fell into that category. Two years later, the same organization found that 44 percent of Americans believed that "God created man pretty much in his present form at one time during the last 10,000 years" (Gallup 1983: 208–213). If literalism and creationism are key tenets of Fundamentalism, then the potential pool of adherents is large indeed.

In both surveys, these conservative beliefs were most prevalent in the South, among nonwhites, and among those least educated.[14] However, one-fourth of college graduates and 40 percent of those who live in the secularized East still adhere to creationism as an explanation for humanity's beginnings; and when those who believe in theistic evolution are added, fully three-fourths of these most "secular" groups acknowledge a divine role in creation. Likewise, even the most educated segments of American society have not so much adopted a secular view of scripture as they have allowed for the possibility that not every word is literally true. In every social category, at least 80 percent of Gallup's respondents viewed the Bible as the Word of God. Clearly, theistic, biblical religion still enjoys wide grassroots support in the United States; and the most conservative version of that religion maintains a strong position within the mainstream. A large segment of American society, then, could hear in Falwell a message with many familiar ingredients. Although they might not all join the Moral Majority or even agree with all of Falwell's politics, his ideas about the importance of the Bible and of obeying God's rules may strike these people as just what the country needs to hear.

After a careful review of the Gallup data on Evangelicalism, Hunter (1983) concluded that those most remote from the forces of modernity were most likely to hold Evangelical beliefs and that Evangelicalism has significantly accommodated itself to the ways of the modern world. Although he makes a persuasive case for the accommodation of Evangelicalism to the structures of modernity, he makes a grave error in equating Evangelicals and Fundamentalists in this regard. As Hunter himself documents, the split between Fundamentalists and Evangelicals took institutional form in 1941 and 1942 (respectively) with the formation of the American Council of Christian Churches (on the Fundamentalist side) and the National Association of Evangelicals (on the Evangelical side). The Evangelical body consciously sought ways to establish a place for itself in the modern world. Rather than accommodating to modernity, however, the other side sought ways to withdraw, to fight back, and to exist in spite of it.

Hunter analyzes Evangelicalism's accommodation to the "cognitive style," the ways of thinking, characteristic of modernity. He claims that Evangelicals have found ways to adopt functional rationality (that is, a dependence on reason and organizational efficiency in all areas of life), structural pluralism (that is, the division of social life into functionally differentiated institutions), and cultural pluralism (the presence of diverse moral communities). As we will see, Fundamentalists, in contrast, reject functional rationality in favor of knowledge based on scripture and prophecy. They also shun the Evangelical's "civil" responses to cultural pluralism in favor of old-fashioned "hell-fire and damnation." Fundamentalists are convinced that their differences from others make them superior not only because they have something better but because theirs is the only truth, the only right way to live. This stance relative to cultural pluralism is linked, as well, to the Fundamentalist response to structural pluralism. As I have already argued, Fundamentalists refuse to

Refuse to relegate religion either to an insignificant segment of life (Hunter's "privatization") or to an individualized system of meaning (Hunter's "subjectivization").

Fundamentalism has not, then, incorporated the cognitive style of modernity in the way that either secularists, religious liberals, or other Evangelicals have. Neither, however, could Fundamentalism exist without modernity (cf. Lechner 1985). Fundamentalism as a movement arose when an old consensual orthodoxy encountered the challenges of critical scholarship and cultural pluralism. And today Fundamentalism is most likely to be found at the points where tradition is meeting modernity rather than where modernity is most remote. It is therefore not surprising to find Fundamentalist churches thriving in suburbia, for suburbia is populated at least in part by people who grew up in small-town religion and find the more agnostic, urban world in which they now live untenable. Fitzgerald notes of Falwell's own parishioners that "many current Lynchburg residents, including many Thomas Road members, literally made the journey between the underdeveloped countryside and the city. Many others, however, made a similar journey without moving at all" (1981:70). For some, the small-town ideal is not so much a memory as a dream, but the point is that neither group now lives in a place where most people share their views.

Those who do live in essentially traditional communities (and there are many of them left, especially in the South) may share many beliefs and practices with their conservative urban cousins, but they do not share the militant separatism that characterizes Fundamentalism as a movement. They may score high on scales of orthodoxy or literalism or "evangelicalism," but in significant ways traditional, rural, often southern, religion is different in kind from the religious expressions of people who must encounter diversity every day. Only where traditional orthodoxy must defend itself against modernity does Fundamentalism truly emerge.

If, then, Fundamentalists are most likely to be found on the growing edges of modernity, why should they be so visible at this particular time in history? What are the sources of Fundamentalism's current strength? Numerous researchers have begun to seek answers to these questions. Some look for explanations in the failures of modernity that have become painfully apparent in the last two decades (for example, Berger 1982, Cox 1984, Horowitz 1982). Others focus on the role of conservative politics in bringing conservative Christians into the limelight (Wuthnow 1983). Still others emphasize that such external factors are not a sufficient explanation; they see the internal resources developed by organizations like the Moral Majority (Liebman 1983) as important factors also. Along with political scientists, such as Lienesch (1982) and Lipset and Raab (1981), these observers have opened our eyes to the persistence of conservatism, despite predictions to the contrary. Although each researcher focuses on a slightly different cultural trend, all point to a hospitable cultural climate in recent years as an explanation for the resurgence of Fundamentalism.

The Nature of This Study

For the people involved in Fundamentalism—the people who call themselves "Bible believers"—a hospitable cultural climate is an irrelevant explanation. As they see it, the modern world is doomed, and the Author of its doom is neither political conservatism nor demographic shifts. Surviving in the interim is not a matter of political organization or social location but simply a daily effort to live a "separated" life and to "share the plan of salvation." For the ordinary believers who will be introduced in this book, the relationship between religion and culture is in the concrete reality of deciding how to relate to their neighbors, how to educate their children, how to explain what is happening in the Middle East, or how to vote. Social scientists have begun to understand the broad social and demographic patterns of Fundamentalism; this book is a look at the everyday world in which those patterns take shape.

This study is an effort to introduce the lives of ordinary Fundamentalists into the larger discussion of Fundamentalism's place in American society. Fundamentalism is examined here not as a cultural or political phenomenon but as a way of life. The primary units of analysis are individuals and the groups to which they most immediately belong. We will learn why Fundamentalism exists by listening to the stories of people who have chosen it. We will listen to how one group of Fundamentalists defines itself and how it gives order to the world. And in so doing we will hope to gain a detailed understanding with which to return to the public issues raised by Fundamentalism.

Understanding the everyday world of Fundamentalism requires much more than a demographic profile. It requires the kind of personal encounter that is possible only when researcher and subjects meet each other and spend a part of their lives together. The view of Fundamentalism presented here comes through the lens of such shared experience. For the year that stretched between June 1979 and May 1980, I became a participant in the congregation I will call Southside Gospel Church.[15] Members knew I was a researcher, but they also accepted me as "one of us." I attended almost every time the church doors were open, sang in the choir, helped in Sunday School and Junior Church, and even helped paint their Academy building. I celebrated their births and mourned their deaths. I listened to them describe and explain the world and tried to hear with the ears of an insider while watching with the eyes of a trained observer. In short, my effort was to get as close as possible to the way Fundamentalism is experienced in everyday life.

I chose participant observation as a method despite possible difficulties in gaining access to a Fundamentalist congregation. For most researchers, doing any sociological study of Fundamentalism is difficult and often nearly impossible. Fundamentalists often distrust secular researchers so much that they will not even complete questionnaires; gaining access for participant observation is even less likely. Part of the problem is that we sociologists are seen as chief among the "secular humanists" who have corrupted traditional ways of thinking. We use secular categories to explain everything, ignoring the actions of Almighty God. Likewise, in the Fundamentalist view, most sociologists are unrepentant sinners who live worldly lives that are unwelcome in a Fundamentalist congregation. Believers simply do not expect anyone who is not saved to be able to understand or empathize with their beliefs (cf. Robbins et al. 1973).

Nevertheless, after visiting a Sunday morning service at Southside, I approached the pastor about studying his church. For all the reasons I have just described, it is not surprising that his first question was "Are you born again?" Because my religious history is Evangelical, I could honestly answer "yes." The religious experiences of my childhood had prepared me for the language and expectations of a group like this, and those experiences opened doors that might have been closed to other researchers. Although I am not a Fundamentalist (and I disclaimed that identity whenever it was explicitly

bestowed on me), I am committed to the Christian faith; and I knew that I could translate much of my experience into terms this group would recognize and accept (cf. Ammerman 1982a). I could speak the language of an insider, and I was willing to live by an insider's rules. Where they had norms about drinking, dancing, and how to dress, I conformed. When they sang, I sang too; when they prayed, so did I; and when they read the Bible, I followed along in a King James Version. Because I was identified as saved and spoke the language of a saved person, I was accepted by most of the congregation and granted access that a complete outsider might never have gained.

I promised in return that I would present an inside view of Fundamentalism that was fair and accurate. Where I describe their ideas and experiences, I hope the people I studied find it so. Where I analyze what I saw, using the categories of secular sociology, I do not expect that they will accept my explanations. Although I would never wish to argue that sociological views of reality are any more true than religious ones (cf. Berger 1969:179ff.), accepting multiple explanations is not a comfortable position for the people of Southside.

While Southside's members may not find my sociological analysis agreeable, other information from this study may be of practical value. I prepared especially for them material on the demographics and organizational structure of the congregation—material that they subsequently used to develop new programs. While the research was in progress, I was careful to avoid disturbing the natural processes of the church; but after I left the field, it seemed only right to give back something of what I had taken.

My attempt throughout the study was to take seriously the world in which these people live, their noncognitive symbols as well as their rational structures and doctrines, the meaning of their experience as well as its form (cf. Bellah 1970, Geertz 1966). I began with the premise that an interacting group of people comes to common understandings (often unstated) about who they are and what the social world is like. What people do and say is built on the assumption that others will understand what they mean by those actions and words. Mead (1934) would say that people understand each other because meaning has been negotiated in a "conversation of gestures." Berger and Luckmann (1966), similarly, would say that a group's reality is "socially constructed." That construction process involves not only explicit ideas and values but the "strategies of action" that make most sense in a given corner of the social world (see Swidler 1986). My aim as an observer, then, was to understand the group's shared meanings and to uncover the subtle assumptions about reality that support and are supported by their everyday lives (cf. Blasi and Weigert 1976, Glaser and Strauss 1967, Truzzi 1974).

Although participant observation offers the best possibility for understanding a group's meanings and assumptions, we can never be quite sure how the observer has changed the world she is observing. Sometimes events seem to flow along undisturbed, while at other times the observer's presence brings an abrupt halt to the action. In this case, the disturbances seemed to be rare. Although I never sought to hide my research role, neither did I go out of my way to advertise it. Even after seven or eight months, people were sometimes surprised to find out that I was not just an ordinary participant. When they found out what I was doing, they treated me with a mixture of curiosity and acceptance—as long as they were sure the pastor approved of me. Most people were never quite sure what a sociologist would be studying, especially in their church and especially since I did not seem to be doing anything unusual. I was always there and often did things to help. I took notes during the pastor's sermons, but then so did a lot of other people. In the public context of church activities, I was more often treated as a participant than as an observer.

My role as observer involved much more than what my subjects saw of course. Besides taking notes while the pastor was preaching and teaching, I recorded other observations as soon as it was possible—often into a tape recorder as I was making the trip home. All these notes were typed, filed, and cross-filed into categories that began to reflect the dominant themes and concerns of the congregation. Out of this body of data specific areas were identified for further exploration in interviews. After about four months in the field, I began selecting a sample and contacting people to be interviewed.

Obtaining this sample was among the most difficult parts of the research process. Not surprisingly, the church did not have an accurate, up-to-date listing of its members, and the church clerk balked at turning over the list she did have. My list, then, was compiled with the aid of the church secretary and the pastor from the mailing list, their membership lists, and a recent pictorial directory. We arrived at an available population of 167 households in which there was at least one member. I used a table of random numbers to select fifty-nine of those households as my sample. Of that number, nine families could not be contacted because they had apparently moved out of the area; and nine others refused to be interviewed. To these were added samples from the 1,000+ mailing list and from the list of people converted in recent months. The final result was completed interviews with sixty-two adult members, twelve adult nonmembers, and four children.

My role as an interviewer often placed an initial distance between me and my subjects that was not present in my role as a participant observer. Those who had been selected to be interviewed received an introductory letter from me and from the pastor and a phone call to arrange a time to meet. But despite our efforts to preempt worries, a good many people approached the interview full of apprehension about what it would be like to be interviewed by someone who was getting a Ph.D. from Yale. After they had cleaned their houses, prepared special food, and even bought new clothes, some still worried about whether they would know the "right" answers and why I had chosen them instead of someone who was a stronger Christian or had been in the church longer or had a more interesting testimony.

Once we began to talk, however, people almost always became more comfortable. They told me how they had been saved and what they do at church. We talked about what it means to them to be a Christian and the things they like most to do. We discussed families, jobs, neighbors, politics, and the state of the world. I guided the conversation and asked enough questions to make sure that certain topics were covered, but much of our talk was not different from what it might have been if they had simply invited a new church member home for dinner. Sometimes they stopped halfway through the interview to ask when the "real" questions would begin. By the time we parted, they often commented about how much easier it had been than they had thought it would be. They felt that we had become friends.

This study reflects both the strengths and the weaknesses of such personal involvement. Its strength is understanding and richness of detail, in Geertz's (1973) words "thick description." Its weakness is the absence of comparative data and quantitative testing, which would place these findings in their proper context. Everyday life in one congregation does not represent that in all of American Fundamentalism. Such congregations pride themselves on their independence, which results in hundreds of major and minor variations in faith and practice. Almost anything one church does may be done differently in another Fundamentalist church somewhere else. Yet, despite their independence, Fundamentalist churches exhibit a remarkable uniformity. The common ground they share makes it possible for them to cooperate with each other in various evangelistic efforts, for members to move from one church to another, for churches to participate in common organizational networks and mutually to claim the name *Fundamentalist*.

Southside Gospel Church advertises itself as "Independent, Fundamental, Premillennial, and Baptistic." Its self-identification (along with its convenient location) initially justified its selection for this study. That selection was justified further by the extent to which this congregation is integrated into the network of Fundamentalist institutions throughout the country. Nearly every major Fundamentalist publication is read; there are ties to many Fundamentalist colleges; and most of the nationally known revivalists have supporters in the church. In addition, the ideas presented from Southside's pulpit never deviated in significant detail from the ideas described by historians, theologians, and sociologists who have studied Fundamentalism. Although not technically representative, Southside can safely be assumed to be fairly typical. Although not randomly selected, its identity and way of life place it squarely in the midst of the larger Fundamentalist movement.

A Look Ahead

This book, then, is about the ideas and habits of a group of people who claim to be "Bible believers" in the midst of a modern world that operates by different rules. We will begin the book by tracing the history of the Fundamentalist movement of which they are a part. We will see that the rumors of its demise have been grossly exaggerated. Whatever "resurgence" has recently occurred has taken place within an already well-established network of Fundamentalist institutions. Next, we will take a close look at the past and present of this particular congregation. It has been in existence almost one hundred years and today occupies a comfortable spot in the suburbs. We will look carefully at the social characteristics of today's Southside congregation to see what, if anything, marks them off from their neighbors.

Having located these people in time and in social context, we will turn to the ideas that order their lives. They often say that a believer must "be always ready to give an answer"; we will ask about the assumptions they make and the conscious principles they use for finding those answers. To use Berger's (1969) terms, we will explore the processes of "world construction" and "world maintenance," also looking at the way theodicies are made and supported. These ideas take form in an often-hostile everyday world. Believers would say that they must "walk in the light," knowing that the light exists in the midst of a world of darkness. We will look at the way in which this group of Fundamentalists interacts with and sets itself off from the non-Fundamentalist world. Throughout, we will look for the ways in which believers shape the world to fit their ideas and the ways in which the world insistently intrudes. We will look for the subtle ways in which official ideology and everyday reality intersect.

Because the everyday world is so often hostile, the activities and relationships within the church assume special significance. The "assembling together of believers" fills the time and focuses the attention of Southside's members. Within the church and through its affiliated institutions, believers construct a Fundamentalist subculture as distinctive as any ethnic one. We will look at the world they construct and at the ways, both overt and subtle, in which that world makes sense of and shapes all they do. If the church is successful, believers will take on a new identity and new expectations for how the social world should run.

The church, however, does not have to undertake this task alone. Christian homes are built around priestly husbands and submissive wives who honor God and God's Word above all. Homes, like churches, are structured according to biblical principles, extending the social boundaries of the world in which Fundamentalist ideas are taken for granted.

Fundamentalist ideas, of course, cannot always be taken for granted. This way of life is most precarious in the places where it is just being introduced, where it must compete with old habits or with alternative views of the future. Believers can maintain their own world only as long as they continue to draw outsiders away from those old habits and to persuade their own children to forsake those alternative futures. Because Fundamentalists are a cultural minority, they must recruit new members if they are to grow. They must constantly be about the business of "bringing them in." As we will see, their successes are distinctly mixed with failures, as are their attempts to bring up their children "in the nurture and admonition of the Lord." Although they carefully surround "church kids" with a biblical world, a large number of Southside's youth, like the youth across Fundamentalism, choose to leave when they reach an age of consent.

Having described the world in which these ordinary Fundamentalists live, we will finally return to assess the impact of their beliefs both on their own lives and as they are part of a larger cultural/political movement. We will look at questions of alienation and power, limitations and potentials, the past and the future. Looking back at the dialogue between these believers and the modern world, we will attempt to look ahead toward Fundamentalism's place in the future.

But first, a look back at the past.

CHAPTER TWO

Fundamentalist Forebears: Warriors Against Modernity

Put on the whole armor of God. . . . For we wrestle not against flesh and blood, but against principalities, against powers, against the rulers of the darkness of this world.
—Ephesians 6:11–12

THE IDEAS that shape Southside's way of life have a history. This church is part of a movement that arose in this country in the latter part of the nineteenth century, but Fundamentalists themselves are likely to trace their roots back much further than that. Most retain some vestige of the "landmark" argument that Bible-believing (especially Baptist) churches can follow "the trail of blood" leading from the present day back through the Middle Ages to the New Testament itself.[1]

But even in that argument, the United States occupies a special place in the history of God's people. Fundamentalists see themselves as the keepers of both the Christian heritage of the first century and the American heritage of the Puritans and the Founding Fathers. Their understanding of American history is not all wrong. Puritans did leave England seeking religious liberty and the opportunity to bind themselves together under a new "national Covenant." "In the early years, this sense of a common calling was strengthened by the widely held conviction that the reformation being carried out in these commonwealths was actually a decisive phase in the final chapter of God's plan for his Church in this world" (Ahlstrom 1975:I:182). This sense of mission would largely disappear within a century of the founding of Plymouth, but its symbolic place in the American religious identity remains. The idea that this nation has a special mission and therefore enjoys God's special providence continues to be a central theme in American "civil religion" (Bellah 1967).

By the time the Constitution was written, the nation's symbolic rhetoric came more from deism than from any doctrinally pure version of Protestantism, but for at least another century "almost all American Protestants thought of America as a 'Christian nation'" (Marsden 1980:11). And the majority of Americans were Protestant. Not nearly all of them belonged to churches or maintained a "godly" way of life, but the early American religious institutions formed what Ahlstrom (1975:I:165ff.) calls a "Protestant empire." He points out that the first and second "Great Awakenings" secured the importance of Evangelicalism in American culture; and, on the frontier, Baptists and Methodists (and to a lesser extent Presbyterians) became the religious entrepreneurs of the day. These days of Protestant hegemony are the golden age Fundamentalists long for. They perceive that before about 1870 their view of religion prevailed in this country; and in this perception they are not entirely wrong.

They are also not entirely wrong in perceiving that about a century ago things began to change. A variety of forces began to alter the rural, homogeneous, Protestant character of American life. After the Civil War, cities and industry began to boom. Science, technology, and business were taking over where tradition, prayer, and faith had left off. At the same time, streams of European immigrants were arriving with their Catholic and Jewish traditions. Religious pluralism was becoming an American fact of life. The second half of the nineteenth century brought what Marty (1969) has called the "modern schism." Old assumptions (mostly Protestant) were replaced by new dogmas of industrialism, historicism, and secularism. Yet *replaced* is not quite right. Although religious assumptions no longer dominated the culture, religious institutions thrived. Marty calls the result "controlled secularity." Religion gradually became compartmentalized in the private, family, and leisure spheres, leaving political, scientific, and economic affairs to the secular experts.[2]

Alongside these social and cultural changes, an intellectual revolution was taking shape. An objective view of the world was rapidly giving way to a subjective one (cf. Marsden 1980). In the human sciences, psychology and sociology began to question the nature of human responsibility, destiny, and free will. In the natural sciences, Charles Darwin's ideas began to change the way scholars viewed the physical universe. In political science, Karl Marx's ideas led people to look for the hidden meanings in religion, politics, and philosophy. And in theology itself, scholars began to analyze biblical material as if it were ordinary ancient literature that reported events that might also be explained in natural, human terms. From every direction, the world was changing. It was no longer what it used to be or even what ordinary people thought it to be.

It was, then, when the world was changing that Fundamentalism began to emerge. For many religious people, the new ideas and strange ways of life seemed too different to ever be reconciled with what they knew of Christianity. If nothing else was sacred, at least religion should be. When, in the late nineteenth century, some denominations began to liberalize their views of doctrines such as the virgin birth, human depravity, the resurrection, and life after death, conservative groups began to fight back (cf. Cole 1931, Dollar 1973, Marsden 1980). At least in part, Fundamentalists are right in claiming to be the preservers of beliefs that once characterized most Protestants. Conservatives began to gain a common identity as they fought to save the historic creeds of their denominations.

But as surely as Fundamentalism grew out of a defense of the old, it also adopted beliefs and practices that were genuinely new. Chief among these were premillennialism. Early in the nineteenth century in Britain, J. N. Darby developed a view of history that came to be known as dispensationalism. As he saw it, God had divided his[3] activity in the world into seven dispensations, each with different rules for obtaining salvation. After Christ's resurrection, the world entered the "church age," in which grace is the means of salvation. The next important event on the cosmic calendar is the Rapture. What seized the imaginations of Darby's readers was that the Rapture would be unknown to nonbelievers, that Christians would suddenly just disappear. In addition, Darby's ideas helped to revive a perennial interest in setting dates for Christ's return. People began to read the scripture as if it were a puzzle containing clues to God's historical timetable. Some (like William Miller) added up the clues and predicted when Christ was due to return. Others simply began to preach the "any-moment Rapture" as a central theme in the gospel. Even after Miller's followers were left standing on a hill waiting for Christ to come, the idea that the Rapture might be at any moment continued to gain in popularity. By the end of the century, this emphasis on prophecy and the Second Coming was among the ideas that would shape Fundamentalism.[4]

Among the other nineteenth-century innovations that Fundamentalism adopted was the revival. These communitywide meetings

aimed at capturing the souls of the masses through the use of enthusiastic preaching and singing. They began on the western frontiers
and in northern cities, but the most successful of the preachers soon
became national figures. And the meetings they held brought together Evangelicals of all denominations in a common effort. Frankl
(1985) has argued that Charles G. Finney, followed by Dwight L.
Moody and Billy Sunday, laid the foundations both for the idea of
measuring success in numbers of souls saved and for the extrade-
nominational organizational structure that was to characterize urban
revivalism (and later televangelism). In the early revival years, the
preacher's concern for the lost and suffering urban masses helped to
create social-reform movements as well as efforts at individual salvation (cf. Smith 1957). But these men were also concerned about keeping their gospel safe and pure. By the end of the nineteenth century,
revivals were a characteristic gathering place for the conservatives
who were about to recognize each other as Fundamentalists.

The cultural and intellectual upheavals of the last quarter of the
nineteenth century were fertile ground for premillennial prophecies
and mass evangelism. As conservatives began to sort out the traditional doctrines for which they would fight, they brought along
these new ideas as well. When the Fundamentalist historian George
Dollar lists the central ideas of these early conservatives, he includes
"the promises to Israel; the any-moment return of Christ for the
Church; the rapture as the next important event; the certainty of the
thousand-year reign of Christ; the separation of Christians from
worldly things; and world-wide evangelism before Christ comes"
(1973:27). However, even Dollar admits that these "Bible truths" had
had a "spotty existence in church history and had never been great
cardinal tenets of a main body of Christians" (1973:27). The theological roots of Fundamentalism, then, lie both in traditional conservative ground and in the soil of popular nineteenth-century religion.

The theological ideas provided only the raw material however.
What remained was the actual work of building the organizational
structure and the sense of identity that would be necessary for Fundamentalism to emerge as a movement.[5] Potentially like-minded
people needed opportunities to share and develop their ideas, and
those opportunities came in a variety of new organizational forms.
Revivals provided local interaction as well as identification on a na-

tional level with other people and churches who had listened to the same evangelists. That national identity was increased with the calling of two well-attended prophecy conferences—the first in 1878 in New York and the second eight years later in Chicago. The emerging conservative coalition was aided also by the founding of newspapers like the *Bible Champion* that served as a means of communication. But perhaps most important, the Niagara Bible Conference and others like it began to provide continuing points for broad national participation.[6] People came from all over the country, attracted by nationally known preachers and by the chance to retreat from the trials of everyday life with a group of fellow believers. They also gained in the process a recognized core of leaders and identification with a group that began to understand and develop its own distinctiveness.

Around the turn of the century, conservative leaders began to make formal statements of the beliefs they saw as central to the Christian faith. In 1890, at the Niagara Bible Conference, J. H. Brookes's "Fourteen Points" were endorsed.[7] At about the same time, at Princeton Theological Seminary, Charles Hodge and B. B. Warfield were fashioning a scholarly defense for inerrancy and orthodoxy. C. I. Scofield's premillennially annotated version of the King James Bible was published in 1909. And from 1910 to 1915, A. C. Dixon edited a series of booklets called *The Fundamentals*, which defended the Bible, conservative doctrine, and the Second Coming. Taken together, such publications began to provide a body of dogma that was distinct from the beliefs of the rest of Protestantism and that circulated in unique organizational channels.

Those organizational channels were, at this point, primarily urban, northeastern, and in the Baptist and Presbyterian denominations. During these formative years, Fundamentalism's strength was in New York and Philadelphia, Boston and Chicago, Minneapolis and Toronto, rather than in Atlanta or Charleston or Birmingham. In the South, liberal theology and social change were not yet factors to be defended against, and Protestantism had not yet been displaced as a dominant community force. The similarities that would emerge between southern Protestantism and Fundamentalism have more to do with styles of personal morality and corporate worship than with theology or organizational ties (Primer 1980). Southerners adopted neither biblical literalism nor premillennialism as tenets of their faith. It was in the North that Christians became convinced that the Rapture was near and that they should organize to keep the gospel pure.[8]

By the time World War I began, the boundaries of Fundamentalism were beginning to emerge; and the war gave an additional push to an already growing movement. Germany made just the right military target for people who were convinced that most of the evil ideas they were fighting had originated in German universities. Might this even be a prelude to Armageddon and the defeat of the anti-Christ? In 1918, a prophecy conference was convened in Philadelphia to explore what the Bible had to say about such perilous times. Even when the war was won, the sense of impending doom did not abate. The formation of a League of Nations and a new burst of ecumenism only heightened fears that the anti-Christ's superkingdom was being prepared and that the Rapture must be at hand. The stage was now set for the battles out of which institutional Fundamentalism would be born.

The verbal duels that took place during the 1920s were lively, to say the least. In the main-line Protestant denominations, liberalism, ecumenism, and the social gospel were the order of the day. Liberals like Harry Emerson Fosdick were as eager to be rid of Fundamentalists as conservatives like J. R. Straton were to purge the churches of heresy. While Fosdick and Straton slugged it out in New York, T. T. Shields in Toronto and W. B. Riley in Minneapolis joined forces with southerner J. Frank Norris to form the Baptist Bible Union, through which they attacked modernism, liberalism, ecumenism, and all the other ills of the days. Although some of these colorful leaders were tainted by scandal,[9] their enthusiasm inspired a following. Beginning in 1919, many Protestant denominations were involved in major liberal/Fundamentalist controversies. Groups of Fundamentalists among the Northern Baptists, the northern and southern Presbyterians, the Disciples of Christ, the Methodists, and the Episcopalians denounced the schools and leaders and publications they saw as suspect. Each battle was unique to the denomination in which it was fought, but in each case Fundamentalists sought to purge the group's institutions of heresy and to "regain" control for themselves.

In each case, Fundamentalists failed substantially to change the denominations, but that failure should not be interpreted as the demise of Fundamentalism.[10] Rather, when they were unable to change denominational institutions, many broke away and formed their own. They continued the organizational process that had begun with the Bible and prophecy conferences. Attempts at a unified national organization (such as the World's Christian Fundamentals Association, founded at the Philadelphia prophecy conference in 1918) never had much success; but a patchwork of independent publishing houses and schools began to thrive. During the 1920s, J. Gresham Machen left Princeton Theological Seminary to form Westminster Seminary; Shields founded Toronto Baptist Seminary and took over Des Moines University; and Riley founded Northwestern Bible School in Minneapolis. More and more churches became independent of their parent denominations or were founded as independent in the first place. They offered a base of support for these new Fundamentalist institutions. Although the denominational battles were mostly over by 1930, Fundamentalists had managed by then to capture enough territory from each of their opponents to create a place for themselves on a revised map of American religion.

Having established an identity and a territory, Fundamentalism proceeded to develop impressive structures within those boundaries. They continued to establish and expand training and support facilities such as the mammoth Moody Bible Institute in Chicago and the Bible Institute of Los Angeles. Summer Bible conferences continued to be extremely popular, and radio broadcasting began to extend the reach of evangelists and teachers. While the main-line denominations struggled to maintain any mission effort at all, the new, independent Fundamental agencies sent out hundreds of new missionaries even during the Depression. From 1930 until the Second World War, Fundamentalist institutions grew and thrived (Carpenter 1980).

By 1941, however, Fundamentalism was no longer a unified movement. That year and the next saw the birth of two opposing parties within the old movement. The conservative wing was organized by Carl McIntire into the American Council of Christian Churches. This was to be a specifically antimodernist voice, a militant organization, speaking out aggressively against compromise in religion, politics, or morality. And almost immediately this militant voice was countered by the formation of the National Association of Evangelicals. The two groups differed not at all on doctrine, but their styles and behavior were vastly different. The new Evangelicals simply refused to separate themselves from other Christians or to adopt right-wing politics as part of their creed. The Fundamentalists meanwhile began to see Evangelicals as even more compromising and offensive than liberals (cf. Marty 1976). While Fundamentalists called Evangelicals weak-kneed and heretical, Evangelicals were calling Fundamentalists hard-headed and obnoxious. The split became most visibly public when several prominent Fundamentalists refused to endorse Billy Graham's 1957 New York City crusade, while Graham equally adamantly refused to denounce his "liberal" supporters who would not sign a pledge of doctrinal orthodoxy (Falwell 1981: 129–131).

Throughout the postwar period, both Evangelicals and Fundamentalists continued to expand. Both groups kept a strict conservative orthodoxy in belief, but differences in style and in response to the world increased. Fundamentalists remained committed to the notion that the modern world and modern theology must be resisted at all costs, that compromise in either doctrine or lifestyle would be devastating. They looked at Evangelicals and saw a dangerous level of toleration. As Falwell writes, "The Evangelicals' acceptance of doctrinal and individual differences became the catalyst that started their drift to the left" (1981:164).

This Fundamentalist refusal to compromise has created fertile ground for schism. When people disagree, they form new organizations rather than accommodating to their differences. Yet this has not apparently weakened the movement. Fundamentalism has never been organized around a single person or institution. Rather, it thrives as a loosely knit, often contentious coalition of independent churches and other independent institutions. These are the people who identify themselves and each other as "true Bible believers," as the defenders of the timeless truths of the faith, as Fundamentalists with a capital F. And despite scholarly and cultural inattention, the Fundamentalist movement not only has sustained itself but has provided the seeds from which the new religious right and its related movements have sprung. The people of Southside are not a new phenomenon. Rather, they are creating a place for themselves in today's world out of ideological and social material borrowed from a movement now a century old.

CHAPTER THREE

Southside Gospel Church: Its History and People

But ye are a chosen generation, a royal priesthood, an holy nation, a peculiar people. . . . Which in time past were not a people, but are now the people of God.
—I Peter 2:9–10

IN THE LATE nineteenth century, as the Fundamentalist movement was getting started, a small congregation gathered in the heart of a growing industrial city in the Northeast. Rather than affiliating with a denomination, they sought to carry on the revival tradition that had given them their start. Their goal was to preach the gospel to everyone and to live the disciplined lives of true believers. By 1916, however, some of the members were growing concerned that "worldly things" seemed to be creeping into the church. When two wayward young members openly attended a movie and no one moved to censure them, a group of concerned members broke away from the original church to form what became Southside Gospel Church. They called the original pastor to join them and vowed to remain true to the gospel and to a life of separation from the world.

For almost fifty years, they met in their central city location. The membership fluctuated between about 50 and 250, depending on the reputation and preaching skills of the pastor. By the mid-1960s, they were thriving and needed more space. They voted to solve the problem by moving to the suburbs. The move and the arrival of a new pastor a few years later contributed to another spurt in growth that has brought the membership to around 350 and attendance to over 500. They have started a Christian Academy, where their children can be educated from nursery school through high school. They have also purchased a nearby tract of land on which they hope to build a complete new church and school complex.

The neighborhood where the church is now located could be a

suburban neighborhood anywhere. Located about five miles from the center of the metropolitan area, it is bordered on the west by the city where the church began, the city that serves as the industrial heart of the region. The town of Valley View is a comfortable, middle-class community of ranch-style and split-level homes with well-manicured lawns. Nearby, a 200-year-old cemetery is one of the few reminders that although the houses and apartments are new, the town is not. Long before it was a suburb, Valley View was a New England village, and the highway that is now its main commercial artery was a link between New York and the upper New England states. The church stands atop a small rise, a few blocks from that main highway. It is an ordinary-looking, one-story, L-shaped, brick building, with a small white steeple. Only the sign in front identifies this church as any different from the others nearby.

But if the neighbors stop to read that sign, they are likely to wonder just what it means to be premillennial, fundamental, independent, and baptistic. Despite the ordinary-looking exterior, they may expect to find some unusual people inside. They may expect the members of a Fundamental church to be mostly poor or uneducated or old or southern. But if they expect any of those things, they are wrong. The people who make up Southside Gospel Church might easily be mistaken for the members of any other church in town. As is common in American churches, there are more women than men in the Sunday morning congregation (see Table 3.1). But unlike many other congregations, this is not an elderly group. There are substantially fewer people over fifty-five than would be expected in this town; and there are almost half again as many young adults as would be expected.

Neither is this a group of marginal or "disinherited" people looking for comfort. Almost no one is unemployed—at least not for long. Many work in offices and factories and machine shops (see Table 3.2). Some are skilled in trades, and some are salespeople. A large number are teachers and health workers, while several work for city and state government. Others work in small businesses, for themselves, and for the large national and multinational corporations headquartered in the area. Of the women in the church, only 17 percent are full-time homemakers. Almost half currently work full-time outside their homes, while the rest work part-time or are retired. Although there are only a few owners and upper-level manag-

TABLE 3.1. Distribution by Age and Sex of Southside Congregation
and Valley View Population

	Southside			Valley View		
Age	Male	Female	Total	Male	Female	Total
20–34	18%	27%	45%	15%	17%	32%
35–54	18	24	42	16	18	34
55+	4	9	13	15	19	34
Total	40%	60%	100%	46%	54%	100%

SOURCES: For Valley View, U.S. Department of Commerce (1982b); for Southside, a head count of the Sunday morning congregation on June 1, 1980, which included 247 adults.

TABLE 3.2. Distribution by Occupation of Southside Congregation
and Valley View Population

Occupation	Southside	Valley View	Occupation	Southside	Valley View
Professionals	32%	15%	Craft/trade workers	11%	11%
Managers	11	12	Factory workers	9	11
Technicians	*	4	Service workers	2	10
Salespeople	4	12	Farm workers	1	1
Clerical workers	29	24	Total	99%	100%

SOURCES: For Valley View, U.S. Department of Commerce (1982a); for Southside, a questionnaire distributed (nonrandomly) to the Sunday morning congregation, May 25, 1980 (106 respondents).
*Not available.

ers in the church, there are also not many members near the bottom of the economic order. The occupational structure of this congregation is decidedly middle class.

Likewise, the incomes of church families are fairly typical of their community (see Table 3.3). In 1980, the town's median household income was $23,143 (U.S. Department of Commerce 1982a). Southside's median was also about $20,000. Three-fourths of the congregation lived on between $10,000 and $30,000 that year. Several of the older members have lower incomes, but none is living in abject poverty. Few, if any, members receive government assistance other than Social Security and Medicare. At the other end of the economic spectrum neither is anyone enjoying great wealth. No one in the church reported a family income above $40,000.

TABLE 3.3. Distribution by Income of Southside Congregation
and Valley View Population

Household income	Southside	Valley View	Household income	Southside	Valley View
< $5,000	11%	4%	$20,000–$24,999	24%	16%
$5,000–$9,999	9	8	$25,000–$34,999	19	26
$10,000–$14,999	13	11	$35,000–$49,999	2	13
$15,000–$19,999	22	16	$50,000 +	0	5
			Total	100%	99%

SOURCES: For Valley View, U.S. Department of Commerce (1982a); for Southside, data gathered during interviews of randomly selected participants (forty-six households).

The educational level of this group might also surprise the outsider. There are more high school graduates than would be expected in the community, and many have had some training beyond high school (see Table 3.4). Only a few, mostly the older members, have not completed at least twelve years of school. Those who have gone beyond high school have been to trade schools, Bible schools, and colleges. Partly because of the large number of teachers and nurses, a significant segment of the congregation has obtained baccalaureate degrees.

Southside's members, then, have incomes, occupations, and educations (the standard measures of status) that are typical of the American middle class and of the community in which the church meets. And in a host of other ways, they are just as typical. Two-thirds of the church's families own their homes, mostly suburban tract houses ranging from new to thirty years in age and from about $40,000 to $90,000 in value. Those who rent live in both new complexes with all the amenities and in older houses that have been turned into apartments.

In the more subtle areas of taste and style, Southside's members are equally mainstream. They are more likely to shop for their clothes at Sears than at either Saks or K-Mart, to follow the styles in *McCalls* rather than in *Vogue*. They favor gospel songs over Bach, *Prevention* magazine over *The New England Journal of Medicine*. They would be equally out of place at New York's fashionable Riverside Church or in a local ghetto storefront, although they might share a

TABLE 3.4. Distribution by Education of Southside Congregation and Valley View Population

Years completed	Southside	Valley View
< 12 years	16%	25%
12 years	41	37
13–15 years	21	18
16 + years	22	20
Total	100%	100%

SOURCES: For Valley View, U.S. Department of Commerce (1982a); for Southside, data gathered during interviews of seventy-four randomly selected participants.

Baptist heritage with both those places. Theirs are the lifestyle and status of middle America.

On almost every variable that sociologists usually use to measure differences among people, this group of Fundamentalists consists of average, middle-class Americans. The differences that do exist place them on the side of the more comfortable and better educated. Although class and education may affect their beliefs in subtle ways, those subtleties would not be detected by any of the usual demographic measures. What makes the members of Southside Gospel Church different is not that they come from a marginal segment of American society.

Neither can this group be called outsiders to the culture in which they reside. They are by no means transplants from the South. There are more native Europeans in the congregation than native southerners. A few are from the Midwest, but the vast majority grew up near their present homes or elsewhere in the Northeast. Just like the surrounding community, this congregation is sprinkled with second- and third-generation Italian and Eastern European ethnics, along with Anglo-Saxon New Englanders. There are even a few blacks who attend regularly, although, to my knowledge, none are members.

This is also not exclusively a group of lifelong Fundamentalists (see Table 3.5). While about 15 percent have been members of Southside all their lives and another 28 percent grew up in similar churches, over half the congregation has come to Fundamentalism from some other religious tradition. The evidence we have from na-

TABLE 3.5. Childhood Religious Preference of Southside Congregation
and Members of U.S. Sects

Southside		U.S. sects	
Fundamentalist	43%	"Sects"	50.9%
(including 18% "Baptist")		"Baptist"	17.5
Other Protestant	12	Other Protestant	19.1
Episcopal	7	Episcopal	.6
Congregational	10	Congregational	.6
Catholic	24	Catholic	6.1
Jewish	0	Jewish	.3
None	4	None	4.9
Total	100%		100%

SOURCES: For Southside, data gathered during interviews with seventy-four
randomly selected participants; for U.S. sects, Kluegel (1980: Table 1).
NOTE: Kluegel's tables are based on data from the General Social Survey. In that
survey, respondents are categorized as "Baptist" based on responses that vary enormously in meaning, from the very main-line American Baptist churches to the various
forms of black Baptist churches to the very sectarian independent churches like
Southside. Groups are categorized as "sects" based on their small membership and
deviance from the American norm, but this category may include everything from
Jehovah's Witnesses to the Unification Church (see Davis 1984, 397–399). These
figures then, should be taken as only an approximation of membership in churches
that are comparable to Southside or in the other conservative, "Baptist" churches
from which its members have come.

tional surveys indicates that this percentage of converts is higher
than is typical of most "sectarian" churches (Kluegel 1980). The religious heritages of these converts are also not typical of sectarians but
rather are typical of the religious patterns of the Northeast. The
community is predominantly Catholic, and almost half of Southside's converts used to be Catholic. Because the dominant Protestant
denominations are Episcopal and Congregational (United Church
of Christ), many of Southside's converts come from those groups. In
religious background, as in cultural and social position, the members
of Southside Gospel Church are not atypical of their community.

Finding that this group of northern Fundamentalists is demographically representative of its community suggests the possibility
that all Fundamentalists are demographically indistinguishable from
the particular regions they call home. Hunter's (1983) evidence suggests that regional variations may "explain away" many of the supposed demographics of Fundamentalism. In other words, because so

many Fundamentalists come from the South, the South's demographics skew the national averages. In the South, Fundamentalists (like everyone else) are likely to be less educated and less urban than the national average and are more likely to come from a sectarian background. Combining a large number of southern Fundamentalists with a small number of nonsouthern ones makes for demographic averages that overrepresent southern characteristics. It thus obscures the possibility that by being typical of their regional culture, Southside's members are more like other Fundamentalists than it first appears. I would argue that it is likely that all Fundamentalists are demographically typical of their home cultures.

The members of Southside who present this ordinary demographic profile are, of course, more than numbers. They are people whose stories constitute the community of Southside. In the pages that follow, they will tell what they think makes their church special and why their lives are different. Sometimes the speakers will be anonymous people from among those who were interviewed and observed. Others will become familiar because they often seemed to capture best the experiences everyone talked about. Among those who will speak most often are these members:

Bonnie Towles is about thirty. Her husband, Sam, has recently begun attending church with her but has not yet joined. They have two children, Jimmy and Sarah, who go to school at the Academy. Sam has a good job with a utility company, and Bonnie works part-time at the church nursery school. They live in a new subdivision near the church. Although Bonnie had gone to conservative churches as a child, her arrival at Southside five years ago marked a significant change in her life.

Bob and Rebecca Hughes are in their mid-thirties. They also have two children, daughters, who go to the Academy. Bob is an inspector in an aircraft company, and Rebecca directs the church nursery school. They live about twenty minutes from church in an older home they share with Rebecca's mother. Bob grew up in liberal churches, and Rebecca was a Catholic, but neither attended church much until they were converted about seven years ago.

Jim and Doris Forester are thirty years old and live about twenty minutes in the other direction from the church. Theirs is a relatively new home in a fashionable suburb. He is a manufacturer's representative, and she stays home with their four children, the older two of whom attend public school. He was a Catholic until about seven years ago, but she grew up in Fundamental churches. They joined Southside recently, when they moved into the metropolitan area.

Steve and Elaine Young are also about thirty and have two daughters who go to the Academy. He is a mechanical engineer, and she works for a bank. With two incomes, they have been able to purchase their first home in a nice older neighborhood near the church. They had been fairly active in a Congregational church until Elaine began church shopping. About five years ago, they were converted and joined Southside.

Joe and Janet Slavin are more recent converts and a bit younger —in their mid-twenties. They were inactive Catholics until their conversion three years ago. He has recently started a job as an auditor, and she works part-time as a retail clerk when she is not taking care of their eight-month-old daughter. When I saw them, they were living in the second-floor apartment of a two-family house in a city neighborhood. Within a couple of months, however, they had purchased a new home at the edge of the metropolitan area.

Harry and Ellen McLean are also ex-Catholics; they have two daughters who are in school at the Academy. They were converted and came to Southside about three years ago. Because they have some extraordinary family expenses, Harry works at two jobs—as a policeman and as a retail salesman. Ellen is a customer-service representative for a credit company. They live in a comfortable, suburban, ranch-style house about four miles from the church.

Ray and Mary Danner are in their fifties; their three children have all left home. They converted to Fundamentalism in the early years of their marriage and have been at Southside since they moved to the area several years ago for Ray to take a job as a regional manager for a chain of grocery stores. Now that the children are gone, Mary works part-time as a receptionist in a doctor's office. Their spacious older home is located in one of the charming small towns that has been incorporated into the metropolitan area.

Howard Otto is in his mid-thirties and has two daughters who are enrolled at the Academy. He, too, was a Catholic until he converted about six years ago. He works as an industrial salesman and was in the midst of an unhappy divorce when I talked with him.

Ann Lazzaro converted from Catholicism when she married

a man who had been a lifelong member of Southside. That was twenty-five years ago, and now the youngest of their three children is in high school, and Ann is working and going to college part-time so that she will be able to teach school. Her husband is a carpenter, and they still live in the modest home near the church that they bought new when they got married.

Connie Meyer is in her late thirties and lives in the new extended-care facility just down the road from the church. She has some difficulty talking and cannot walk, so she gets around in a wheel chair. She comes to church whenever there is someone to pick her up (which is almost always). Before her conversion at Southside three years ago, she had rarely attended church at all.

This group is representative of the people most committed to Fundamentalism, not necessarily of the congregation as a whole. They will help us to see the distinguishing marks of their view of the world. On the surface they have lived lives much like those of others in their area. Only as we look and listen closely will we discover the differences.

Although the people of Southside might easily be mistaken for their non-Fundamentalist neighbors, their church and its activities are far from typical. Those who live nearby undoubtedly notice that the parking lot is full at least three times a week, with an almost constant stream of smaller groups coming in and out. Southside is a busy church. When neighbors venture from their outside vantage point into a Sunday service, they will be handed a bulletin in which more space is devoted to weekday activities than to the Sunday order of service (see the Annotated Guide to the Week's Activities at Southside).

Sunday visitors also discover that Southside neither looks nor sounds like the main-line Protestant churches typical in the Northeast. The sanctuary is a large rectangular area divided by a center aisle. The style is typical of the late 1960s, when the building was built—simple, angular lines and little ornamentation. There are straight rows of padded pews on the main level and in the small balcony above. At the front, a piano is on the right, a Hammond organ on the left. At the center of the raised platform in front is the pulpit, with a communion table at audience level immediately in front of it. Except when the Lord's Supper is observed (once a quarter), a large Bible is centered on the table. The preacher and song leader sit on

An Annotated Guide to the Week's Activities at Southside

SUNDAY

8:30—Bus Routes. Four teams composed of a driver, captain, and one or more workers get their buses from the leasing company and pick up ten to forty children each. On the way back to church, they sing choruses, and the captain offers a brief devotional on the importance of being saved.

9:30—Sunday School. Children are in classes with others their age. They learn Bible verses, hear Bible stories, sing, play, and do Bible art projects. Adults have a choice of three classes: the pastor's Bible study, a Bible study discussion led by a deacon, or a class of older adults taught by another deacon.

10:45—Preaching Service. There are congregational songs, prayers, announcements, special music, an offering, and the message and invitation.
—*Junior Church.* Children through fourth grade have the option of remaining in the Sunday School area, getting a new team of teachers, and continuing with Bible-learning games, stories, and songs. For this hour, however, they sit in rows, are expected to be quiet unless called on, and are given an invitation—"just like in big church."

2:00—Teen Service at Open Hearth. Once a month a group of three or four teens leads a worship service at this rescue mission. They sing, give testimonies, and one boy often preaches. On other Sundays they sometimes do similar services at a nearby nursing home.

5:00—Deacons' Meeting. About once a month, the deacons meet to discuss church business, set policy, deal with problems in the fellowship, and interview new members.

5:30—Teen Bible Club. A group of six to ten teens follows a format outlined by Word of Life, an independent education and publishing agency. They spend a good deal of time singing, then are coaxed into a time of testimonies, prayers, and lessons in Christian living. During the week, they are encouraged to memorize scripture and to keep a daily spiritual journal.
—*Soul-Winning Class.* Whenever there is enough interest, Spence Schuster, an influential deacon, schedules a six-to-eight-week series of classes to teach witnessing skills.
—*Sign Language Class.* This series of weekly classes, offered period-

ically, is taught by one of the church's interpreters to other aspiring intepreters.

—*Missionary Committee Meeting*. This and other committees meet about once a month to discuss their respective tasks.

6:00—*Choir Practice*. The adult choir meets twice each week for rehearsal.

7:00—*Evening Service*. This service has the same format as the morning gathering, but it has a more informal style, a smaller crowd, and a focus on Christians rather than on the unsaved.

8:15—*Fellowship*. Occasional receptions and fellowships are scheduled, especially to celebrate the comings, goings, birthdays, and anniversaries of the church staff.

MONDAY

Morning
7:00—*Prayer Meeting*. A small group of men gathers at the church to pray before starting the week at work.

Evening
7:30—*Southside Bible Institute*. Various teachers from Southside and neighboring churches offer in-depth courses about the Bible and Christian living. Students pay a small tuition, have textbooks and homework, and attend class each Monday night for a semester.
—*Committee Meetings*. Scheduled as needed.

TUESDAY

Morning
9:30—*Ladies Visitation*. Women who are available during the day visit unsaved women, prospects for the church, new Christians who need encouragement, and so forth.

10:30—*Southside Senior Fellowship*. Once a month, forty or so seniors meet in the Fireside Room of the church to sing, hear a devotional, plan parties and outings, and eat lunch together.

Evening
7:00—*Church Visitation and Teen Visitation*. Members go out in pairs to visit those whose names they have been assigned from the prospect files.

WEDNESDAY

Evening
7:00—*AWANA*. The name is an acronym based on II Timothy 2:15— Approved Workmen Are Not Ashamed. It is a club for children

from kindergarten through junior high, complete with uniforms, a flag, and scoutlike awards for achievements in Bible knowledge and church attendance.

—*Mid-Week Service.* After an opening period of singing favorite songs, the pastor delivers a brief Bible study or lesson on Christian living. People then present prayer requests to add to the printed list. The congregation breaks up into groups of three or four, and the groups spend about fifteen minutes praying. As the pianist begins to play, the prayers are concluded, and someone offers a closing prayer for the whole congregation. About once a month this routine is interrupted for a presentation by a missionary, describing work being done in far-flung lands and asking for support.

8:00—*Choir Practice.*

—*Committee Meetings.* Scheduled as needed.

—*Sunday School Planning.* Teams of teachers who work with children meet to plan the next Sunday's activities.

THURSDAY

Evening

7:30—*Ladies Missionary Fellowship.* Women who are interested in missions meet once a month to hear about the work of their missionaries and plan projects to aid and communicate with the missionaries.

—*Academy Parent-Teacher Fellowship.* Southside's version of PTA meets once a month.

—*Committee Meetings.* Scheduled as needed.

FRIDAY

Evening

7:30—*College and Career Bible Study.* Members are mostly students in community or Bible colleges or those working in entry-level jobs. They are generally in their twenties and single and are led by a married man in his thirties. They have an extended time of sharing, testimonies, and prayer requests, and a brief time of Bible study. Afterward, they have refreshments at the church or go out to eat. They also have frequent parties and outings together.

—*Teen Fellowship.* At least once a month some creative activity is planned, and a large group of teens attends.

SATURDAY

—*Bus Visitation.* Bus teams knock on doors along their routes to recruit new riders and remind the old ones to be ready the next morning.

—*Church Family Outing.* Several times a year, the whole church (but especially the young families) gathers to spend the day on a picnic or trip of some sort.

—*Word of Life Marathon.* Several times a year, the Word of Life organization sponsors sports competitions for teams from Fundamental churches. Winners go to regional and national "marathons."

short pews facing the congregation, with the choir arranged in rows behind them. Neither the pastor nor the choir is robed. Behind the choir is an opening through which the baptistry can be seen. When new converts come into the church, this is where they are immersed, a ceremony usually observed on Sunday evening. The central fixtures to which attention is drawn, then, are the baptistry, the pulpit, and the Bible on the communion table.

The pastor who leads this congregation is Ronald Thompson, an attractive man of thirty-five, who has been at the church for nearly seven years. He is the son of a preacher and "surrendered to the ministry" himself at the age of eleven. He was educated through high school and college at a Bible Institute in the Midwest. He met his wife, a graduate of Bob Jones University, while doing church work; and they have two adopted sons. He exudes enthusiasm and good humor, playing the role of friendly big brother to the congregation as he welcomes them to the service. Only when he begins to preach does his enthusiasm become more intense, more passionate. Never, however, does he approach the fervor of a Jimmy Swaggart; his style is more polished, more like Falwell. He looks successful and happy, sounds certain of what he says.

When the pastor, youth minister, music director, and choir file into the auditorium on Sunday morning, the service begins with a rousing chorus from the choir, reminding the congregation that Jesus is coming soon. Throughout the service, although everything is led by those on the platform, there is a feeling of spontaneity and participation. There are no recited prayers or responses, no prayer of confession or words of assurance, no formal call to worship or prayer for the world. The primary components of the service are singing, unrehearsed prayers by the ministers, and preaching. Even the pastor's sermon is not written out in advance.

For those acquainted with the popular revival music of the late nineteenth and early twentieth centuries, the sounds of Southside will be familiar. The opening prelude, played on either piano or organ, is much more likely to be an old gospel song than a piece by Bach or Handel. Likewise, the music sung by congregation and choir bears more resemblance to country and folk styles than to classical. The melodies and harmonies are easy to sing, and the congregation's participation is hearty. Their enthusiastic singing of old favorites like "Have Faith in God" or "Love Lifted Me" or "Power in the Blood" can be contagious.

The newcomer will notice not only the informality and the congregation's enthusiastic participation in singing but also that nearly everyone has brought a Bible. There are no lectionary readings during the service, but when the pastor begins to preach, the members follow his sermon with open Bibles. Rather than focusing on any single biblical passage, he is likely to direct their attention to a dozen or more verses from all parts of the scriptures. His sermon will be organized around three or four easy-to-remember points, the designations for which are often alliterations. A sermon on the hope of the Second Coming, for instance, spoke of that hope as cleansing, comforting, continuing, cautioning, and condemning. It took the twenty-fourth chapter of Matthew as its springboard, but included references from I John, Titus, Daniel, Revelation, I and II Thessalonians, and II Peter.

Along the way, the pastor is likely to remind his hearers that the world is in a sorry state, that divorce and delinquency are rampant, that movies and television are full of pornography, that the teaching of evolution and secular humanism has taken over in the schools, and that despite its proud heritage as God's chosen nation, the United States is in grave danger of destruction. The only answer to any of these problems is to trust Jesus. He can save people from their sins; and before the world reaches its worst state, Jesus will return to rapture his children home to heaven.

As the pastor approaches the end of the sermon, no matter what the previous focus has been, he turns his attention to the "plan of salvation." He pleads with his hearers to examine their hearts and know that they are sinners unworthy to stand before God unless they have trusted in the saving blood of Jesus Christ. They will be reminded that the decision to accept Christ as savior is the only way into heaven. Not only is such a decision essential for salvation, but it must be made now because no one knows when the Lord may come or when death may cut off the opportunity to decide. The service climaxes with the singing of an invitational hymn, during which sinners are urged to walk to the front of the auditorium to declare their willingness to repent and be saved.

When the service closes, the newcomer may notice that many in the congregation remain to visit with friends. The pastor and his wife stand at the back door, greeting those who leave, but the line moves slowly. On cold winter Sundays, it can come almost to a complete halt as people greet each other, retrieve coats from the racks, pick up babies from the nursery, and slowly make their way outside.

The newcomer may leave Southside with a mixture of impressions. On the one hand, the people she has seen seem perfectly "normal." They hold ordinary jobs, have comfortable incomes, live in average houses, have the usual ethnic and religious backgrounds, and have a typical amount of education. On the other hand, neither the style nor the content of their Sunday morning service is at all typical. The newcomer is likely to hear ideas that sound strange to the modern ear. What distinguishes this group of people is not demographic categories but their participation in a social and ideological world that becomes for them all-encompassing. These ordinary people are shaped by the ideas and expectations that have come to be known as Fundamentalism, and those ideas give them their extra-ordinary identity and way of life.

CHAPTER FOUR

Being Always Ready to Give an Answer: Explaining a Distinctive Way of Life

But sanctify the Lord God in your hearts, and be ready always to give an answer to every man that asketh you a reason of the hope that is in you.
—I Peter 3:15

THE RELIGIOUS community of Southside Gospel Church is, among other things, a community of shared ideas. The people who make up that community identify themselves as "believers"—people who have learned both the right questions to ask about life and the right answers. Peter Berger suggests in *The Sacred Canopy* (1969) that such a system of religious ideas can be understood as a dialectic between the ordering of the world it creates and the everyday social interactions of the people who inhabit that world, ideas and social interactions each influencing the other. Bennett Berger reminds us that "ideas are human creations . . . created for purposes, in contexts, and are definable in time and place, by living people who invested themselves in *these* (rather than *those*) ideas" (1981:20, emphasis in original). Understanding this community of shared ideas, then, will involve both exploring the ideas themselves and examining the community processes and everyday habits of life that embody and sometimes modify those ideas. We will begin here by asking what these believers assume to be true and how they arrive at those conclusions, what principles they use for explaining the events of their lives, and how those principles survive in the face of challenges.

World Construction

One of the favorite scriptures at Southside is Romans 8:28: "And we know that all things work together for good to them that love God, to them who are the called according to his purpose." The members of Southside take that verse to mean that God has a purpose for everything and that because they are Christians they will be able to discover and live by God's orderly plan. Just as they are sure that the universe did not originate by chance evolution, so they are also sure that nothing in today's world happens by chance either. Believers can know that God causes everything as surely as they know that day follows night and that for everything there is a season.

In fact, when the people at Southside look at people who are not Christians, part of what they pity is the chaos in which those people seem to live. Believers do not like living with uncertainty. When they have a question, they want an answer. A member who works in state government talked about his colleagues: "The people I work with won't ever make decisions. They like to live in the gray area, and I don't like to live in the gray area." Another member expressed her dissatisfaction with the psychology she had been studying by saying, "I don't find too much satisfaction in 'sharing' when there's not an answer to the problem." In the outside world, there are no rules, no absolutes, no answers. It seems that nothing makes sense any more, that punishment no longer follows crime. An older woman reflected that "nobody seems to know what's immoral." And Janet Slavin said, "There are no lines, I guess, there. You are totally free. And now I realize that lines are definitely better because you'll go too far, as much as you think you won't."

In contrast to the chaos of the outside world, the believer's life is full of order. The ideological world in which Southside members live comes with a detailed and well-marked road map for living the Christian life. Some behavior is required, and other behavior is prohibited. The task of the believer is to find God's will and to follow it to the letter. If God says to be a housewife, be the best one possible. If God says to hire a new pastor, do it with haste and enthusiasm. If God says to build a school, it must be done. And if God says to vote for Ronald Reagan, there can be no other Christian response than to follow God's leading. We will return to the matter of just how believers know God's leading; what is important here is the fact that they are sure God does have a plan and that God's plan leaves little room for individual variation and quibbling.

Not surprisingly, the deity Southside's members worship is equally predictable. Believers relate to God by contract: If I do this, God will do that. At the most basic level, salvation itself is an exchange of belief for eternal life, and the Christian life is an exchange of right living for blessings in this life and the one to come. The more detailed content of the contract is the 7,834 promises members have found in the Bible. These cover everything from safe travel to health and child rearing. God's promises form a kind of rule book for explaining the way the world must work. Believers are confident that God will keep his promises because their God is exact, orderly, and predictable.

Knowing what is right and wrong, what is God's plan and what is not, provides a structure that believers treasure. They know that obedience, trust, and discipline are the virtues God rewards with blessings. Howard Otto talked about how important order and discipline are for him: "Everything is measured against a certain standard, a Christian standard, and the Holy Spirit leads you. . . . That's what I need right now. I need a regimen. I need something to give me guidance." and Joe Slavin put it this way: "I love the absolutes. . . . I'm glad I serve a living God that is absolute. He has all the answers. I don't have responsibility. He gives us all the answers. He makes the decisions for me, and that is great!" Because God's plan is absolutely perfect and totally comprehensive, the response demanded of believers is equally absolute and total: "You either believe God all the way or not at all. Then it begins to add up. If you can believe him on one thing, you gotta believe him on everything." The rules of the Fundamentalist world are clear, and having such rules makes the believer's life more livable than it might otherwise be.

God's plan, then, is not mysterious; it does not require expert interpretation. Ordinary believers can understand and explain it. They claim not only that there is a reason for everything but that they are able to know the reason. One woman said, "Being a Christian, I have a better outlook on the world. I can understand what's going on in the world." Having an explanation for everything is a vital part of being a Fundamentalist. Listen as Jim Forester, Ray Danner, and Bob Hughes explain why certain events happened the way they did.

The Lord moved us here for—there's a reason we live thirty minutes from the church. Why didn't God move us right next door to Southside Gospel Church? There's a reason we live in Westfield. Now certainly the Forester family is not going to evangelize Westfield. But at the same time, if we're following the Lord, if we're in the Lord's will, God can use our testimony in our community to possibly lead somebody to the Lord.

The Lord's hand was in it. I could have married somebody who wasn't interested in spiritual things. . . . Just before the invasion I was given a ship to go over, and I couldn't make that ship. Because I couldn't, I was put on a certain base, and I came in contact with Mary. So I believe the Lord orders things ahead of time, even though you are not saved but will be in the future.

When I was a kid I always used to have the question in my mind, "Why me? Why am I in this body looking out on everything else?" Of course nobody could answer my question. I would ask my folks. They couldn't really give me any solid answer. Now I know Jesus Christ. I can understand why I'm me—because I'm created to be what I am, and everyone else is too.

These people are claiming a special knowledge that is theirs as a result of knowing God so well. Life is not a puzzle at all, at least not if you know the ways of the puzzle maker. With the absolute truth of the Bible and the guidance of the Holy Spirit, any believer can discover the explanation for the events in his or her life.

Believers not only claim special knowledge about their own lives but also claim to understand the history and future of humankind. What they know about the past is that God is the author of everything, and his truth is unchanging. Jesus Christ is "the same yesterday, and today, and forever" (Hebrews 13:8); what is stable and familiar is more likely to be "godly" than something new and different. "Old-time religion," for instance, is the only good kind. The fact that the world outside is always changing only proves just how evil it is.

What Southside members know about the present and the future is that this world will soon come to an end. That one fact explains almost everything else. This exchange with Connie Meyer was not unusual.

INTERVIEWER: Why do you think the world is the way it is?
CONNIE: Because it's coming to an end.

INTERVIEWER: What do you think would make the world a
better place?
CONNIE: Well, the Rapture.

Believers understand that the world's sad state indicates only its impending demise. As one man said, "We *know*, we know where the
end is gonna be."

Many of Southside's members enjoy reading about prophecy
even more than they enjoy reading their Bibles. And when they read
the Bible, they like to turn to Revelation or Daniel or to the prophetic notes provided throughout the Bible by Scofield or Ryrie. For
believers, the Bible is a history book for both past and future. It reports accurately the events of the past, and it presents detailed predictions of things that are yet to come. To discover and interpret
these biblical prophecies, members read books like *The Late Great
Planet Earth* (Lindsey 1970) and weekly newspapers like *The Sword of
the Lord*. They watch the nightly news and remark, "It's just like it
says in the Bible." For the most avid, the day's events can be cross-
referenced by chapter and verse. Three of Southside's members
offered these explanations.

Just the way the nations are aligning now are exactly the way
Ezekiel spoke in Chapter 38. The nations are gonna come
against Israel. And he mentions Ethiopia, Libya, Egypt,
Togarmah, which you know is considered to be Turkey, and the
lands of Gomer and eastern Europe—Poland, Hungary, you
know, all of the countries that have been taken over by Russia.
In particular it mentions . . . Gog and Magog, Meshech and
Tubal. All that means Russia.

We believe in the Second Coming. We believe that a lot of
things that are going on in Iran and Israel really show that the
Lord will be coming really soon, and I am looking forward to
that day.

The time is really close. It's building to a crescendo with the
missiles and the Arabs and the oil, and rebel groups having
atomic weapons, and the wars in Africa, and the movement of
communism today.

Reading the Bible with an eye toward prophecy is not the same
as reading it for its literal meaning. The principles of dispensational

premillennialism are used as an interpretive scheme through which scripture is understood. For the prophetically knowledgeable reader, the words of scripture do not always mean what they seem to mean. For instance, in the book of Daniel, a vision is recounted of events that will take place over a period of seventy weeks. To harmonize the vision with their understanding of history and the future, Fundamentalist readers interpet the seventy weeks as seventy periods of seven years. The years are not 365-day periods, but twelve thirty-day (or "prophetic") months. By assuming a precise date for the return of the Jews to Jerusalem from Babylon and another precise date for Jesus's entry into Jerusalem before his death, sixty-nine of the seventy revised "weeks" fit exactly between. The seventieth week in most prophetic schemes is assumed to be the Tribulation, a seven-year period (usually expected after the Rapture) in which great catastrophe will befall the earth. Because the Tribulation has not yet come, an indefinite gap must be assumed between the sixty-ninth and seventieth weeks to account for the current period in history (see Pentecost 1958). Although this reading of scripture is certainly not literal, it is characterized by the same order and detail that Fundamentalists expect of all God's doings.

One Southside man had carried this meticulous logic to a rather unlikely conclusion. As an amateur mathematician, he was more likely than most to see the promises and analogies of the Bible as like equations. He started with the assumption that these are the "end times" and reasoned backward that Noah's times must have been like these: "The times are right. 'As in the times of Noah, so shall the end times be.' I take that very strongly and without reservation. I believe in the times of Noah they were doing greater things with computers and whatever else than we are today. And when we reach that point —as in the times of Noah—that will be the time when the Lord will reappear." When I questioned him further, he explained that he is convinced that these are the end times because of "the promiscuity of women, the lack of morals, and the freedom. The world knows that a country can rise no higher than the morals of its women."

Although most Southside members do not lay all the blame on women, they do share the feeling that the world is so bad that judgment cannot be far away. One woman saw no alternative to the Lord's quick return. She said, "The way things are going, he's got to. How much worse can it get? He promised it, didn't he?" Her sentiment is echoed by a variety of others.

This is all pointing to the end times. You know, it's hard to talk about our children in college. You know, I don't think they'll ever make it to college. I don't think we'll be around. 'Cause you look at the world, and you say, "How much worse can it get?"

I'm looking for the Rapture. I mean this world is getting so bad that I won't read a newspaper. . . . My brother and I were discussing how close the Rapture is, how near it is. He was saying, "I'm really looking forward to it because it is just so bad that I almost can't stand it any more."

I have been reading *The Sword of the Lord*. He said in the end times men would be lovers of themselves; there would be signs in the sky, different changes in the weather, earthquakes. Just see the way men are living. I see people dancing on TV, and they remind me of Sodom and Gomorrah. . . . I just know that the Lord is not going to let this go on much longer without some kind of judgment.

Perhaps it all points to the fact that this is the last days. Sometimes we who are Christians know that things won't get any better, and this is the only comfort we have as we see things getting worse—that it all points to the fact that Christ is coming.

For the believer, God is in control of the world—past, present, and future. Everything is explainable, even if the explanation is only that things are bound to get worse until Christ returns.

The world Southside members construct, then, is a world in which God is in charge. It is seen as an orderly, well-mapped territory in the midst of an uncharted, chaotic, modern wilderness. In the outside world, the rules are subjective, imperfect, and always changing. Inside, God provides a plan that is clear, objective, and timeless.[1] There are clear rules and understandable answers for all of life's questions.

Assumptions of orderliness and knowable truth pervade the everyday conversations of believers. Just as Eskimos have many words for snow, Fundamentalists have many ways to talk about God's will. They speak of a plan, a purpose, or a reason. They use the image of a jigsaw puzzle in which all the pieces fit or of a metronome or pitch pipe that establishes a perfect standard. When they talk of the future, they add "if God wills," and they attribute the events of the past to a grand heavenly design. When they pray, they ask only for what they hope is in God's will anyway. The existence of a divine plan is the cognitive foundation on which all the believer's assumptions about the world are built.

Knowing that there is a plan does not tell us what is in that plan. What believers assume to be in God's will can be discovered in a variety of ways, but one convenient measure is to listen to how they pray. What they pray about is what they presume God to care most about, and at Southside the most prevalent concern is salvation. Members almost always begin their prayers with thanksgiving for their own salvation, and they would feel remiss if they did not know some unsaved friend or relative for whose salvation they could pray. Members are sure that God's plan for the world and for individuals rests on the universal need to accept Christ as personal savior. Everything is organized around that one fact. Autobiographies are dated "B.C." and "A.D.," and believers often celebrate their spiritual "birthdays" as well as their earthly ones. Jim Forester described how he can now see that God had his life under control even before he was saved: "Looking back upon my, you know, my first exposure to the gospel, I'm amazed and very appreciative of how the Lord kept after me, even though I wasn't saved. I could see how the Lord kept after me. He kept bringing people into my life that were Christian people that would witness to me and be a friend and be someone I could talk to. And they always were Christian people."

Being saved is the first step in God's plan. It opens all the doors that make understanding the rest of God's will possible. In the Fundamentalist theology, God hears the prayers of saved people and watches over their every need. The Holy Spirit becomes available to those who believe, helping them understand the Bible and what it says about God's plan. In sociological terms, the saved are members of the fellowship and participate in constructing explanations about God's will. Being saved provides assurance that one's eternal destiny is in heaven and offers membership in a group that confirms that assurance. The individual exchanges old, selfish, human desires for a socially supported effort to live according to God's will.

Not surprisingly, then, the second most important part of God's plan is that believers should participate in a local church. Once saved, converts should be baptized, join the church, attend at every opportunity, and give generously to all the church's programs. They should use and develop their talents as workers and leaders in the church; and they should witness to their unsaved friends by inviting them to come to church. When Southside members hear sermons about God's will, they are likely to hear about their responsibility to the church.

The importance of the church is also reflected in the prayers of the people. When members present requests at church meetings, the personnel and programs of the church are high on the list. But even when they talk privately about their concerns, they often mention the pastor, the missionaries, and the work of the church. It would seem absurd to believers to suggest that God might not want them to be a part of a church or that Southside should be different from what it is. One of their underlying assumptions about reality is that the basic institution out of which believers build a Christian life is a local church.

That the church should be at the center of the world Fundamentalists construct is not at all surprising. But the divine plan they believe in does not stop at the church door. Southside members search out direction from God on most of the details of their everyday existence. They pray about decisions as important as marriage and vocation and as mundane as what the day's activities should be. They are sure that God cares about what happens to them and, in fact, knows what should and will happen.

When believers talk with each other and address God in their prayers, everyday divine activities are very much in their minds. If they are not married, they look for God's will among the potential mates they know. If they are unemployed or unhappy in their work, they listen for clues to God's vocational plan. Almost anything, good or bad, can be explained as God's doing. God keeps dishes from breaking and locates things that are lost. He supplies friends and offspring. He makes sure cars get fixed at affordable prices. He arranges convenient overtime work schedules and makes hiring and firing more pleasant. He provides clothes and food when they are needed, as well as less essential items like tickets to a rodeo or a pet dog for the children.

Whatever the believer is doing, God is one step ahead, working things out. One family talked about their trip to Europe: "Every morning we prayed for a place to stay that night, and there always was a place. One day we got ahead of schedule, and the Lord wanted to slow us down, and we forgot the clothes and had to go back!" Another family told about a chance meeting that they were sure had been arranged by God.

> We went to Maine for a week, and John had gotten his motorcycle license. We didn't want him to drive home by himself . . . so he wrote a slip of paper with the route on it, and then the next day we would take the same route so we could stop [together]. So, he didn't follow the route, . . . and he had gone three or four hundred miles further than us. The next day, it was just getting dusk, and his motorcycle konked out on the Massachusetts Turnpike, and we were there at the same time. And that has to be the Lord. We couldn't have planned it.

No logic can account for such stories, but God can.

Whenever money is needed, God can be trusted to find it. Ellen McLean told of getting an unexpected tax bill for more than they could pay, but it was followed by an unexpected pay raise for exactly the amount of the bill. Bonnie Towles recounted needing extra money for piano lessons.

> When I started praying for a new job I asked the Lord for something extra this time. . . . Jimmy is showing an interest in piano, so I asked that when the Lord provided the new job that he would provide money to buy a piano and pay for lessons for Jimmy. So when I got the offer at the nursery school, I was just sure it was gonna cover everything, and it didn't. . . . First I was a little bit downhearted, and then I said, "Well, Jimmy, the Lord doesn't feel that this is the right time for you. Maybe next year." A couple of weeks after school started I got two phone calls about taking care of children, and so there it is.

Another of the things God plans is where people live. Connie Meyer claimed that God had arranged for a new nursing home to be built near Southside so that she could live near church. An older woman who had just moved into a new apartment said, "I really think my prayer was answered. If you keep at it, you'll get what you pray for eventually if it is what he wishes for you to have." And Bonnie gave all the credit to God for their new house.

> This house is directly put here by the Lord. We were in Centerville for six years, and four of those years I was traveling back and forth to Southside. . . . For two years straight I prayed and

several people with me about moving to Valley View. . . . I remember saying to pastor one day, "When the Lord decides
we're gonna move, our feet are never gonna touch the ground."
And it was like that. Our house sold in four days. . . . By the
time we saw our direction and we came to the builder, this was
the only lot left, and somebody else was already showing interest in it. But because we could spend must have been just two or
three hundred dollars more than this other family, that's how
we got here. It was all the Lord's timing.

The world believers construct is thus one in which God has an
orderly and absolute plan and knows exactly what will happen. Life
has rules and reasons; the believer's task is to live according to the
rules and understand the reasons.[2] To the extent that the individual
person's will is surrendered to the divine will, "all things work together for good." To the extent that anyone seeks to live without
God, chaos results.

For the individual, knowing what is expected often provides a
kind of structure and discipline that brings life under control. Joe
Slavin explained it this way: "It is a great feeling to know that when I
fall into sin . . . he is not going to let me get away with it, and that is
great. I need chastening. And I need his powerful hand to come
down upon me when I make mistakes. I need his blessing, too, when
I do something right, that peace and joy that you get." Fundamentalism provides clear definitions of right and wrong that sharpen
the conscience and make such feelings of remorse and joy possible.
People who struggle for years to find some meaning in life or to understand the conflicts in their own souls may find in Fundamentalism a set of answers that by definition resolves their anxieties. For
those whose private hell was uncertainty, the command to believe
without doubting is their salvation. For others, whose hell was lone-
liness or depression, the command to be faithful members of a local
church provides relationships and activities that become their salvation. Connie, for instance, talked about how church helped her to
"stay out of the dumps" by keeping her busy "doing his will as much
as I can." Although Southside's theology proclaims that salvation is
by grace, their practice more nearly resembles the disciplined observances of Old Testament Judaism. It is, in fact, in obeying the rules
that believers experience God's favor.

For the members of Southside, the orderly world of Fundamentalism is indeed a sheltering canopy, a defense against the terrible chaos they perceive in the modern world and sometimes feel within their own souls. Berger's description of religious world building is especially apt for them: "The sacred cosmos, which transcends and includes man in its ordering of reality, thus provides man's ultimate shield against the terror of anomy. To be in a 'right' relationship with the sacred cosmos is to be protected against the nightmare threats of chaos. To fall out of such a 'right' relationship is to be abandoned on the edge of the abyss of meaninglessness" (1969: 26–27). The social constructions of Fundamentalism enable believers to protect themselves from a world that denies that absolute order is possible. Where explanation is not possible, God does not exist; and without God life would be unthinkable. The social world of Fundamentalism, then, is built on the assumption that explanation is possible, and it extends wherever a community of believers is able to share in the process of sustaining those explanations.

World Maintenance

In a world where the rules for living are absolute and clear for anyone to see, it is not surprising that the authority supporting those rules is equally unequivocal. When Southside members are asked —as they often are—why they believe as they do, they turn immediately to the Bible. For them, it *is* God's Word, and it contains the answer to whatever questions they or anyone else might have. Because it is God's Word, it is complete and true. As one man put it, "It's not a fairy tale. It's something that actually happened." The stories of the Bible are not to be confused with the mythologies of other peoples: Biblical stories are about the one true God and are not the product of human imagination. Likewise, because God is the timeless author of every word and story, the Bible need not be interpreted in a historical or literary context. Each word is equally valid, and each sentence is equally timeless and useful. The way one man said it reflects the belief of the whole group: "I believe the Bible is the inspired word of God, from the first word to the last."[3]

Believers recognize that a great deal of what they hear and see in everyday life seems to contradict scripture. They know that most people believe things that seem completely out of keeping with the

Bible. Non-Fundamentalist Christians often attempt to reconcile modern ideas about the world with biblical accounts. These other Christians see no inherent conflict between the findings of biology or geology and a belief that the Bible is also true.

Not so with Fundamentalists. If Genesis says "day," it means twenty-four hours. If it says that man is created in the image of God, then human beings can have nothing in common with any lower animals. According to the members of Southside, anyone who contradicts the "plain words of scripture" is doing the work of Satan, whether they know it or not. As one man put it, "Satan attacks the word of God anyway. He starts off attacking in Genesis, particularly Genesis and Revelation. In Genesis his downfall is prophesied, and in Revelation it is completed; and he doesn't like either one. So he tries to throw out the beginning by bringing in evolution, and throw out the ending by saying that man does not owe anything to God. And then, there you come up with the atheist."

The Bible, however, is not just to be believed; it is to be lived. To say that a preacher "never strayed from the Bible" is to give him the highest compliment. Believers judge their own conversations by how "biblical" they are—in their words, "to make sure that I'm saying something scriptural," to "explain with scripture, not just using my own words." Knowing the Bible is the highest measure of one's success as a Christian. To "know the Bible all the way through" is the goal of those who want to be better Christians. In sum, the Bible is the standard by which all conduct should be judged.

> Our line is drawn. If it is against what we believe and what the Bible says, we will not do it.

> Of course, when you accept the Lord, you accept the Bible, and you accept God's Word. And if God says it, then there's really no argument.

Statements such as these reveal the symbolic importance of the Bible to this group. The words *scriptural* and *biblical* are synonymous with *good*. The ultimate authority to which believers turn in everyday practice is not the God of scripture but the scripture itself.[4] The world they construct is maintained through constant application of biblical "mortar."

A reverence for the idea of scriptural authority does not, however, say much about how that authority takes shape. The Bible, after all, is a large and complex book from which a variety of arguments can be made about how one should live as a Christian. Even the fact that the Bible comes in various translations reflects the ambiguity of some of the original texts and of the translation process. But at Southside ambiguity is greatly reduced. At Southside, the King James Version is *the* Bible, with some referring to modern translations as "perversions." Although many members read the New International Version, the New American Standard, or even the Living Bible, they always refer back to the King James as the standard.

> Perhaps the newer version, the way they have gotten it written up today, you might be able to understand it better, but I mean to read it as it is written [in the King James Version].

> [I bought a modern] version, an English version, but it's a little too summarized, so I go back and read the Bible—the two together.

To read the bible "as it is written" is to read the King James Version. In it are found "the exact words of scripture."

Referring to one translation as authoritative helps in clarifying what the Bible says, but that still does not explain how all the sometimes contradictory words of even one translation get transformed into simple rules for living a Christian life. To understand how Southside members actually use scripture, it is necessary to know what they mean by a "proof text." The name comes from the idea of supporting an argument by finding the "texts" that are the "proof" of God's answer. Any portion of scripture, no matter how small, can be used. In fact, small portions (verses or parts of verses) are most often cited. The pastor's sermons are usually built on a word or phrase from the Bible. People memorize verses for each day or week. And it is to individual verses that people turn when they are looking for answers to questions. Although they often read the Bible from cover to cover, believers rarely refer to the themes of the whole Bible or even to whole books or stories. Rather, they "search the scripture" to find the word or phrase that seems to answer the question at hand.

Those discrete units of scripture, then, contain the crucial elements of God's message to the believer. In addition, because the Bible is timeless, each word is as true today as it was when it was written. One man shared with an adult Sunday School class how God had given him such a timeless message. He had been worried about whether to buy a new tent from Sears because the last one he bought there leaked. He was just about to leave for the store when he sat down to search the scriptures one more time. He turned to Deuteronomy 14 and began to read. In the fifth verse, among the list of animals that Jews would be permitted to eat, he found the name "roebuck." Because roebuck was on the list of things God approved of, the man concluded that he should indeed buy his tent from the Sears Roebuck Company.

Connie Meyer had a similar experience in trying to decide how to get to a revival meeting one night: "I knew my mother would be all upset if they knew I was taking a taxi instead of the van. So, before I made up my mind completely to take the taxi—I had my mind almost made up—but I opened the Bible. And would you believe what my eyes fell on? The verse that says that if I shall set you free, you are free indeed. Now that was the answer to that prayer, right there. So I knew I was right. So I took the taxi." Another family struggled with whether to tell their children about the child the husband had fathered while separated from his wife (and before he was saved). They kept coming back to John 8:32: "The truth shall make you free." That verse was God's message to them that they should make the past known and then deal with the consequences. For Howard Otto the Bible had been a source of advice and comfort.

> In the last year, with my problem, I've had to search the scriptures to find comfort and to find direction. I've memorized a number of verses that just seemed to be comforting. . . . Mostly they tend to be on waiting: "They that wait upon the Lord shall mount up with wings like eagles. . . ." "Be anxious for nothing, but in all things through prayer and thanksgiving make your requests known to God."

Each of these people went to the Bible to find something specific. They expected to find there a word or verse that would apply directly to their situations, that would give them an authoritative answer.

But any of the verses through which they heard God's message could have contained a different message for another person in another situation. The Bible can prove itself a flexible book, informing, shaping, and then ratifying decisions that need to be made. As long as the choice being made conforms to other basic guidelines, the range of possible "biblical" decisions is broad indeed. Once made and connected to scripture, the choice becomes absolute and authoritative, but that position masks the personalized, flexible process by which individual needs and biblical material are brought together.

The Bible provides not only practical and ethical guidance but also scientific information about the physical universe and the history of the world. Biblical truth concerns both what "ought" to be and what is and was. Everything God wants people to know is contained in scripture. As one young convert put it, "The Bible is the ultimate scientific approach."

Conversely, whatever is accepted as true must, of necessity, be in the Bible somewhere. Believers, for instance, do not suppose that the world is flat or that there are oceans above the skies. They accept as true the common understanding that the earth is round, but they are unwilling to think that theirs is a new truth, unknown to the writers of the Bible. After all, God wrote every word, and surely God knew that the earth is round. That dilemma is resolved by finding in the Psalms the phrase "the circle of the earth." That phrase proves to the believer that the earth's roundness is a fact contained in scripture. There simply are no truths for human beings to discover that are not already revealed in the Bible. Again, the Bible proves a flexible enough authority to accommodate much that is new in the world.

Given this attitude toward the Bible as a scientific authority, it is not surprising that the people of Southside have a mixed attitude toward education. As is typical in American society, they hold college graduates and postgraduates in esteem (and some awe). Especially respected are those with technical skill or people who have written books. However, believers are equally likely to see higher education as somewhat useless. An educated preacher was described thus: "He'd get up there every week, and he'd philosophize about these twelve-letter words, and he'd get off on his own little trip. You needed a dictionary to find out what was going on." The knowledge that really counts comes from the Bible and is available to all those who have the Holy Spirit to guide them.

Biblical authority is thus the basis for what believers know about the world as well as for how they choose to live. Still, that does not entirely answer the question of how the rather massive volume of scripture gets translated into everyday rules. It seems at times that messages almost leap off the page. Sometimes people actually open the Bible and point a random finger, believing that God will guide them to what he wants them to read. More often, however, individual searching of the scripture is guided by some other source of authority. The believer is not simply left alone with the Bible and the Holy Spirit to work out a way to live the Christian life. The authority of the Bible takes concrete form in the human authority of the church and its leaders.

By far the most important of the human authorities in the believer's life is the pastor. The pastor provides both specific interpretations of scripture and a model for applying the Bible to the dilemmas of modern life. Faithful members can hear the pastor's expositions four or more times a week—in Sunday School, two Sunday sermons, a Wednesday night devotional, plus radio messages and talks to various small groups. By shear quantity of influence his authority would be strong, but for Fundamentalists the matter is also one of principle. The pastor is mandated by scripture to be the "shepherd" of the flock. Although he may incorporate democratic procedure and gentle persuasion into his means of governance, the pastor expects to be the leader.[5] And when Fundamentalists join a church they expect to submit themselves to the authority of the pastor.

This pattern of authority and submission is seen as the biblical model for all social institutions. At home, there are husbands and fathers to be obeyed; at work, there are bosses; and in the government, there are duly elected officials. The ideal is for each of these authorities to be acting in concert, with God's will in mind. But even if that is not the case, Christians must still obey. In the long term, believers are likely to try to discontinue their relationships with ungodly authorities, but in the short term they must submit. For instance, when Joe Slavin was confronted by his boss about witnessing on the job, Joe knew that God was telling him to get a new job; but, in the meanwhile, he said, "I have to follow his orders because I was working for him. I can't disobey orders." It is God's will that on earth some people make decisions and give orders, while others must obey. When members of Southside are asked why they do what they do, they may answer that someone in authority told them to do it. If they are asked further why they should obey that authority, they will say that the Bible says they should, and no one may doubt the word of God.[6]

Referring to scriptural and pastoral authority is one of the primary ways that the people of Southside maintain and repair the world they have constructed for themselves. When challenged or puzzled, they know how to find an answer. Yet no one stops to think about every decision. Most of what everyone does every day is done by habit, simply because it has come to be expected. The members of Southside are no different, except that even their reflexes and habits have come under the influence of the Fundamentalist world of which they are a part. The very words they use to describe their lives come from the Bible and from the pulpit. When asked how they know that something is God's will, they are likely to say that they "just know." The principles by which God's will operates have become so ingrained in their thinking that they no longer need any aids to making decisions. In many cases the socialization into this religious world view is as complete as is humanly possible. Many have literally lost the ability to imagine themselves living by any other rules.

It's hard for me to think of how I would be if I weren't [a Christian].

Now it's a part of me, you know.

I can't imagine! I often wonder where I would be, what I would be doing if I wasn't a Christian.

Although the big decisions may still take some reflection, the day-to-day ones come by experience and reflex.[7]

That does not mean that on the whole finding God's will is easy. After taking account of what the authorities say and what has been learned by experience, the believer may still find God's will by looking for "signs" and relying on a great deal of hindsight. God rarely delivers precise, detailed instructions in advance. I met only one person who claimed to receive verbal messages from God, and she has left the congregation to join a Pentecostal church. For most Southside members, deciding what God wants them to do may be a matter of judgment; and sometimes, they admit, it is just plain hard to know: "See, that's my biggest problem. I really don't know. The only thing I can do is to live my life as best I can, in accordance with the teachings of the church and the Bible, and put myself where I belong. And then I assume that whatever happens is the Lord's will." Sometimes, only the church and the Bible stand between the believer and total uncertainty.

The role of hindsight in this process cannot be overestimated. It is most often as they look back that believers see the patterns in their lives. Order becomes apparent only after all the facts are in. In the midst of a situation, God's hand may seem almost hidden. One woman talked about her frustration in arranging the timing between the sale of her house and the opening of the apartment complex into which she moved: "I developed a nervous stomach because I wanted the sale of the house to go through at the same time these were ready. . . . And I couldn't get into here, and, oh dear! But it worked out beautifully. Heavens, the Lord was just good to us. He smoothed it all out in the end." Only in the end could she celebrate God's control. Rebecca Hughes admitted that she was not sure of the Lord's leading when she took her present job: "I went in because I thought, 'Well, if I don't take it, somebody else will.' And I don't think I was more led to take it because I felt the Lord leading me. But now I know he was leading me." Her husband, in turn, talked about how he knows when his prayers have been answered: "Anything that I ask him that's in his will, he'll give it to me. I mean, if I'm asking something for my own selfish reason, I guarantee I'm not gonna get it. But if I ask in keeping with his character and something I know is his will or revealed in his word, then it's good." Again, the Bible helps, and—although Bob does not say it directly—so does hindsight. At the time he makes the request, he assumes that it is in God's will, else he would not bother asking. Only after looking back can he know that the things he has not gotten must have been selfish requests.

Such dependence on hindsight and habit as indicators of God's will leaves open enormous space for human interpretation. Because all of life is expected to fit the pattern of a master plan, the habits and exigencies of everyday life can be sanctified in retrospect. What people do as a matter of economic and social necessity or choice becomes as much divine imperative as what they do in response to direct biblical instruction. As a result, many of the things believers see as God's will are not at all at odds with "selfish" ends. For instance, several families had struggled with how to buy a house when prices and interest rates were so high. Even though they were sure that God intended for women to be full-time homemakers, they concluded that the greater good of owning a house outweighed the temporary problems of going to work. Elaine Young explained how they made the decision: "We had umpteem discussions. Is it all by faith, and we just keep being faithful, serving in the church, doing what we should be doing, and I can stay at the nursery school and let the Lord provide? If he wants us to have a house, he will. To the other extreme of: Well, God works in everyday measures, and what does it take nowadays for people to get a house? It takes both working." Janet Slavin was sure that God wanted her to go back to work: "We knew that one day we would like to have a home, and we weren't going to be able to save without something a little extra. I wasn't really looking for another job, but one day I believe the Lord had me look at the help-wanted page. I happened to look there, and it said, "Maternity Warehouse opening up at the Knox Corner Shopping Center." And here I was pregnant, and who else would hire someone who was pregnant!" In neither case was the goal of buying a house questioned. In both cases finding God's will meant finding a way to pursue that goal.

Finding the right church presents similar problems. Believers are sure that God wants them to belong to a local church, but the choice often depends on the mundane considerations of distance, friendships, the pastor's style, or the particular programs that are offered. The individual needs and tastes of the members help them determine what seems to be God's will: "He wanted us at Southside, and maybe God let all that happen to show us and to make us appreciate more the ministry of Southside. And looking back on it, I think that's exactly what he did. . . . What matters is the Lord's will and serving the Lord and the ministry that's right for us and for our family." Again, hindsight is important, but so are the desires of the believer.

When the members of Southside are searching for God's will, they often say that they are looking for "open doors." They are looking for opportunities that seem too good to be coincidental. Sometimes these opportunities confirm in their minds that the decision they have made is the right one. At other times, an "open door" may prod them in a direction they might not previously have chosen. Happening to look at the want ads and seeing the perfect job seemed too good to Janet not to be God's leading. Similarly, Joe's move from truck driver to accountant was hastened by happenings that seemed too good not to come from God. Janet told the story:

> I saw the Lord's hand intervene. Joe happened to be talking about the Lord again, I guess, in Winston, in one of the

schools. And one of the women who was a cafeteria person, who was also a Christian, couldn't believe she heard Joe talking about the Lord. "You're a young guy talking about the Lord!" And she was happy about that, and she said to Joe, "What's your major anyway? Did you go to school?" And he said, "Yeah. I'm an accounting major." She said, "You are? And you're delivering milk here? I'm going to talk to my husband. He is in the city. I'm going to see if he can get you an interview, just to get you in there." . . . It was unbelievable. That woman called back, or had her husband call, and said, "Come in Monday morning for an interview." Joe went that day, and it was the next day or the one after that they called that he was accepted!

Looking for open doors does not always lead to such happy results. When I asked Jim Forester what was most frustrating about his life, he quickly answered, "My job. I don't care for it. Well, I appreciate it. It must be the Lord's will because, when I left my previous employer in Ohio, I quit the job. I resigned without another job to go to. And we prayed that the Lord would help me to find another job, so here it is." There are clearly perils in interpreting every seemingly good opportunity as God's will.

Another way to find God's will is to accept that God also closes doors: "Sometimes it will be that things will happen. Maybe if we are praying, and it is impossible to have it. Or, you ask the Lord to show you. I don't know; it is different in every situation. . . . I feel strongly about it, or really peaceful about it. Or, I ask the Lord to close the door to that or open it. Not literally, he doesn't, but he will make it possible, as far as if you want something, and he doesn't want you to have it." Again, the closed doors are sometimes seen in hindsight. The McLeans, for instance, talked about how he had pursued what looked like an attractive job. In fact, it seemed that "the Lord dangled it in our faces." But it did not work out, and only then did they discover (or admit) that it would have meant more traveling than he wanted and therefore must not have been the Lord's will. Another family talked about almost taking a job, then not being able to find a house. After God closed that door, they discovered that the job was not such a good one after all.

Sometimes it is clear that God has help in closing doors. Jim Forester not only admires Pastor Thompson (and dislikes his own current job) but also entertains thoughts of becoming a preacher himself. From time to time he responds to invitations at church to make public his willingness to preach "if God calls." He explained: "As you can see, I'm not a preacher today, but it's not something that never enters my mind. . . . I talked with my wife about it, and I also believe that if the Lord calls me, he's gonna have to call her. It just can't be me. . . . She doesn't feel that definitely right now. I'm not saying that I do either. But what I'm saying is that if that is what the Lord wants me to do, I'll do it." The more we talked, the more it became apparent that Doris feels definitely indeed that she is not called to be a pastor's wife, and her desires help God to keep that door closed for Jim.

In another instance, it was the pastor who closed the door. Janet Slavin has a college degree in early childhood education and was slated to teach at Southside Academy when she discovered she was pregnant. The pastor decided that her contract should be terminated. She recalled the conversation with him: "The pastor said, 'You are an answer to prayer. We have a deficit, and eliminating one teacher's salary, yours, will help us out. . . . We'll combine two classes together.' For a split second I was hurt, and then I realized it was the Lord's will, that I was going to be trained to be a mother now, not a teacher." Even in this potentially disturbing situation, she could maintain her faith in God's orderly plan for her life by accepting the authority of the pastor. In addition, the Bible had taught her to value the role of mother, and that decision would be enthusiastically supported by other church members. Even when God closes a door, the community of believers provides the explanations.

God's will, then, is discerned in cooperation with fellow believers and with "spiritual eyes" that are trained to see God opening and closing doors. That process was particularly apparent as Bonnie described how she got her job at the nursery school.

I think it was around April or May I began to just, you know, on a daily basis just ask that he keep me right where he would have me. And in June my boss told me that he had changed jobs. I was out of a job because he wouldn't be getting a secretary with his new job, and so that's that. So where would the Lord have me to be? It is not there; that's clear. But where would the Lord have me to be? I wanted to only be in Christian service. . . . So that when I lost that job I knew whatever job I got next, it would be somehow in service for the Lord. . . . I also knew that the Lord wouldn't have me to not be here for the children. I feel that it is important for me to be with them. Several girls from the nursery school said, "Well, we're gonna pray you into the nursery school. Do you mind?" And I said, "Let the Lord have his way." And that's how it worked out. So that's why I'm here.

As a part of the community of believers, she had learned to value being in Christian service and being available for her children. When she left the job hunting in the Lord's hands, her fellow church members helped the Lord open a door. Such everyday communication in an organized group of believers often provides the answer to prayer. The will of God is discovered through participation in the community of faith.

It is tempting to be cynical about this tailoring of divine plan to individual desire, but such fitting of ideas to circumstances is the stuff of which all social life is made. Neither practices nor ideas can long exist in isolation from each other. When the existing ideas do not seem to match the existing circumstances, what is needed is "ideological work" (Berger 1981). Such work is particularly necessary in situations—like that at Southside—where ideology plays a primary role. Swidler (1986) points out that in "settled" lives, ideology takes a back seat to habit and routine. But the people of Southside are inhabitants of a world they see as "unsettled" and in need of new explanations. In such times and places, leaders and followers alike work especially hard to make sure that ideas are tightly linked to each other and to action. If Fundamentalism is to replace competing explanations and patterns of behavior, it must do its ideological work carefully.

Building and maintaining a world where God's will can be discovered is a difficult business. Living with absolute rules and explainable reasons does not always seem to work, especially when there are constant challenges from a skeptical outside world. Southside members may not always know the answers, but they at least know where the answers can be found. For believers, the ultimate and absolute authority is scripture. And scripture is brought to life in the words of the pastor, church leaders, and Christian friends. All these things working together help them to know when God is opening and closing doors and what they should do in response. To refer to scriptural authority, to respect and learn from the pastor, and to look for signs of God's activity are the habits of mind that support a world where there is order and reason. They are the principles that maintain the believer's world and legitimize it.

The Problem of Theodicy

Knowing that God has everything under control may be comforting, but it can pose serious theological dilemmas. As Berger (1969) points out, theodicy is a particular problem for people who, like Fundamentalists, posit a God who is both all-powerful and all-righteous. If God could change things and wants to change things, why does God allow evil to persist?

Such theoretical intricacies, however, are rarely of concern to the people at Southside. Most of their efforts at dealing with suffering and death are pretheoretical—that is, they are likely to draw on whatever explanation seems most appropriate to a particular situation without having worked out a comprehensive explanation for the presence of evil in a world created and run by God. One theologically educated Sunday School teacher tried for several weeks to introduce his class to these broader questions, totally without success. They were quite content to use the partial answers they had already learned, searching out individual reasons for individual tragedies.

The most common explanations believers give for suffering are that humans are sinful and that Satan is present in this world. Believers see the world and their lives as arenas for the battle between good and evil, God and Satan, their saved natures and the unredeemed humanness that remains. Because human beings chose to rebel against God in the beginning, all of us are doomed to living in an imperfect world. The suffering that besets us is at least indirectly a result of our fallen condition. When a drunk driver runs off the road and kills himself, his sinfulness seems clearly to provide the explanation for his death. When he also kills an innocent family, the explanation, although less clear, still holds. In a world where Satan has power, sin brings evil consequences. Believers may be sure that un-

forgiven sin will be judged by God. That, for instance, is the reason
Bonnie gave for her father's death.

> My dad had a heart attack at Christmas time. So he came home
> from the hospital, and he went back into the same type of life
> that he was leading. And I feel that the Lord gave him a second
> chance. He gave him three weeks, and at the end of three weeks,
> right to the day, he was dead. And it was on his way to church.
> . . . He would sing a solo most Sundays, and on Saturday night
> he would sing at a restaurant where there was drinking and
> stuff. And I think the Lord decided that he gave him that gift of
> singing, and he wasn't going to allow him to misuse it any
> more.

Sometimes, however, the person who suffers is not a person
who willingly participates in Satan's activities. Believers expect, in
fact, to be attacked by Satan and made to suffer just because they are
Christians. Such suffering is not a result of their sinfulness; on the
contrary, it is a kind of badge of righteousness. Those who are most
faithful to God are singled out by Satan for his worst attacks. Also,
new converts should expect to be persecuted.

> There are a lot of things that you can warn them against, the
> fact that Satan is going to try and discourage you right away.
> You have to warn new Christians right away so they will be
> prepared.

> When we were married, right away my husband became sick,
> and then we had three children right in a row. Our last child
> was born with a birth defect. Being a new Christian, with hardly
> any time to grow, I was so busy raising a family that I became
> sick myself, nervous and all, because of so many trials. Satan was
> really trying.

When there seems to be no other reason, it may be that good people
suffer because Satan is persecuting them. This "theodicy of dualism"
—God versus Satan—enables Southside members to avoid attribut-
ing their pain to an all-powerful, righteous God or to their own sin.

The activity of Satan is particularly apparent to Southside members in the special kind of day-to-day suffering they endure when

they encounter opposition from nonbelievers. Members rarely keep their differences in belief and lifestyle a secret. They often speak up for what they believe by witnessing to their friends and colleagues. Such interaction with outsiders is often described as a battle, with Satan providing the power for the opposition. When believers live the way God wants them to live, they expect Satan to attack in the form of ridicule and hostility from outsiders. Rather than retreating or calling a truce, believers plunge into the fray, glorying in the knowledge that this suffering is the special lot of the strongest believers: "You know, we Christians think sometimes—oh, we have some of our hard days. We have problems here, maybe witnessing, maybe we've been humiliated and things like that. But you know, it says in scripture, we think we have suffered a lot for the cause of Christ; but like it says, we haven't suffered nothing at all yet."

Although it is Satan who does the attacking, it is God who allows the trials to come; and the lines of causality are not always clear in the thinking of Southside members. They speak of their difficulties as "battle experience" and see them as a necessary part of the Christian life. And because the trials may result in good, the trials themselves are often attributed directly to God. Believers say that God sends suffering to make them strong or to test their faith. As one woman said of a friend's illness, "The Lord has to give us something to keep us trusting him, to test us." Although the theologians may have worked out ways to explain how a righteous God could be the originator of suffering, the people at Southside do not worry about the philosophical niceties. Their concern is to find a reason that places their suffering in the divine scheme of things. If God is truly in control of everything, he must be in control of suffering too: "A lot of people think that everything that happens to them is just their misfortune. They don't realize that it is the Lord that is doing this to them."

As with everything else in their lives, the people of Southside approach suffering and death with confidence that there are knowable reasons, that evil events somehow fit into God's plan. At heart, this is the "theodicy of masochism" that Berger describes (1969: 55–58). Believers are eager to surrender their own selfish desires to the will of God, no matter what that will may be. If God's will includes suffering, so be it. It is better to die on the mission field, if

God so wills, than to live in luxury at home, if God does not will. It is better to be ridiculed and ostracized for speaking out than to be loved by ungodly people.

Yet, certain elements here moderate the blindness of the believer's surrender to God. Although God's will may determine their destiny, Southside members believe they can know the rules by which God acts. Only when they find themselves without an explanation, not knowing a reason, do they feel despair. Without an explanation for suffering, God's presence seems remote, and doubts arise. That is what happened to Doris Forester when her mother died: "I always thought that there was a reason for this; there has to be a reason. Maybe it was because my uncle, her brother, who was an alcoholic, maybe he'll turn to the Lord because of this. But it was not any great earth-shaking thing that happened because mother died. So for a few years I was pretty turned off on God. This isn't fair that my mother should have to die when there's evil people in the world that are still alive." If there had only been a reason, she would have felt satisfied that God was still on his throne, that the world was still working as she understood it should.

At the opposite extreme, Connie Meyer, who has been handicapped since birth, can suggest several explanations for her condition: "But I just know that he made me this way; and well, here I am. I mean, if he wanted me running around, I could run around." This explanation reflects a kind of blind surrender, but she also reaches for a more tangible reason: "If I wasn't handicapped, who knows if I would have been saved or not." Because it is God's will that everyone be saved, anything that leads in that direction must also be part of his plan. Likewise, it is God's will that saved people tell others about their salvation. That need to witness helped Connie explain another of her difficulties: "I lost my voice. Well, it was like this: I lost it for a reason, and when he became number one to me, he gave it back to me for another [reason] . . . to tell people about him, what else?" Part of what makes suffering endurable is knowing why it happened.

The idea that any given instance of suffering can be explained as God's will is far more important to Southside members than having a logically consistent theory about the presence of evil in the world. Their explanations grow out of a larger understanding that God has an orderly plan and that his plan includes individual salvation, witnessing, going to church, and living by scriptural rules. If people step outside that plan, they can expect to suffer the consequences. But even if they are living as they should, they may still suffer. If their difficulties are not a result of sin, they can still be explained as part of some larger good. Even (or perhaps especially) in the midst of hard times, the people of Southside know they can find reasons that will make sense of their lives.

I found, unfortunately, that I'm much closer to him in time of personal turmoil than I am whenever things are going along just fine.

It's been a good life—ups and downs—but if we didn't have the downs, we wouldn't appreciate the ups.

Again, Connie talks about the good that has come of her suffering: "I'm not trying to brag at all, but I know in my heart that he means more to me than he does to the rest of you. I know that because I can sit around and see him. I just see him." Bonnie reflected that years in an unhappy marriage had helped her to grow: "I left my husband. I went back to my home town, and I found that I was just as miserable there as I was at home with my husband. . . . Like I said, I had no really spiritual growth. I didn't have enough sense to know that I wasn't in his direct will, . . . but he allowed all of these things to happen, and only so that he could bring me to where I'm at now." No more explanation is needed. If the believer grows in faith, learns patience, learns to trust God more, the trials of life are bearable. To fail to find such an explanation for suffering is, by definition, to fall from the faith.

To succeed in finding an explanation for suffering has the added benefit of increasing believers' ability to tell others about their faith. If they have endured, and in fact grown from, hard times, they feel they have more about which to testify. They are able to identify with the struggles of others and to answer objections. One young man recalled the problems he had had with alcohol and drugs before his conversion. He regretted having lived such a hard life, but he saw his previous experience as a way to convince others that God can change lives. Being such "living proof" is reason enough to justify suffering.

To say that believers look for the good that will come out of their suffering is not to imply that they find suffering easy. They recognize that trials can cause some people to lose their faith, to fall into doubting. They know that only the strong survive with explanations about the blessings that have come from suffering, and the explanations may come only with time. Those who survive to find those explanations are the people who have learned to draw on the divine and social resources that are available through the church.

While people are in the midst of their suffering, the only resource the church may be able to offer is what Berger calls a "theodicy of incarnation" (1969:76–78). Because God himself became human and suffered, human agony can become more bearable. Howard Otto seemed to understand that: "It hasn't been pleasant. I don't know why the Lord has allowed this. But as my attorney said, he says, 'Howard, my savior suffered for me; who am I not to suffer?'" Incarnation means that God understands the depths of human woe. That God could walk beside the believer through "the valley of the shadow of death" can be immensely comforting. The people of Southside are sure that no trouble could ever be too big for God: "You're not supposed to carry it on your own shoulders. You're supposed to give it to the Lord. He has the strength to carry your troubles." A woman who came to the United States after World War II was especially eloquent in recalling her experience.

> My family owned a lot of property, and one day they lost everything, and they were left penniless and homeless. The only thing, their bodies were covered. So it is something that we made sure, that God is something we can't lose. . . . You know he is there, in your moments of despair or loneliness, like I went through—like I was homesick and in a way depressed, and it was a strange country for me, . . . but I knew that God was there, and I knew that I could talk to him. I could pray to him, and I knew that after each prayer I felt I gained something, like you have real black thoughts and then it seems like it is lighter once you get through.

Sometimes when Southside people are in the midst of suffering, they pray not so much for understanding or comfort as for a miracle. They are confident that if it is his will, God can always remove any problem; and when the suffering is over, they are sure to give God the credit. When people get well, they believe that God has provided a cure (although they still take their medicine). Whatever the problem, God promises to provide a "way of escape," even if that escape is simply good sense or hard work.

A final resource Southside members have to survive their difficulties is the hope of heaven. We have already seen that the outside world is described as inherently evil and full of suffering, ripe for the return of Christ. Believers are sure that God will not permit this vale of tears to continue much longer. Christ's imminent return will change every trouble into joy in heaven. This "other-worldly theodicy" (Berger 1969:70–71) is at the heart of every other explanation they offer: "If we didn't have heaven to look forward to, it would be a pretty gloomy world. . . . That's one of the reasons the Lord has given us eternal life." A woman who cares for chronically ill and dying patients says that she often tells them, "There will be riches untold in heaven, and no more gnashing and crying. There'll be peace." And Connie reflects on her current suffering by comparing it to the future: "A lot of people may think that a handicapped person may feel inferior. Maybe in some ways you can't help it, a little bit. . . . I look at people walking around, and I wonder what it would be like, believe me. . . . And I hope when we get to heaven, I'll be walking around too."

For the members of Southside, then, even funerals can be a time to rejoice. The reasons they rejoice are reflective of the various theodicies they employ. If the person who has died was a Christian, they find glory in the thought that their brother or sister is no longer bound by earthly pain and woe and is now in the paradise of heaven. To this extent, theirs is an other-worldly theodicy. If the deceased died after a debased life, they can explain the evil of his or her life and death in terms of the struggle between God and Satan and take comfort in knowing that God will eventually win. To this extent theirs is a theodicy of dualism. For those left behind to sorrow, there is the comfort of casting their cares on Jesus, who can understand all the problems of human existence. To this extent, theirs is a theodicy of incarnation. And, finally, believers search for reasons that place this death within God's perfect will. Even if no reasons are immediately apparent, they will still trust the wisdom of God's plan.[8] To that extent theirs is a theodicy of masochism.

Whatever explanation believers choose, the most important goal is simply to place potentially disturbing events under the canopy of God's plan. Whatever happens is just part of God's strategy for bringing individuals to salvation, strengthening their faith, and bringing the events of history to a climactic close. Suffering and death are explained by the same principles that explain every other daily event. And the explanations are sustained by the same processes that support the rest of the believer's view of the world. The answers for suffering and death can be found in the same way other answers are found, from scripture tailored to meet individual needs and from the church and its leaders. Out of this social cloth, and with the aid of hindsight, an explanation can be woven. Bonnie described the process of dealing with her father's death this way: "I thank the Lord now. At the time I didn't realize what had happened. I couldn't understand it. But being at Southside, even after the first couple of years, different times pastor had spoken on different things, and I began to see what had happened. And I thank the Lord for it." When Connie had to decide whether to expect God to use a faith healer to make her well, she also turned to the church for advice: "I decided I wanted to talk to Pastor Thompson about the whole cotton-pickin' thing. . . . I really didn't know if the way I felt about the healing bit was right or wrong." The ultimate authority is scripture, so the individual believer is likely to spend a good deal of time looking for verses that contain reasons and comfort. But the pastor's sermons and advice help, as do conversations with fellow believers.

The process of developing explanations was especially apparent when a freak autumn tornado struck another suburb. Much of the next Sunday School hour in one adult class was spent trying to discern just what God had in mind by sending such a storm. Everyone was sure that so unusual an occurrence must bear a divine message, but not everyone agreed on what that message might be. If they were to keep their ideas about God's will alive, they would have to do their "ideological work." As they discussed the situation, some simply noted that it must be one more sign that the end is near. But others sought more specific explanations. Ray Danner proposed that it was more than coincidence that his store in the area was spared. But another person quickly objected that her fine Christian friend had been in the motel next door and had nearly been blown away. Ray then revised his ideas to say that perhaps the saving of his store would give him a chance to witness to others about God's power. Other class members proposed that the sins of the people could account for this supernatural punishment. Still others noted that the event was likely to cause some to repent and turn to God. People seemed willing to live with the explanations posed by others and to revise their own ideas. The only intolerable possibility was that the whole thing was "merely natural." Explanations do not have to form a logical whole, but there must be an explanation, one that includes divine activity.[9] No single explanation covers all possibilities; often more than one explanation is employed at a time. But believers are confident that an explanation is possible. That faith underlies everything they do. It is the foundation on which their world is constructed, the belief that separates them from a subjective and disorderly modern world.

CHAPTER FIVE

On Light and Darkness: Living in an Alien World

Be ye not unequally yoked together with unbelievers: for what
fellowship hath righteousness with unrighteousness? And what
communion hath light with darkness?
—II Corinthians 6:14

THE IDEAS that make Southside a distinctive community of
faith are built on the principles of order and authority.
They are sustained by regular searching of the scriptures and
listening to spiritual guidance. But they must be sustained also in dialogue with everyday life in the modern world. Believers must make
sense not only of their own life histories and the ways of their church
but also of the lives and actions of people and institutions that do not
share their beliefs. They learn at church to recognize and maintain
clear boundaries between themselves and what they come to see as
an alien outside world. They learn to walk in the light but to stay
constantly vigilant against the forces of darkness.

The people at Southside, in fact, are eager to tell anyone who
will listen that they are different from the rest of the world. At the
heart of the matter is the fact that they are saved and the rest of the
world is not. They have their names "written in the Lamb's Book of
Life" and can look forward to an eternity in heaven. The rest of the
world is lost, separated from God, and headed for eternity in hell's
torments. For believers this difference is like that between light and
darkness; it affects how they identify themselves and how they relate
to everyone else.

We have seen that salvation is the cornerstone of God's plan for
how people should live. Although it is important to know which job
is in God's plan, which house God wants you to buy, or which person you should marry, it is even more important to know that you
have passed from darkness into light. Salvation is the fact around
which everything else is organized. What Southside members read in

the Bible, what they hear from the pulpit, and what they talk about with their fellow believers constantly affirm the importance of being saved. Even when someone is sick or dying, believers worry about physical recovery only after they are sure the person's eternal destiny is secure. In every sense, the people of Southside see personal salvation as their most important identifying characteristic and the boundary that divides their domain from the outside world.

If you asked Southside members to explain personal salvation, they would probably point you to the Bible for an answer; but they might also tell you about their own experiences or give you one of many official statements on the subject. Because salvation is the most important experience in their scheme for organizing the world, they have developed an extensive vocabulary for describing just what happens in the transition from darkness into light. They might start by saying that they were "rescued from sin by the blood of Christ." They might quote Romans 6:23: "The wages of sin is death; but the gift of God is eternal life through Jesus Christ our Lord." They might next point out that they did nothing to earn this salvation, but received it by the grace of God. Ephesians 2:8−9 says, "For by grace are ye saved through faith; and that not of yourselves: it is the gift of God, not of works, lest any man should boast."

The one thing that is required, however, is that a person believe. As Romans 10:9 says, "If thou shalt confess with thy mouth the Lord Jesus, and shalt believe in thine heart that God hath raised him from the dead, thou shalt be saved." If, then, a person is willing to repent of his or her sins, accept the sacrifice of Jesus on the cross as God's forgiveness, and believe in the resurrection as proof of eternal life to come, that person can be saved. The Gospel of John summarizes it this way (1:12): "But as many as received him, to them gave he power to become the sons of God, even to them that believe on his name." The Apostle Paul says much the same thing in II Corinthians 5:17: "Therefore if any man be in Christ, he is a new creature: old things are passed away; behold, all things are become new." The people of Southside are likely to describe the experience as being "born again."

Becoming a new creature implies a great deal more than mere intellectual assent to a group of doctrines. Believers often say that what is required is "heart knowledge," not "head knowledge." To become a believer in Jesus means to turn your life over to his direction and let him "live in your heart." It means that you are willing to turn your sinful nature, including your pride and your will, over to God in exchange for a new life full of peace and joy and the assurance that you are going to heaven.

In fact, believers see confidence about this life and the one to come as evidence that a person has been saved. They feel so much better about life and about themselves that they are sure it must show on their faces.

> Here's all these kids, every one of them Christian. What a marvelous atmosphere! The kids were all beaming, nice, clean, scrubbed faces. They glowed with what they were!

> I just felt like I'd been born again. I really did. And I have a little foster daughter that I have brought up, and she said, "Gladder, it shows in your face." You know, it's just so wonderful!

And when believers describe what produces the glow on those faces, they often mention the inner peace and joy of knowing where they will spend eternity.

> Living according to the Word means joy and peace. It means absolutes. It means eternity. Whereas living in the world brings nothing but misery and discontent and unhappiness.

> It's hard to imagine my life without Christ. I can't even fathom it. I'd be the most miserable person, I think, to begin with, because of no hope of eternity, no nothing.

The promise of heaven means for Southside members that they should be able to face life with a smile and endure hardships with a song in their hearts. One of the most persistent themes in the pastor's sermons is that Christians ought to be happy. When they find themselves worried or lacking in enthusiasm, they reflect that they must not be as close to God as they should be, and they pray with the psalmist that "the joy of their salvation" will be restored. Being visibly happy is one of the ways Christians see themselves as distinctive. Joe Slavin remembered that about the friend who had witnessed to him: "I didn't really know the guy, and every day I used to see him, and he was always smiling and always really happy and content. I could never figure out why because he had a harder job than I did. Yet he was happy." Being confident and happy is part of the heritage claimed by Southside members when they join God's family.

The Outsiders

Being a group of saved sinners who joyfully direct their lives according to rules found in the Bible gives identity to the people of Southside and thus sets limits on the behavior they are willing to tolerate in those who claim to be believers. As Erikson has written, "A human community can be said to maintain boundaries, then, in the sense that its members tend to confine themselves to a particular radius of activity and to regard any conduct which drifts outside that radius as somehow inappropriate" (1966:10). He goes on to suggest that it is deviants within the community who "venture out to the edges of the group [and] are met by policing agents whose special business it is to guard the cultural integrity of the community" (p. 11).

In the case of the Southside community, however, it is the daily task of virtually every member to "venture out to the edges of the group." Because they are a minority in the midst of an alien culture, they need not look far to find whole masses of people deviating from their norms. Because they must live with these outsiders, the task of boundary maintenance is a constant one. To keep their identity as a separate and distinct group, all members of Southside must become "policing agents," being continuously on guard against doubts that might destroy their own faith or compromises that might destroy the identity of the church. In order to know what one is, it is also important to know what one is not.

That basic fact of social life has, from the beginning, been a central feature of Fundamentalism. One of its defining characteristics has always been "separation from the world." From its inception, Fundamentalism has gained much of its identity from its insistence on being aggressively different, on establishing clear boundaries where others saw only shades of gray.

And, as has always been the case with militant Fundamentalists, Southside's most well-defended boundaries are those that divide it from its closest neighbors, those with whom it would seem to have the most in common. The pastor's righteous indignation is far more likely to be directed at the clergy and members of other Christian churches than at thieves, murderers, pagans, or atheists. At Southside the greatest public sins are failures in belief and lifestyle. Durkheim might almost have been thinking of this congregation when he wrote, "Imagine a society of saints, a perfect cloister of exemplary individuals. Crimes properly so called, will be unknown; but faults which appear venial to the layman will create there the same scandal that the ordinary offense does in ordinary consciousnesses" (1895: 68–69). Like their Fundamentalist forebears, the people of Southside declare the greatest of scandals to be modernism. They vehemently decry any effort by other Protestants to introduce "modern compromises" into the Christian faith.

Southside's opposition to modernism is explained not only by history but by the fact that each community's forms of deviance are shaped by the values they hold most dear. As Erikson points out, "Every human community has its own special set of boundaries, its own unique identity, and so we may presume that every community also has its own characteristic styles of deviant behavior" (1966:19). Fundamentalists claim being born again and belief in the Bible as their identity, and it is violation of those norms that they condemn in modernists. They hear from the pulpit that liberals and modernists distort the Bible, do not use it in their churches, and make it an object of ridicule. Many members have noticed in attending other churches that the Bible does not seem to get as much respect and attention as it does at Southside.

> I was raised in a liberal federated church that was a combination of liberal Baptist and Congregational put together. And, you know, they had the same typical liberal thinking, like that the Bible *contains* the word of God. . . . That's the way liberalism is. What do you learn from it? You've got to get into the Bible and learn something. That's what's important.

> I didn't like the way the Catholic church seemed to hold back the Bible, keep it away from people. They read the missal every week, but they never say, "Go out and read the Bible."

> When we have our services we look at the Bible. We're like participating. I don't think most churches are like that. It's a routine in other churches.

The other major sin of modernists is failing to "preach salvation." Southside members are sure that other churches never gave them the message of salvation as Southside does. For them, the most important message of the Bible is "the gospel, pure and unadulterated," and the gospel is that everyone must be saved. Connie Meyer pointed to the preaching of the gospel as the mark of a good church.

INTERVIEWER. What do you think was the difference between Southside and the Congregational church? What made Southside better?

CONNIE. Because it's the real McCoy.

INTERVIEWER: How do you know that it's the real thing? What do they do differently?

CONNIE: They preach the gospel. They tell the truth.

The Foresters felt the same way:

We attended an American Baptist church once in Shaker Heights, in Cleveland. . . . It was—we didn't know what kind of church we were in. We were looking real hard to find something about the gospel in that strange sermon that was delivered.

The world outside is full of people who simply do not know the gospel. But those who are most dangerous to the people of Southside are the ones who say they know the gospel but believe and act differently. These are the people who have "fallen away into apostasy" and now "teach lies as if they were the truth." The way Southside members understand things, without the right beliefs about salvation and the Bible, liberals not only doom their own souls but threaten to steal the souls of the innocent people they deceive.

Even if liberal churches changed their beliefs about the Bible and about salvation, however, most Southside members would still not choose to attend. They just do not seem to be "real churches." This judgment comes in retrospect, but believers do perceive that some important ingredients are missing in liberal churches. For instance, many of the people who now enjoy the participatory style of Southside's services describe their old churches as "cold" and "formal" and "routine": "The Christianity that I knew was not real. . . . It was just a real formal ritual that I went through in the Catholic church. I thought that was Christianity because nobody ever taught me anything, through the Word, what Christianity was all about."

The conviction that their old churches were not teaching them "through the Word" is closely related to a feeling that they were not growing as Christians. Believers want to have opportunities to learn more about the Bible, and they want to be challenged to live according to the principles they find there. None of that seemed to be present in liberal churches.

> I went to Episcopal Sunday School. It was a social hour, with coffee and smoking. And they didn't know any more than I knew, and I didn't know that much at the time.

> I tried to tell them there was nothing coming out of the preacher, that we were not being fed. There was nothing there for us to grow on, and I left.

Most of all, liberal churches never offered their members the warm spirit of fellowship Southside members claim as the mark of a real church.

> I never got one thing out of it [the Methodist church]. . . . Not a soul spoke to you except the minister.

> In the Catholic church, you didn't look at anybody or talk to anybody, and everything was so, you know, what do you call it—regimented. If you're going to compare the service at St. Paul's Catholic Church with that at Southside or any other Fundamental church—. At the end of the service at the Catholic church, they can't wait to get out. Do not stand in the door, or you'll be trampled to death! But at our church, or any Christian church, you got—in order to leave—you got to wait until everybody's through talking!

Southside members have come to expect that church and friendship and everyday life will form a seamless whole. They expect the people and activities of church to dominate and define their lives. In liberal churches they miss participation in a community that shares multiple, overlapping life experiences.[1] In part they feel uncomfortable because of differences between themselves and liberals in age and class, which are often just as real as the theological differences they have with liberals. Southside members have chosen a church in which they find people with whom they feel comfortable sharing their lives. In this northeastern city, not many churches are populated primarily by young, middle-class families. That dimension, however, is rarely acknowledged by members beyond the admission that they enjoy a "fellowship" at Southside that they did not find in other churches.

But the perception that liberal churches are not "real churches" entails more than just class-based differences in life experience. At Southside, church is not one among several valued commitments but the one central commitment that gives others their value. When Southside members come to church, their goal is not private worship disconnected from the secular realities of modern life. They do not draw lines between sacred and secular, private and public. Part of the "modernism" they reject is the presumption that there are issues to which the church should not speak. They would rather hear a biblical word about society than a social word about the Bible.

The differences believers perceive between themselves and other Christians are indeed profound. They have to do with lifestyle, worship, theology, and authority. As a result, Southside members become convinced that liberals are not really Christians and that liberal churches are not really churches. Their doctrines are seen as heresy, and their practices are at best a hindrance to Christian living. Those who merely attend liberal churches are pitied for their unsaved condition. Those who are committed to liberal ideas are sometimes suspected of complicity with the devil himself.

When people at Southside use the term *liberal*, they include most of the Protestant churches in the Northeast. Congregationalists, Methodists, and American Baptists are the prototypes because they were once "fundamental," but have now "fallen away." Most Presbyterians also fit that model, although a few have "kept the faith." Episcopalians and Lutherans have always been so different in liturgical style that Fundamentalist believers have little sense that they were ever part of the same family. A person who goes to any of these churches is assumed not to be saved.

The other people most commonly assumed not to be saved are the Catholics. Most of the members of Southside are not so rabidly anti-Catholic as their Fundamentalist ancestors were. There are simply too many Catholics in the community to allow indiscriminate anti-Catholic broadsides. Mostly Catholics are treated as similar in kind to liberal Protestants. Notice that many of the same criticisms have been leveled at both. Again, the basic problem is that Catholics do not really believe the Bible, and they do not preach salvation.

Catholic ideas about the Virgin Mary, the saints, the pope, and so forth, seem rather strange to Southside members, but mostly they condemn the emptiness of the ritual and the church's misplaced priorities.

The boundary between the Catholic church and Southside is a particularly interesting one because so many people have crossed it in the direction of membership in the Southside community. Most of these ex-Catholics are aware that there is now a barrier between them and many of their family and friends. If we listened to what was said at church, we might think that liberals were the most troublesome outsiders. Although liberals may be the most theologically dangerous, Catholics are the greatest everyday problem to ordinary members. At least half the outsiders Southside members meet every day are likely to be Catholic; so knowing what is wrong with the Catholic church is essential for maintaining the believer's identity.

Southside members, in fact, find it frustrating to be surrounded by so large a group of outsiders who seem so impermeable to change.

> It's terribly hard to talk to a Catholic person. . . . In fact, my mother-in-law, I used to talk to her all the time, and she would listen to me patiently and she'd say, "Yeah, I know you are right, but you were brought up your way, and I was brought up my way." She felt she couldn't leave it.

> If I was going to fight something here in this life, the thing I'd fight the most is the Catholic church, all its teachings. So many people I've witnessed to, and Steve's parents, are just so wrapped up in Catholicism. Sometimes you feel like you're going against the impossible there. You know the Lord wants them to be saved, but teaching them to come out of that church — boy, I could wring their necks!

Catholics and liberal Protestants are especially dangerous outsiders because they openly challenge Fundamentalist definitions of Christian belief. They have the audacity to refuse to recognize their own lost state.

The final group of religionists with whom believers must dispute the boundaries of the kingdom are esoteric groups such as Jehovah's Witnesses and Mormons. Although there are dramatic differences in their belief systems, their similarities in style and structure make them a clear threat to Fundamentalists. In Valley View, Witnesses are the most visible danger. Like the members at Southside, they are conservative, interpret the Bible literally, and are concerned with Jesus's return. Both engage in vigorous missionary activity, and both draw converts from the same neighborhoods— Kingdom Hall is literally only a block away. Southside members fear that someone who is receptive to their own message of salvation will be snatched away when Jehovah's Witnesses come knocking at the door. Rebecca Hughes recalled talking to an unsaved neighbor: "I said, 'Whatever you do, Michelle, don't let them in tomorrow.' . . . I said, 'This is just a good stepping stone for them to get into your home and to get you into their Bible study.' You know, it *all* sounds good to an unsaved person or even to a new Christian."

The boundaries between true belief and falsehood are most strictly patrolled, then, in the neighborhood where falsehood takes the form of other Christian doctrines. These other "believers" are the ones most likely to be held up to ridicule and condemnation from the pulpit; and it is against them that believers must defend themselves in everyday confrontations. Precisely because these outsiders also claim to be Christians and say they are headed for heaven, Southside members must devote a good deal of energy to defining their own distinctiveness. When they look for differences, they find enough to conclude that many other "Christians" are not part of God's family.

Also condemned from Southside's pulpit are another group of theological neighbors: neo-Evangelicals, Pentecostals, and charismatics. Although they share most of Southside's central beliefs, they differ in many matters of faith and practice and are condemned as having wrong beliefs, wrong lifestyles, or wrong associations. Although the pastor rarely declares that such folk are actually unsaved, he makes it clear that they are allowing Satan to work in their lives and that believers should be careful to avoid them and their mistakes.

Southside's members, however, see the issue with no such moral clarity. They may agree with their pastor in theory, but they are quite unwilling to draw such battle lines in practice. They feel that they need all the allies they can find, and they are unwilling to turn some of those allies into enemies. In practice, people are treated as insiders if they accept personal salvation in the same way a Southside member would. As one believer put it, "If it doesn't affect salvation, I don't think it's that important." In fact, salvation is enough to qualify some seeming outsiders as candidates for marriage. "I don't think it would be very difficult to establish a Christian life with the fellow you are going with," a mother told her daughter. "He has accepted the Lord, even if he's not of your faith."

In a variety of instances, believers are willing to let their own experience create exceptions to the rules about where boundaries should be drawn. In some cases, they themselves were saved in churches that are officially condemned at Southside: "It was basically a Pentecostal church, Assembly of God. . . . And I think it was the second time I went to a service I got saved. He preached a biblical message." And, in many other cases, they know people of whose salvation they are sure who do not belong to approved churches.

> I feel that there are a lot of people that are saved, even though they don't think our way. They don't seem to have enough nerve to step out from their traditional church or whatever.

> Even though she was saved, she stayed with the Catholic church. We've talked about that, and now we just don't talk about that difference any more. We just figure we will talk about what we have in common.

Just as they would readily condemn the most apparently conservative preacher who did not "preach salvation," they willingly embrace strangers who nevertheless share their status among the saved. In some cases, they even find common bonds with racial and ethnic outsiders. Ray Danner explained that he had no objections to a Jewish daughter-in-law because "she was raised a Christian." Another man talked about his relationships with the blacks who come to his store: "We have an awful lot of Negro customers, more than any other store. I can relate to them better than many of the whites because basically we have a Fundamental background." Ultimately, salvation is more important than race.[2] For believers, salvation marks the boundary between darkness and light, between misery and joy, between orthodoxy and heresy.

The Visible Signs of Salvation

Eternal destiny is not an easily measured quantity. Neither, for that matter, are peace and joy. As a matter of practical necessity, in everyday life, one's invisible status before God must be measured with visible social and behavioral yardsticks.

At the most basic level, those who are clearly accepted as among the saved are those who actively participate in the Southside community. People who do things with other believers and act according to the norms of the group are assumed to be saved. When believers declare that the only legitimate expression of the Christian church is a local body, they are giving an ecclesiological name—local autonomy—to a social reality. The people about whose eternal destiny they can be sure are the members of their local congregation.

However, a declaration of faith and membership in the church are not an automatic passport into the kingdom. Some people are judged to be outsiders even when they claim to have been saved. These doubtful cases, in fact, illustrate just where the behavioral boundaries are drawn. In a general sense, believers expect salvation to produce a change in a person's life. They appreciate sincere words, but they also want to see "outward signs." This criterion can also work in reverse. As Bonnie Towles said of her husband, "He still maintains that he is not saved. If you ask him outright, he says, 'No.' But he's so totally different that I think only the Lord could do that." And as behavior vacillates, the believer's estimates about salvation may also vacillate. Bob Hughes talked about one of his co-workers: "I'm not totally sure whether Herb's saved or not. One conversation when he speaks, you know he's saved, for sure you know. But then he'll say the next day that he knows he's not. . . . He loves to come to service, and he loves to talk about the things he's learned, which you don't get from someone who's not saved. But there's a lot of things in his life that haven't been cleared out yet."

The members of Southside have specific ideas about what things in a life "need to be cleared out." Because they see their own lives as characterized by confidence, they are suspicious of people who have not given up their worries. Connie Meyer says, "My mother says she is saved, but I have my doubts because they worry all the time." And Rebecca Hughes recounted this conversation with a friend: "He was upset over something, and she said, 'Well, the Lord will get us through.' And he said, 'How can you have so much faith? How do you believe that?' So I don't think that he is saved." People who do not trust God to take care of them live outside the territory in which Southside's members are at home. This might be called a "sin of omission"—something is left out of their lives.

There are, however, also "sins of commission" that are far more grave. Foremost on Southside's list of forbidden activities is drinking. More than anything else, alcohol will cast doubts on the most sincere claims to salvation: "I have one [brother] that's an alcoholic, and I really don't know where he stands. I thought he had accepted Christ. He was baptized. I don't know if it's—is it possible to backslide that much?" Another member did not even hesitate. He cited drinking and going to saloons as evidence for saying of his grandfather, "He wasn't a saved man because he would go and do things of the world." In the most concrete terms, the line between the saved and the damned is drawn at the door to the saloon.

When Southside members talk about drinking, they picture in their minds the direst cases of alcohol abuse: the man who drinks up his paycheck and comes home to beat his wife and children, the derelict living on skid row, or drunken teenagers who kill people on the road (cf. Peek et al, 1979). To drink is to inhabit the same world that those people inhabit; there is no middle ground. Just as there are only saved people and unsaved people, there are also only two categories for the use of alcohol: abstinence and drunkenness. Alcohol belongs to Satan.

Drinking is also at the heart of what is wrong with today's world. As one member put it, "I think if we had a little less drinking and taverns and more church going, we might not have the trouble we have in the world today." One woman wished drinking would be completely eliminated "so we wouldn't have to be worried about our kids." Believers and their children must remain separate from the world where drinking is accepted. New Christians are quickly advised that they must give up drinking. Janet Slavin recalled, "They taught us right from the word of God, and they weren't afraid to tell us about things like smoking and drinking. . . . You have to emphasize it at first to some people because it gives them the idea right off the bat that maybe they should start disciplining their lives. You have to tell them, in a loving way, that's what it means to be a Christian. You don't smoke or drink."

People on the outside, then, are likely to drink too much, while people on the inside have the courage to say "no" to drinking and to other "sins of the flesh." Believers are admonished, for instance, that the only proper place for sex is within the bonds of matrimony. A "Christian marriage" is one that is chaste before the wedding and sexually exclusive "until death do us part." Women should avoid temptation by being modest in appearance, and men should beware of their wandering eyes.

It is clear to believers that lust is a characteristic of the outside world. As quickly as they list drinking as one of the chief evils of the world, they add "sex sins" as equally heinous: "People don't want to be told that, for instance, having what I call pornographic and obscene magazines on the counter shelves anywhere is wrong and that allowing strip-tease joints and go-go bars is wrong." Southside members are horrified at the permissive sexual ethic of the postpill generation. To the vicarious pleasures of pornography, to adultery, and especially to homosexuality and "casual sex," believers shout a resounding "no". Whatever does not conform to the monogamous standards they see as biblical is condemned as un-Christian. In recent memory, the only formal dismissal of a Southside member from the church was for adultery. To be an accepted member of the community of the saved, sexual propriety is a must.

One of the many influences members blame for corrupting people is rock music. If Satan's favorite activities are drinking and sexual license, then rock music is his prime tool for getting people involved. Recall how disco dancing was described as one of the signs that the end must be near: "I see people dancing on TV, and they remind me of Sodom and Gomorrah. . . . I just know that the Lord is not going to let this go on much longer without some kind of judgment." The way of life portrayed in most rock lyrics is offensive to believers, and they are also unwilling to accept "Christian" rock. As they see it, music with a strong beat is inherently seductive, and no amount of good intentions can turn one of Satan's tools into something a believer should enjoy. Students at some Bible colleges are protected from the evils of rock music by being forbidden to listen to anything but Christian radio. And the training begins much earlier. A second grader described a speaker who had come to Southside Academy: "There was this guy that came to our school last year, and he was telling us about, you know, that rock group Kiss and how bad it is. Well, they just want kids to get involved in all that kind of icky stuff." Listening to rock music and getting involved in "icky stuff" are other habits that distinguish the unsaved from the saved.

An immediate indicator of a nonbeliever's status, however, is the way that person talks. People who use "filthy language" are definitely not insiders. Swearing and vulgarity are also among the chief sins in today's world.

> They'll use words that I was brought up not to use. . . . You know, I mean, here it's their normal language. Like my sister has picked it up working in the warehouse, and so a lot of the things she says I don't approve of.

> I wasn't used to all the swearing and everything. Every time you turn around there's a swear word. I'm not used to being around women that swear that much or that smoke and this type of thing.

They are not used to swearing because people who have been saved are careful to avoid even the hint of a curse: "I used to think at one time that there was no problem with even swearing, but now I realize that it is something that is definitely grieving God."

Believers are constantly having to let people know that they will not participate where "bad language" is used.

> They always resign themselves to the fact that they have to keep their language proper. They know that if I go, they've got to, not because I tell them to do it, but it is automatic. They don't want to do it around me. They have that kind of respect, I guess.

> Of course, you get all kinds when you're out in the working field, but I praise the Lord they knew where I stood, and they were very careful what was said around me.

The fact that believers do not swear or allow swearing in their presence marks them as different from the unsaved people with whom they live and work. A deacon talked about the differences other people notice in him. He said, "Language is another big one. Your co-workers say, 'How come you don't swear?'"

The difference in language, however, is not all one sided. Outsiders are not the only ones who are recognizable for the way they speak, and insiders are not different only because they refuse to swear. Insiders are also different because they have developed their own distinctive vocabulary for describing the world as they understand it. They are sometimes as offensive to outsiders as outsiders are to them.

When Christians get together, it's almost like we speak another language, . . . and if you had an outsider sit in on it, they'd probably think to themselves, "Woa! Listen to them talk!"

Somehow you're around people and you're talking and they get to know you, and I guess, without realizing it, people find out that you're a Christian.

In everyday interaction, language often most clearly identifies Southside members as a separate and distinct group.

Religious groups of all kinds develop a jargon to fit their particular practices and liturgical traditions. Southside Gospel Church is no exception. The congregation has a jargon that describes their organizational structure and their pattern of worship. They take "love offerings" and give "invitations." They send missionaries out "on deputation" to gather "faith promises" so that they can journey to the "mission field."

The language of Southside, however, is not confined to the four walls of the church. It also pervades the everyday worlds of its adherents. When they are sick, they are "suffering in beds of affliction" or perhaps have a "thorn in the flesh." Parenting is "bringing them up in the nurture and admonition of the Lord." To test an alternative is to "put out a fleece," and to arrive at a decision is, of course, to "find God's will." To converse or eat with church members is to "fellowship," while stirring up trouble is "murmuring," which will undoubtedly lead to "backsliding." The everyday life of a Christian should consist of "bearing fruit" by "witnessing" and "winning souls." And there are special words to identify insiders and outsiders —"saved," "born again," and "Bible-believing" versus "unsaved," "liberals," and "modernists."

The origin of most of the unique language used at Southside is the King James Version of the Bible. They read it daily, memorize its verses, and hear the pastor preach from it; and gradually it works its way into their conversations. They come to think of God's true language as containing old-fashioned grammar and archaic forms of address, and when they talk to God in prayer, that is the language they use.

Members of Southside have created a language that is adequate to describe the things that are important to them. Accepting Fundamentalist ideas and practices goes hand in hand with speaking the proper language. Berger reminds us that "the fact of language, even if taken by itself, can readily be seen as the imposition of order upon experience. . . . On the foundation of language, and by means of it, is built up the cognitive and normative edifice. . . . To participate in the society is to share its 'knowledge'" (1969:20–21). Learning to call things by their correct names is part of the process of becoming a member of the community. Insiders sound like insiders.

In a variety of ways, then, saved people can be recognized by their disciplined lives and their refusal to indulge in frivolous pleasures. Believers do not approve of drinking or promiscuity or dirty jokes, and they seek to avoid anything that would tempt them in the direction of those sins. Southside members are particularly enraged that television has now invaded their homes with the same "filth" for which they have always condemned the movies. In fact, it seems to many believers that television is largely to blame for presenting evil ways of life as if they were good. A man who is a deacon complained that he would like to see television programs "a little bit cleaner . . . [than] they have on, and, of course, the living together without marriage. The soap-box operas portray that, like the worldly magazines do, that this is an acceptable way of life." Mary Danner expressed her frustration as well: "We watch very little TV, but sometimes the last hour of the day we will look at the program to see if there is anything on that we would like to watch, like from ten to eleven. And we turn it off ourselves. We have no young children who are watching that we are being careful of, but the whole way of thinking is wrong . . . somebody lived with somebody else, and he lived with this one, etc. And it has become a way of life with the world."

A number of people in the congregation have simply given up on television and packed theirs away in the closet. They have become convinced that nothing worthy of a Christian's time is coming over the airwaves.[3] More typically, Southside families respond by limiting their viewing and that of their children. Jim Forester talked about how things might be different if he were not a Christian: "I think that probably we would be more permissive as far as our children's habits are concerned, like what they watch on TV. . . . To me, watching television—it's almost forbidden around here." To the extent that television represents the evil ways of the unsaved world, believers remove it from their lives. Saying "no" to television is another of the ways believers discipline their own lives and distinguish themselves from the indulgent world around them.

When believers look at the world outside their territory, they see people whose choice of pleasures they cannot approve. They are eager to declare themselves different, "separate" from a world where drinking and dancing are considered fun and where casual sex is a prelude to casual marriages. In addition, Southside members are horrified at the violence, dishonesty, and corruption that seem to surround them. Although these are not sins that often tempt believers personally, examples are never far from home.

> This world is getting so bad that I won't read a newspaper. I may watch the news at eleven, but that's about the height of what I get. I hate to get the newspaper 'cause all I see is knifings and killings and shootings and muggings, and in the paper there's nothing nice to read.

> I don't mean it has to be a dream world, but at least a little bit better than what it is, where you can go out in the street at night and not be afraid.

Terror in the streets helps to reinforce in the minds of believers the total "otherness" of the world outside. To be unsaved is to be part of the realm of darkness, where Satan does his awful deeds. To be saved is to have escaped to the realm of light.

The corruption of the outside world hits closer to home when believers encounter unsaved people who are simply selfish and mean spirited. Becaues believers try to be polite and pleasant, they cannot understand the coldness and lack of concern with which some unbelievers treat their neighbors and co-workers. "Hating the neighbors" was part of the evidence for Connie Meyer's declaration that she had grave doubts about her mother's claim to salvation. When believers talk about what nonbelievers are like, selfishness of all sorts is almost always on the list.

> Their whole attitude is "do whatever you want to do; do whatever makes you happy." And it doesn't matter how it is done or who it hurts or whatever.

> Power-hungry people—you get those that they're only out for how much power they can get under their control, and they don't care who they step on to get there.

When members of Southside passed from darkness into light, they left behind an ethic of looking out for number one and exchanged it for an ethic of caring for others. For them, the formula is J-O-Y: Jesus first, Others second, Yourself last.

The line between selfish behavior and unselfish behavior is not nearly so easy to draw as that between drinking and abstinence or between chastity and promiscuity. In fact, none of these behavioral boundaries between the saved and the unsaved are either perfectly defined or universally agreed on and obeyed. A small number of people in the congregation, people accepted as believers, will at least privately admit to having an occasional glass of wine with a meal. Although no one advocates divorce, a few have been through the ordeal and have even remarried. No one likes smoking, but a few believers do it. Even if disco dancing gets uniform disapproval, ballet and square dancing are not automatically taboo. And selfishness is something that creeps into everyone's life now and then. Despite the orderliness of the list of rules, Southside's members must still live in the imperfection of the real world. In that, they are no different from the rest of us.

What distinguishes Fundamentalists, however, is both the location of the boundaries they draw and their insistence that a line can be drawn. Although there is some disagreement within the ranks on where to draw the line between "Christian" and "worldly" behavior, there is still an underlying agreement that a line must be drawn. Saved people are different from unsaved people. Those on the outside have no standards, no sense of right and wrong, no concern for others. They fail not only to believe as they should but to live as they should. It comes out in big sins like drinking, sexual immorality, and dishonesty. But it also comes out in the numerous little actions that indicate to believers that a person "does not have a Christian attitude." Both belief and behavior separate the members of Southside from the outside world. Whether the outsider is a Presbyterian or a Catholic, a drunkard or a teller of dirty jokes, he or she is separated from believers by an abyss no less than the one that separates heaven from hell. On the side of the saved there is right doctrine, right living, and God's eternal favor. On the side of the damned there is apostasy, promiscuity, and eternal separation from God. It is a difference of which believers are very aware.

> When you're with someone who's not saved, you can almost sense a total difference. Sense? I think that's the word. Not feelings or vibration, but like a sixth sense.

When people write in your yearbook, they always say, "You're so different."

Encountering the Darkness

Although they are different, believers must live in the same world with unsaved people. Relating to outsiders is inevitable, and the most favored way to do it is to witness, to try to persuade outsiders to be saved. The Southside congregation is constantly reminded that their world is a mission field, that there are unsaved people wherever they go. Members need go no further than their families, their neighborhoods, and their jobs to find people as pagan as any "African heathen." The souls of the unsaved people they know are the responsibility of Southside's members.

They approach this responsibility with a variety of methods, from the silent witness of their differentness to aggressive attempts to persuade the unpersuaded. Basically, believers claim that the quality of their lives is the best argument in favor of salvation. If they do not live by their faith, they know others will be unmoved by their words. They are keenly aware that nonbelievers will be eager to catch them in hypocrisy. Because they are told that their lives "are the only Bible many people will ever read," they are scrupulous in their faith, honesty, and uprightness. They publicly exhibit their standards of morality and regular church attendance, hoping that their example will induce others to inquire about what motivates such discipline. They fear that if they fail to live as they should, someone they love might reject Christ and end up in hell.

Living such an exemplary Christian life is sometimes the only means for witnessing that believers feel they have at their disposal. Some people do not feel capable of putting the gospel into words, and even those who do sometimes feel constrained by their environments. Sometimes a boss forbids them to witness, or a husband refuses to listen. In those cases, the rules of the situation are stronger than the command to witness in words. The only alternative is to hope that the way one lives will be testimony enough.

I make it clear that my life is the Lord's, but I try not to choke it down anybody because I'm there to work.

I think sometimes when you're working and saying little, you make a better witness. They can't be paying me for talking.

Especially at work, witnessing is less likely to be verbal and more likely to be by example.

Almost everyone admits that they are much more diligent at living the gospel than at putting it into words. Not everyone exercises the power to witness they are told God will give them. Talking about salvation is difficult. People are often afraid they cannot explain what they believe. They expect outsiders to challenge them, and they worry that they might not be able to convince such doubters. Avoiding the hard questions is one reason Rebecca Hughes prefers working with children: "I know the Lord has me in nursery school. That's a joy—to see these little ones that you can give your opinion to and they won't contradict it. They're still at an age where they will accept what you say. You know, they don't think, 'Well, she doesn't know what she's talking about.'" Verbal witnessing requires that believers feel confident of their explanations and powerful enough to ask someone else to listen. Even when they know that they should put salvation into words and that God's power will help them do it, believers sometimes simply do not have the courage. Bonnie Towles confessed:

> I asked the Lord to put us where he could use us, and so many times somebody's been brought into our home. But then to get up the courage to say that to them, to say that we are glad to be of help and that, you know, that we feel that we are here because we feel that this is where the Lord has brought us—I'm so afraid that they'll say they don't want to hear or something. . . . I don't want to go where I'm not welcome. I just can't bring myself to knock on somebody's door and force myself upon them. But I know we're supposed to.

One method for overcoming this difficulty is to use the words of others. When Southside members do not know how to open a conversation or do not think they will get an opportunity to talk, they are likely to use a "tract." These pocket-sized pamphlets tell about salvation in a style designed to arouse the reader's curiosity and sometimes fear. Bold headlines ask provocative questions, interesting people offer their stories, and the way to salvation is explained. Believers hope that unsaved people will read the tract and either spontaneously accept salvation or seek more information. Some members regularly hand out tracts to nearly everyone they meet: "I made up six or seven tracts to a pack and to the best of my ability use the 'This belongs to you' or 'Did you get yours?' sort of thing, with the one that would make them want to open the rest of them on the outside. And I handed out thousands of them to cashiers, waitresses, clerks, you name it—throughout my area of the state."

Others use a tract as a supplement to their own conversations with outsiders about being saved. Still others place tracts where they are sure to be found by someone who has been otherwise unreceptive. The woman who does not want to be paid for talking nevertheless admits to leaving tracts around sometimes. Connie Meyer does the same thing: "I leave tracts around. I try to talk to some of the aides and some of the patients, but they're difficult to talk to." Southside members know they have been commissioned to tell everyone about being saved, but not every social encounter is conducive to religious persuasion. When the encounter is too brief and impersonal, or when personal conversations seem fruitless, written words from some other Christian provide a useful way to introduce the subject of salvation.

In addition to providing printed words with which to witness, Southside also offers its members practical ways to increase their skill and confidence in talking about salvation. The church conducts ongoing classes in how to witness. People are taught to create and seize opportunities to talk about salvation and the words to use when they do. They rehearse with each other and then attempt a trial run with an unsaved person. As a result members gain practical training that makes talking about salvation a great deal easier than it might be.

The church also offers its members incentives to witness and rewards when they do. Every time they go to church, believers are reminded that witnessing is the Christian's first and most important responsibility, and they feel guilty if they do not "bear fruit." They are convinced that if they care about people and value their own salvation, they should witness. Within the fellowship, those who witness are richly rewarded. They have stories to tell and prayer requests to make. They can stand before the church and report on their activities; and when they do, they gain status in the eyes of their fellow believers. They provide practical models of how to witness and examples of how rewarding it is to have the approval of God and of your fellow believers. It may be important to live a circumspect life, but the members of Southside know that they have not completely succeeded as Christians until they have talked explicitly with someone about salvation and convinced that person to be saved.

What Southside members learn from expert soul winners and in soul-winning classes is how to talk about why they are different from the rest of the world and how life changed when they were saved. They learn to give a "personal testimony" and to lay out the theological argument for being saved. They use a simple four- or five-step "plan" of salvation, with each point backed by scriptures that prove it. They memorize the argument much as a salesperson learns a pitch, and they conduct the.encounter in a way designed to "make the sale." They want the unsaved person to make an immediate commitment, to seal his or her eternal fate that very day.

The ideal-typical model for witnessing is to present a personal testimony, outline the "plan of salvation," and invite the person to be saved. Although they may do it in bits and pieces, this is how believers define "really witnessing." Janet Slavin talked about witnessing to her workmates: "I have witnessed there in some way or another to everybody. . . . I don't know of anybody who was saved, but I was able to share the whole plan with them, and they did see something different in me. And they referred to me as a Christian when they wanted to ask a question. I don't know if they are making fun or not, but they do see something different, and they do respect me."

Believers live under the injunction to demonstrate to others that they are different, and they are taught to create verbal arguments to support the case. As a result, the very activity they define as central to being a Christian—witnessing—has boundary maintenance as one of its consequences. Believers do not cross the abyss to live among the people of the world. Rather, they stand firm on their own ground while tossing a lifeline to lost strugglers on the other side.

Church members look for opportunities to witness by inserting religion into ordinary conversations and seeking out occasions when outsiders may be most vulnerable, such as when they are facing illness, death, or personal troubles. Believers may wear religious jewelry, display religious art, or pointedly listen to Christian radio in the hope that someone may notice, comment, and leave the door open for witnessing. At Christmas and Easter, they are eager to tell why those holidays have special meaning for them. Believers do not give up easily. In some cases they will keep looking for opportunities, giving their testimonies, and talking about salvation to the same people for years. Ann Lazzaro converted from Catholicism over twenty years ago, but she is still working on her family: "A lot of people in my family are not saved yet, my relatives. Although they call me 'pastor,' I still have to reach them. It is a hard thing to do to witness to them."

Ann is right; witnessing is hard. Relationships are difficult to maintain when one party insists that there is something wrong with the other. It is not surprising that few Southside members reported any close friendships with unsaved people. When they talked about their relationships with old friends and unsaved relatives, they reported either that they were maintaining the relationship in order to witness or that they had ceased seeing much of one another. For these people "separation from the world" has meant leaving loved ones behind. Mary Danner reflected on her family's experience: "We couldn't have the form of fellowship; we knew it was different. Their thinking was different, and we knew that if we were serious, we would have to change that. And we said, 'It is going to be sad to lose all of our friends.' But to tell the truth, as time went on the new friends that we got were really wonderful. There were so many, and they thought the way we did, what they wanted to do. We still kept in contact with the old friends, but the fellowship ended." Losing old friends may be sad, but it cushions members against the cognitive dissonance of loving someone who does not share their view of the world.[4] It is extremely difficult to maintain an intimate tie across the gulf between the saved and the damned.

The gulf is felt most acutely when it cuts through the lives of families. Members often feel like outsiders in their own homes. They worry about whether to go to weddings and family reunions because they know that everybody else will be drinking and dancing and urging them to join in the worldly pleasures they have forsaken: "When we're not with Christians—let her go to a wedding or a family party or something, or anywhere where there are non-Christians, a lot of them—I get nervous. They're all smoking; they're all drinking; they're all loud; they're all carrying on. And I don't fit in there, and I feel very nervous about it." Parents and siblings and aunts and uncles may not understand why the believer is no longer the person they used to know.

When the old relationship was a close one, the believer's conversion is likely to bring grief. Janet's story is especially poignant.

> My brother used to be like number one in my life. He was very close with me. . . . We're almost on different ends of the spectrum now, whereas we were very close being brought up. He just doesn't understand now why certain things have to be left out, whereas I don't understand why he has to include certain things. . . . To be able to say "no" to him, "No, Ken, I'm not going to go," is very hard for me, very, very hard. Music in our family was just always there, and jazz, and I was really caught up in it. I was crying when I was breaking my beautiful jazz albums. I was crying. I mean, here I am still calling them beautiful; I can see that I still have a problem. It's something I know is not good in my life. The Lord has shown me that, but it's taken concentrated effort to always keep away from it. I have to stay very close to the Lord, and if I falter at all with it, you know, with my walk with the Lord, then I definitely want all of a sudden to play around, or I definitely want to have a drink, or I definitely want to go hear my brother play.

Giving up the ways of the world can thus sometimes mean giving up important family relationships. When people become committed members of Southside Gospel Church, they often exchange one family for another. They begin to understand what the Apostle Paul meant about having brothers and sisters in Christ and what Jesus meant about leaving father and mother to follow him.

Separation from family members is perhaps the most painful portion of the boundary between the community of faith and the unsaved world. Believers come to understand that their true "brothers" are their brothers in Christ. They simply do not have the kind of concern and understanding for outsiders that is reserved for those who are saved. As Weber put it, members "set the co-religionist in the place of the fellow clansman" (1922:211). Just as fellow clansmen owed each other assistance, so fellow believers care for each other in sickness, health, poverty, and wealth. However, neither clansmen nor believers find it necessary to extend such services to those outside the family. Biblical injunctions to feed the hungry or clothe the naked are seen by believers as commands to care for their Christian brothers, not as commands to love the people of the world. Although they are often reminded to "hate the sin and love the sinner," their love for a sinner is above all a concern for that person's soul.

Believers also know what Jesus meant when he said, "I came not to send peace, but a sword." Those who are not brothers are sometimes enemies. The people of Southside are often reminded that the Christian life is a battle, that Satan is the enemy, and that the Bible is their "sword." The theme of "fighting the good fight" is sounded almost every time the congregation gathers. The battles of the Old Testament are among their favorite stories, especially those where God orders the enemy completely destroyed. And, in the New Testament, they keep returning to Paul's command to "put on the whole armor of God" (Ephesians 6:11ff.). Until Jesus returns, believers expect to be at war with the world.

In part, they mean that their own lives are never quite empty of sin. Bob Hughes talked about his daily petition to God: "Most importantly, he can keep me from sinning, so I'll not have fellowship broken with him. I admit it's a war, all day long. The worst thing that can happen to you is to think you're all right." Believers must constantly battle their own sinful desires, always strive to grow and learn out of each time of trial. Whenever they face the temptations of the world, they feel as if Satan has attacked them with a mighty army, which they can defeat only through prayer, Bible reading, and the wisdom offered by fellow Christians. At least in part, the battles they experience are within.

But believers also fight more visible battles. Simply by being a part of Southside, they identify with a church that "takes a stand against sin." They participate both directly and vicariously in rhetorical battles between God's way and the ways of Satan. They especially identify with the pastor's verbal attacks on Satan's representatives. When he preaches against alcoholism, pornography, liberalism, humanism, and permissiveness, his words seem to be arrows aimed at the enemies outside the gates of the sanctuary. When, on occasion, the pastor engages opponents in direct debate, the congregation would be no more excited if it were a duel of swords rather than of words. One woman reported on a local television debate between the pastor and a gay liberationist by saying that the pastor "beat him all to pieces!" Whenever their pastor or they publicly declare what they as a church believe, Southside members stand.verbally on God's side in the battle against an evil world.

Believers also fight Satan by "taking a stand" against the ordinary, everyday evils that surround them. By making their own lives an example or by asking others to change, believers seek to fight back Satan's attacks. Almost every member of Southside can tell about some time when they had to ask someone to stop doing something—drinking, cursing, or just being mean. Jim Forester explained, "That is another frustration: having to work at a job where the people there are not Christians and having to listen to their philosophy. I try to block it out as much as possible; but sometimes I hear, and it just makes me sick. I just pray that when someone at work really tells me something dirty, I can look at them and say, 'I really don't want to hear that!'" Believers do what they can to prevent Satan's ways from being victorious in the everyday world where they live.

Even when they do not seek a fight, members cannot maintain their distinctive lifestyle (in conscious opposition to the ways of the majority) without creating conflict. Outsiders rarely seem to accept the believer's lifestyle without some resistance. For instance, refusing to drink is often not easy to do.

> My own family gives me a hard time about that. You know, they have different names for me. It's really important, and they can't understand why. . . . I won't serve it to them. They will say, "Get me another beer, or fix me a drink." And I say, "I'm sorry, but I'm not going to fix something for you that I myself would not drink." They think it's really funny.

> They know I don't drink, and, believe me, in all these years that they know I don't drink, they tried their level best to coax me into a drink. Every time, every time!

To the extent that believers continue to interact with people who are unsaved, they are likely to face ridicule and pressure to conform. Sometimes they bring conflict on themselves with a belligerent manner; but, just as often, it is they who are attacked for living by the wrong set of rules.

Given the level of opposition they face on the outside, one might expect a solidly united front among believers, but such is not the case. The distinctions Southside's members make between themselves and the evil world ironically leave them vulnerable to conflicts within their own ranks. The enemies who stalk Fundamentalism from the outside often seem to creep within. One faithful member observed that Fundamental churches seemed to have more than their share of fights, but she took that as reassuring. After all, she explained, Satan is unlikely to attack the churches that are already in his camp. Only the churches that are really preaching the gospel should be expected to suffer from such divisive attacks. Believing the church conflict is inspired by Satan, members are unlikely to be kind to those with whom they disagree (cf. Richardson 1975). At the least, the other side is likely to be accused of immature Christianity. For instance, one member explained his irritation with some Southside members by saying, "After all, everyone who accepts Christ doesn't have Christ foremost in their life."

Those who lead public opposition to the pastor may be seen in an even worse light. At Southside, during this study, there was open conflict between Pastor Thompson and his choir director. During the months before the choir director left, it seemed more than coincidence that the pastor frequently reminded the congregation that Lucifer (the future Satan) had been in charge of music in heaven. Sometimes the battles Fundamentalists fight are against Satan's efforts to weaken their ranks through disloyalty and compromise.

The Fundamentalist spirit is thus a crusading one. They battle against their own imperfections, and they engage in verbal campaigns against evil wherever it may be found—even in their own ranks. Their most visible battles of late, however, have been in the political arena. They have always been fighters, willing to "put on the whole armor" and go into battle against the forces of Satan. If that means picketing a theater or an abortion clinic, they are willing. If it means boycotting Seven 11 or voting against gay rights, they are ready. Their battles are becoming more public and better organized than they were in the past.

However, they have no expectation that the final victory in these battles will be theirs, at least not in this world. Until the apocalyptic events of Armageddon and the millennium, they know that Satan will never be completely defeated. No actions of theirs can ever "bring in the kingdom," and no amount of reform—religious or political—can change that fact.

Their relationship to politics, in fact, has always been an ambivalent one. It brings out all the inherent tensions in a theology that stresses both evangelism and the imminent return of Christ, both human responsibility and fatalism. Believers have never been quite sure when to fight and when to wait for the Lord's return, when to try to change the world and when to simply let it go its own way. The problem becomes particularly acute when defeating evil involves the long, complicated, and messy business of working out legislation. At that point, they would sometimes rather retreat than fight. When those they see as ungodly claim a constitutional right to protection under the law, the members of Southside can envision no middle ground on which to meet. When the world does not seem to want to be convinced of its evil ways, and compromise is not a possibility, believers often simply tire of the fight.

The fact of the matter is that relationships with outsiders, whatever the situation, are sometimes so difficult that most Southside members would simply rather not face the battles. Despite the injunction to witness, they would rather spend their time inside the fellowship. They feel more relaxed around other Christians and find many nonbelievers positively offensive. They no longer feel good about either the people or the activities they once enjoyed.

> At work, they'll ask me, "Aw, come on! We're all gonna go to this . . . club." And I feel a—just a sick withdrawing inside, and I say, "No."

> They were so bombed. I mean they were hollering across the room for some old man over there and swearing. And, you know, I felt so out of place. I just wanted to get up and go home.

Sometimes they do get up and leave. Other times the decision comes more slowly. Both the Danners and Bonnie talked about groups they avoid.

> Mary: I tried the Women's League because I was asked to be in it, and it's quite a respected group in town. But I tried it and, as a Christian, I really didn't fit in, not personally, but there were so many things that I couldn't be wholeheartedly for.

> Ray: And I can't get involved in the volunteer fire department here because all they have is meetings and drinking, beer parties and all this sort of thing. So we try to be good citizens, but you have to sort of stay away from some things.

Bonnie: I was in a club for a year with these other ladies, you know, unsaved ladies; and there was another girl from church with me, and we both felt that this might be, you know, a ministry-type thing. But, you know, it's pretty hard to be in something like that. It seems that when you are in a large group, it seems like you go in with the intent of bringing them up, but what happens is they seem to bring you down.

In part believers are afraid that outsiders will "bring them down," but more commonly they simply lose interest in unsaved people as Fundamentalist ideas and lifestyles take hold. Bonnie described her experience: "I really don't see much of my other friends. These are the girls who when I have gone back to being burdened for them [worrying about their salvation] and gone back and tried to witness to them, you know . . . I just don't share the same things even in what we like ot talk about or what we like to do, so there isn't very much contact. . . . I don't want to go to just waste an afternoon talking about worldly things."

But friends are hard to leave—almost as hard as families. Sometimes being separated means feeling very alone: "It's just like a feeling in the back of my mind that I don't fit in with some of the other people . . . because I feel like a lot of things people do I just don't like. . . . I don't think it's right, and a lot of the times I'll get left in the corner." A Southside father tells his children, "As long as you feel you are right, the majority isn't right. In good conscience, don't be afraid to be by yourself."

In the final analysis, concern for the souls of others is often not strong enough to overcome the believer's sense of alienation and isolation from the unsaved world. Their own words express the feeling best.

Our family is an island, and if other people like the way you do it, fine; and if they don't, it's okay.

It just seems like I'm in a separate world.

It's almost like we're on the spectator end of a demonstration, like when you've gone to the aquarium and you're watching through the window everything that's going on inside, and you're protected from what's in there. It's like the Lord's put up a hedge around us.

I live in this little world—my little Christian world, my little
work world—and everything else seems sorta pointless.

The theological idea of separation thus takes concrete social form in
the daily lives of believers who know that they do not "fit in" with an
alien outside world.

For the members of Southside Gospel Church, the outside
world can be dangerous and unpleasant. Nonbelievers laugh and try
to lead the believer into sin. Liberals and Catholics and Jehovah's
Witnesses distort the very ideas believers hold most dear. And the
whole world seems to be wanton, permissive, and selfish. They venture into that outside world only to try to snatch away the few people who seem open to salvation. On the inside, those who are saved
form a tightly knit family, a brotherhood that is distinct in belief,
language, and lifestyle from the unsaved world outside. For most believers, the orderly world inside is so much more attractive than the
chaos outside that they choose to retreat into the protective shelter
of the fellowship. They leave behind nonbelieving friends, family
members, and organizations to devote all their time to the Bible, the
church, and Christian friends.

The members of Southside know that there is one social world
in which their ideas make sense and another in which nothing makes
sense. There is one social world where they feel at home, and another
where they feel alien. There is one social world where they know
what to expect of each other and of God, and another where none of
their rules seem to apply. They have chosen to leave the world of
outer darkness to enter the light of God's salvation, although they do
not often understand that the ideas they have chosen for shaping
their lives exist in a specific social structure. The difference between
insiders and outsiders is a matter not only of eternal destiny but also
of membership in an earthly social community. It is to the nature of
that community that we next turn.

CHAPTER SIX

The Assembling Together of Believers: Building a World to Call Home

Let us hold fast the profession of our faith without wavering: (for he is faithful that promised); And let us consider one another to provoke unto love and to good works: Not forsaking the assembling of ourselves together.
—Hebrews 10:23–25

FOR THE MOST devoted of its members, Southside Gospel Church is the dominating institution in their lives, a presence not unlike the parish church in a medieval village. Although they may not hear church bells calling them to morning prayers or evening vespers, their days and weeks and lives are no less regulated by the church's cycle of events. It dedicates their newborns, sanctifies their marriages, and buries their dead. They awaken each day to a time of prayer and Bible reading, and they spend many waking hours witnessing to their neighbors and co-workers. When evening comes, they attend church meetings, make visits, and conduct family devotions. On Saturday, they make more visits, prepare Sunday School lessons, and perhaps go on an outing with another church family.

All this activity points toward Sunday; and from Sunday members draw strength for the week.

> You need a good home church where you can feed your soul. For me Sunday is something great. A good Sunday service gives me something for the whole week.

> I love to get to church. I thank God every Sunday that I get there. I thank him first that I found it, and found him again, and that I can get there.

For most, going to church is the highlight of the week. On Sunday, they wear their best clothes and serve their best meal. Members attend Sunday School, the morning and evening preaching services, and a variety of organizational meetings in between. It is truly "the Lord's Day."

The church's most important rituals take place on Sunday, but its activities are by no means confined to that day. Every day of the week, Southside Gospel Church surrounds its members with a structure of activities and relationships that gives order to their lives and makes a Fundamentalist world view possible.

Going to Church

A look back at the Annotated Guide to the Week's Activities at Southside (in Chapter 3) makes apparent the breadth of the structure the church provides. Because many of the activities require advance preparation at home and because everyday witnessing is not on the agenda, even a schedule of meetings does not fully reflect the time a member can spend on church work. One leader asserted that a truly committed believer should be at church at least four times a week. Although only a minority of Southside's members achieve that standard, over half attend more than once a week (see Table 6.1), and most of those are there three or four times. In addition, over half give at least 10 percent of their income to the church and hold at least one church job. Thus, somewhat more than half of those who are part of the church form a core of "highly committed" members, projected from the sample to amount to about 110 adults.[1] Even the remainder of those who participate (the "moderately committed") maintain a comparatively high level of involvement by attending most Sunday mornings and giving some money to the church. The 30 percent of the official membership that does not attend are those who have effectively left the church. Although the church has not removed their names, many have joined other churches or moved away; they do not consider themselves members. People who claim membership but are truly inactive are scarce indeed.[2]

As Kanter (1972) has argued, material and temporal sacrifice is a vital ingredient in the commitment of members to an organization. In practical terms, the more time and energy spent on church work, the less there is available for competing activities and therefore competing ideas. As long as members are with fellow members, doing the work of the church, they exist in a social world where their

TABLE 6.1. Measures of Commitment among Those Currently Active at Southside

Attendance		Giving		Church work	
More than once a week	58%	More than a tithe (10%)	37%	More than one job	3%
Once a week	27	A tithe	20	One job	53
Less than once a week	15	Less than a tithe	43	No jobs	44
	100%		100%		100%
	N = 62		N = 49		N = 62

SOURCE: Data were gathered during interviews of randomly selected participants. Only those currently active are included here. Data on giving were not available for all those interviewed.

theological ideas are assumed to be true. The pastor often reminds members that to avoid backsliding they need to be faithful in church attendance and avoid spending too much time with "worldy" people. No matter what the theological rationale for such advice, it is sociologically sound. The most committed believers are the people who are bound to the world of Fundamentalism by their extensive involvement with the people and activities at Southside.

Southside's core members build their worlds around the church. It helps to shape almost every decision they make. Some have chosen their place of residence because it was close to the church. Recall what Connie Meyer and Bonnie Towles had to say.

I moved here to be closer to Southside. That's the reason I moved here. Funny, I believe He built this place right here for that purpose.

We were in Centerville for six years, and four of those years I was traveling back and forth to Southside. Three years I was traveling back and forth to the Academy. We were here six days a week and twice on Sunday!

Bob Hughes claims that he would not take a new job unless the necessary Christian institutions were available—that is, "a good local church to go to, one with an approved Christian school as well. I would put whatever the monetary fee that was offered me in the second place. I mean if the location we were going to had a Fundamental church with a Christian school, then I would consider a job there. Otherwise, I stay right where I am." For committed members, the Academy has become as much a necessity as the church. Even though it sometimes means financial hardship, nearly nine out of ten of the church's core members who have children are sending those children to Christian schools and colleges.

For many, almost every spare minute is spent on activities related to church. The church *is* their leisure activity. If they bowl or play softball, they join the church teams. If they are handy at crafts, they make things for the nursery or Sunday School. If they like to read, they devour books about the Bible and the Christian life. Even their radio and television consumption is dominated by Christian programing. If they have jobs to do in the church, those jobs spill over into their time at home and can even become a source of family friction, especially if there is an unsaved husband in the house. That was Bonnie Towles's experience: "I was teaching Sunday School for a couple of years—two-year-olds—but there was a lot of preparation to do at home. That in addition to AWANA and helping the kids with their homework, my husband felt that it was, that I always had something else to do. You know, I don't think that the Lord intends for us to get too busy either, which is hard not to because you keep feeling like you should be or you want to be doing something." Ann Lazzaro, whose husband is very supportive, talked about how busy she is with teaching in the nursery school, going to college part-time, taking care of her family, and going to church. In addition, she said, "When I have spare time, if I do, I'm taking a correspondence course for evangelistic teaching for Christian schools, and I like to practice my sign language if I have a chance."

The other side of involvement in church is the loss of time for involvement in anything else. Many members give up nonchurch leisure and sporting activities, as Jim Forester did: "Now I don't play golf any more, and I don't miss it either. And I prayed about it. Golf was getting to be a vice. When I wasn't working, I was on the golf course, and it just wasn't right. So I prayed about it, and I asked the Lord to take that wanting to play golf away, and he did." They soon lose time for and interest in community affairs, as Ann Lazzaro did: "As far as the community, the only thing I did was to do volunteer work in the hospital. Although it was very interesting, and I enjoyed it, I knew that—I kept praying that 'if you don't want me here,

Lord, just let it happen that I don't come here any more.' And then, before I knew it, I was so busy I couldn't get there any more." Elaine Young talked about not having any time to get acquainted with her neighbors: "There's very little time for much in the community. When we moved in, I was working full-time, and with being out full-time and with Steve doing his church bus route on Saturday morning, when we were home, most of our neighbors were gone." Like most committed Southside members, Elaine finds secular activities just not worth the time. The Lord's work is too important to be neglected in favor of secular pursuits.

The Importance of Fellowship

For the members of Southside, this dizzying round of church activities can effectively shut out the influences of the world. At church believers are sheltered by the Fundamentalist ideas that make of the world a sensible place. But to remain alive, to become a part of everyday reality, those ideas and words must make their way outside the walls of the church. The word of God, as heard through the words of the pastor, must become the everyday conversation of the parishioner. In that way, the pastor's words can become the human link between God's inscrutable will and the everyday rules into which it must be translated.

Berger reminds us of the importance of words and conversations in maintaining our understanding of reality: "An individual's nomos [understanding of the world] is constructed and sustained in conversation with significant others. . . . The world begins to shake in the very instant that its sustaining conversation begins to falter" (1969:21–22). Bonnie Towles expressed much the same thought in different words: "You get caught up in the world as soon as you get away from a good Bible-preaching church and when you are not under the Word, the preaching of the Word. It doesn't take long before you get everything turned around." Continually hearing others interpret the events of the world in Fundamentalist language is crucial to maintaining the individual believer's understanding and sense of orderliness.

These sustaining conversations occur in a variety of forms and settings. The most formalized is the pastor's sermon. He attempts to address issues of the faith as they might be faced by a typical believer.

Less formal, and more practical, are the testimonies and prayer requests that the members themselves offer during church meetings. When they tell each other stories about their successes or ask for prayer about their needs, they are placing the events of their lives in words and categories that will be recognized by fellow believers (cf. Beckford 1978; McGuire 1977). Having a testimony is seen as evidence that a person is living in God's will. One of the leading church members used to say that if you did not have a testimony, you should watch out because God might give you one. He meant that God might impose suffering that would remind you of how much you needed divine assistance. Whether or not he was right about God, his instincts about people were on target. Unelss a person is adept at explaining life in terms of God's will, the rest of the Fundamentalist world will not long remain plausible. The person without testimony may soon be lost to the faith.

Conversely, the people who most frequently demonstrate skill at discerning God's will in their lives are likely to rise to places of leadership in the religious community. They are looked up to because their testimonies provide advice and examples for other believers. When leaders tell how God helped them find a job or a house or even a button, the rest of the congregation learns another lesson in finding and following God's will; and everyone is reassured that the world does work as it should.

When people come to church they expect to find help in interpreting and applying the Bible. Sermons and testimonies provide authoritative answers, but informal conversation among believers provides basic daily maintenancc of the faith. Before and after every church service, members gather in informal groups to catch up on "what the Lord has been doing in their lives." They "praise the Lord" for their triumphs and promise to pray for each other when times are difficult. They ask each other's advice and refer each other to parts of the Bible that might help. Even when members are talking merely about the weather or the latest problem with the car, the underlying assumption is that God has everything under control.

These conversations spill over into the hours spent outside church. For most members, their best friends are other members or at least others who attend a similar church. They share meals together, go on outings together, and do all the things that friends always do. But Christian friends can be depended on to understand

and to give advice that others could not give. Believers know about God's will, and they know how to pray and search the scriptures. Bonnie recalled her friendship with Elaine Young.

> All through those first couple of years when I first came to Southside but was still having a hard time, all I needed to do was call Elaine, and she would just hear my voice, and she would say, "I'll be right there." She would get in the car and come over, and she would open the Bible, and whatever it was that I was struggling with or discouraged with, she would not back down. She would not let me say, "I give up." . . . She always came back to the Word.

The two are still good friends who help to sustain each other. They share prayer concerns with each other, and they work together to witness to friends and strangers. When they find themselves with spare time, they are likely to spend it visiting prospects. This is the kind of Christian friendship that Southside members refer to as true fellowship; Janet Slavin echoed the feelings of many when she said, "Having fellowship with believers is what really gives us the confidence in our salvation . . . good fellowship, getting together with fellow Christians and sharing with them, sharing what the Lord is doing in your life, admitting problems, and the other person can give you some encouragement. . . . We try to fellowship with Christians as much as possible. We feel that is very essential." The more formal means for learning God's will—sermons and testimonies and Bible reading—cannot bridge the gap between divine intentions and everyday events with nearly the power of a friendship.

In addition to institutional ties, then, Southside's most committed members are bound to the church by friendships with others in the congregation. They eagerly seek each other out when they arrive at church, and they get together for "fellowship" afterward. Throughout the week they are in touch by phone, go visiting prospects together, and eat in each other's homes. Their relationships are friendships in all the usual ways, but the focus of their lives together is the church.

This is not the case for every member of the church. For the moderately committed of Southside's members, Fundamentalism is a less central part of their identity. They are less likely to have friends in the church, are less likely to have church jobs, and therefore come less often. They simply spend less time among church people. Conversely, they are more likely to have friends outside the church and to be involved in nonchurch organizations and activities, and they are less likely to see these involvements solely as opportunities to witness. The moderately committed seem more willing than the highly committed to tolerate the different religious choices of others. They are still unlikely to feel comfortable with really "worldly" people, but, for them, the boundaries of brotherhood are much wider. For almost 40 percent of Southside's active members, neither relationships nor activities are defined solely by church membership.

The church, for its part, would like to increase the attachment of these people to the beliefs and activities of the church community. Southside recognizes the need for fellowship as a part of that task and likes to think of itself as a friendly church. Members are encouraged to smile and greet visitors on Sunday morning, and the church attempts to provide structured opportunities for fellowship in the form of after-church socials, potluck dinners, and special outings. For those who are already well integrated into the church, such gatherings further extend their time with Christian friends.

For those who are looking for friends, however, fellowships may not be the place to find them. One new family eager to find some fellowship in the church went on the fall foliage trip. They reported with disappointment that they met only one new couple, whose names they had since forgotten. This family will more likely eventually find fellowship in a class or committee of some sort. Regular time together in small groups is far more effective in establishing fellowship relationships than are large-group, occasional events. Both the Senior Fellowship and the College and Career Bible Study, for instance, flourish because they are relatively small, meet regularly, and allow lots of unstructured time for people to get to know one another. Although fellowship is sometimes described as if it comes automatically when one is with other Christians, the experience of most of Southside's members is that they must work hard to find and develop the kinds of Christian friendships in which fellowship means more than a friendly smile.

Some of the moderately committed, in fact, would readily make a more complete commitment if they could only experience such fellowship. They simply cannot seem to find a way into the inner circle at Southside. And at least in part the problem is that they are so-

TABLE 6.2. Age and Marital Status of Highly Committed Participants and Moderately Committed Participants at Southside

		Age			
	Marital status	18–34	35–54	55 +	Total
Highly committed participants	Single	3%	3%	3%	8%
	Attend without spouse	0	5	5	11
	Attend with spouse	42	37	3	82
	Total	45%	45%	11%	101% N = 38
Moderately committed participants	Single	21%	12%	25%	58%
	Attend without spouse	4	4	12	21
	Attend with spouse	8	4	8	21
	Total	33%	21%	46%	100% N = 24

SOURCE: Data were gathered during interviews with randomly selected participants. NOTE: Highly committed members are defined as those who meet at least two of the following three criteria: attend more than once a week, give at least 10 percent of their income, hold at least one church job. Moderately committed members are those who regularly participate but at lesser levels. Some rows or columns do not total correctly because of rounding.

cially different. Income and education do not make much difference as long as the person does not have an extreme amount of either. What does make a difference is not being a young married adult with a family. The most active, core members are overwhelmingly married, with children at home or in college. They are likely to be under thirty-five, and almost certainly are under fifty-five (see Table 6.2). Those who are married but whose spouses do not attend are more active than singles (although they do not give as much money) but much less active than those who attend as a family (see Table 6.3).

The strong family ethos in this church is enhanced by the youth and vivacity of the pastor. People who do not fit the young-family pattern are likely to feel different and are not likely to be sought out by the young families who are now the teachers and committee chairs and planners of events. For seniors, the problem is partly one of incapacity and is mostly overcome by the relationships and activi-

TABLE 6.3. Measures of Southside Participants' Commitment by Age and Marital Status

Degree of commitment	Age			Marital status		
	18–34	35–54	55+	Single	Attend w/o spouse	Attend w/spouse
Attend less than once a week	8%	0%	47%	29%	11 %	8%
Attend once a week	20	32	33	53	44	11
Attend more than once a week	72	68	20	18	44	81
	100%	100%	100%	100%	99%	100%
	N = 25	N = 22	N = 15	N = 17	N = 9	N = 36
Give < 10%	38%	37%	67%	58%	100%	23%
Give 10%	10	37	11	8	0	30
Give > 10%	52	26	22	33	0	47
	100%	100%	100%	99%	100%	100%
	N = 21	N = 19	N = 9	N = 13	N = 6	N = 30
Hold at least one church job	72%	64%	20%	6%	56%	81%
	N = 25	N = 22	N = 15	N = 17	N = 9	N = 36

SOURCE: Data were gathered during interviews with randomly selected participants. Information on attendance and jobs was available for sixty-two individuals; and information on giving was available for forty-nine individuals.

ties that the Senior Fellowship provides. For singles, the answers are not so simple. One woman in her late thirties finally left the church when she could find no place for a person like herself. Another single woman, in her twenties, said, "If I had a family of my own, I'd probably go to the church, and I'd probably want my children to have that background. But for myself to go. . . ." Although Howard Otto was still involved in the church, he found himself increasing lonely as his divorce became final: "I tend to shut myself off from fellowship in this particular instance because unless you've paid your dues, you don't really know where I'm coming from. That may be my problem in perceiving that there's this major difference, but unless you've established your credibility with me, how can you know, how can you tell what I've been through?" Being different often means not being fully integrated into the life of the church.

One other factor has increased the number of unattached and

lonely people in the church: the size of the congregation. It is hard to find a place to belong when the group in which one sits on Sunday morning consists of 400 or 500 people. My own experience may be common. In the two Sundays I visited before I made a research commitment, I was quite able to walk in and out without anyone speaking to me. People I met at various church activities often did not remember me a few weeks later unless they had been told that I was writing a book. Rarely did anyone seek me out with an invitation. In short, the place I made for myself in the church was made at my own initiative. People did not avoid me because they knew I was a researcher; they simply did not know who I was. Because my husband was not with me, and I did not have children, I looked like an unattached single woman. However, when my social status visibly changed to mother-to-be, my place in the congregation also changed. Women went out of their way to strike up a conversation with someone they could perceive as like themselves. What I had not been able to accomplish in months of hard work at getting acquainted was done overnight when I became more socially similar. In such a large group, finding a niche may require both initiative and similarity.

Those who have been at Southside the longest are the most likely to notice the differences size makes. Over and over the old-timers mentioned that they just do not have the fellowship at church they once had. As the church began to grow, a woman who had formerly been willing to fight her husband to come lost her own sense of belonging and quit coming herself. A man who has been a faithful member for decades reflected on the changes he has seen: "Now I guess we're about one of the wealthiest churches in the area, and I see that as somewhat of a detriment spiritually. There's not the closeness there of the church to the Lord, like there once was. . . . With the increase there's been a multitude of people, whereas before it was smaller, more personal." He talked about financial stability and spiritual maturity, but the key was the lack of fellowship. He was not alone in worrying that the lack of closeness in the church might indicate a lack of closeness to God. He recognized that in a large church it is easy for people to drift in and out without becoming committed.

If they are lucky, a few of those people on the fringes meet someone in the church like the Danners. Ray and Mary have two married children and one in a Bible college, so they are eager to fill their "empty nest" with spiritual children. Theirs is a home full of warmth and hospitality, and they are especially sensitive to the lonely and troubled people in the church. Mary reflected on the needs she sees: "It seems like there are a lot of needy people in the fellowship. That seems to be a way of service too. Of late, the Lord seems to have given me the ministry of encouraging . . . new believers and just people you remind of their mother or aunt or something. . . . We miss our children greatly, and the Lord seems to supply that need. So we have been able to minister in a small way and encourage them." Her husband added, "It is really mushrooming for us lately —adults with problems in the church that invite us over. And we have to be careful because there is a fine line: You don't want to offend someone in the church because the deacons are supposed to be doing that. But if they request you, we go." People like the Danners become examples and interpreters of the faith for people who might otherwise drift away because they find themselves too different or not aggressive enough to make a place for themselves. A remarkable number of people mentioned this one couple as among their best friends in the church, having found in the Danners a way into the fellowship.

Establishing firm social connections to the congregation is essential if the believer is to continue to live in the faith. Within the everyday conversations among friends, Fundamentalist ideas are sustained. The activities and relationships of the church are the plausibility structure on which their Fundamentalist world view rests.

The Larger Fundamentalist Network

When the members of Southside speak of the "body of Christ," they are referring to their local congregation; but believers can participate in Fundamentalism beyond the local church as well. Southside may not belong to a denomination, but it has connections to a network of institutions that link it with other Fundamentalists in this country and around the world (cf. Carpenter 1980). Locally (within about fifty miles) there are perhaps a dozen other churches that are recognized as sound. Southside members assume that members of these other churches are saved, and they recommend their sister congregations to people who move. Church staff members exchange services and sometimes plan joint church events. Each church supports the others' revivals, Bible Institutes, and the like. All the churches are independent, but that does not mean that they are isolated from others like themselves.

This web of connections has expanded enormously with the growth of Christian print and broadcast media. Those outside Fundamentalism might once have dismissed such evangelical productions as insignificant, but, with Jerry Falwell's rise to national prominence, the extent and power of their products have become apparent. That Hal Lindsey's premillennial tome, *The Late Great Planet Earth* (1970), was the number one best seller in the 1970s should have warned those who are now alarmed. Christian publishing, broadcasting, and selling are, very simply, big business.

Southside members are connected to the evangelical media in a variety of ways. Although Christian television is a relatively weak influence, almost all the members listen to and support the local Christian radio station. They enjoy it primarily because it surrounds them with pleasant religious music that they "can feel good about listening to." For many, it is Christian Muzak. Those who listen to the radio preachers say they are constantly learning something new about the Christian life. With Christian radio, believers need not worry about being seduced by sinful rhythms or ungodly ideas. Their view of the world is supported rather than challenged.

Another of the important institutions in the Fundamentalist network is the Christian book store. Southside members shop at a couple of stores in the metropolitan area where they live. There they can find gifts for their Christian friends, supplies for Sunday School, and all kinds of good reading. There are Christian novels and story books, Bibles, and books about the Bible. There are books about Christian doctrines, Christian history, and Christian politics. Fundamentalists are voracious writers, publishers, and readers. One woman reported, "We fight over the books from Moody! We read this summer Sterns's *History of Religions*. It was 700 pages long. It was excellent; it reads like a book rather than a history—very easy reading. We were fighting over it, but we finished it. And, of course, it was something we could discuss." Another person confessed, "I tell you I never in my life read so much as since I became a Christian. . . . I get *Moody Monthly*, which I enjoy. All in all, I haven't enjoyed any secular books since I've been a Christian. I don't know, I just find that there is so much wealth and knowledge in Christian books that you don't need secular books." Almost all I met were eager to recommend the latest books they had read, and the books were always from within the nonsecular world. Fundamentalists are people for whom the Word is everything; so it is not surprising that written words, especially religious ones, are a powerful part of their lives.

Even more persuasive than Christian books are the magazines, newsletters, and cassette tapes that flood the mails. The most popular at Southside is a little monthly devotional booklet called *Our Daily Bread*. Almost everyone reads the scripture and meditation it provides for each day. Following that, the most widely read publications are probably *Moody Monthly* and *The Sword of the Lord*. *Moody Monthly* is an attractively produced bimonthly that identifies itself as "The Christian Family Magazine." It contains inspiring stories about the faith of others, articles on doctrine and current religious issues, and hints for improving one's family life and work in the church. *The Sword of the Lord* is in newspaper format, is much less up to date in appearance, and is primarily sermonic, especially concerning signs of impending Rapture and judgment. Once a family is on the mailing list for one of these major publications, it will likely also receive occasional products from other Fundamentalists who feel they have a message worth publishing. Sometimes only one issue ever appears, but if a preacher is able to raise enough money for printing and mailing costs, he is likely to put his message on paper—or on cassette tape—and send it into the homes of believers. Southside members, then, have ample reading and listening materials available to make secular sources almost unnecessary. Church women can even cook from Christian cookbooks.

In addition, believers have opportunities for Christian recreation that nearly eliminate the need for secular entertainment. Rather than going to secular movies, they go to Christian ones in their own and other churches. Rather than sending their children to summer tennis camp, they send them to church camp. Instead of a secular resort full of sinful pleasures, families can choose Schroon Lake, in beautiful upstate New York. There a Christian family can enjoy skiing in the winter and boating in the summer, while taking in a Bible study or two and being inspired by evening preaching services. If Schroon Lake is not handy, Bob Jones University or PTL's Heritage USA offer similar programs. The network of services is large indeed, and with the Christian Yellow Pages to help, even visits to the doctor and dry cleaners can be conducted without venturing into the truly unregenerate secular world.

Perhaps even more important than these everyday services are the institutions that educate Fundamentalist children and train their leaders. As we will see in Chapter 10, the Academy is a vital link in creating and maintaining the faith of individual believers. But the most important institution in creating and maintaining the character of Fundamentalism as a whole is the Christian college. What pastors and missionaries learn there shapes their ministries and therefore the churches they lead. There are no Fundamentalist seminaries; Bible schools and Christian colleges fill that role. Although many are accredited by secular authorities, their primary credentials come from the Fundamentalist parents and pastors who keep a vigilant eye on what their young people are learning. Even a hint of heresy can quickly deprive a school of its Fundamentalist clientele.

Because these colleges expect to be able to enforce rules of Christian conduct, they do not cater to nonbelievers. They do all their recruiting through Fundamentalist channels. During the summer, teams of students put on programs in the churches and spread the word about their schools. Christian colleges advertise in *Moody Monthly* and similar journals. But, most importantly, they are judged by their graduates. If young people have been impressed with a pastor or a special speaker, they are likely to inquire about his college. And once one person from a church has gone, others are likely to follow. Although the pastor at Southside is a graduate of a Bible college in the Midwest, only a few have ventured to that part of the country to study. The current favorite among his youth is Pensacola Christian College, a new school, in a warmer climate. A few have also gone to Bob Jones University, while others are attending Tennessee Temple College, Pillsbury and Maranatha Baptist Bible Colleges, and especially Moody Bible Institute. At least a dozen of Southside's youth were attending Christian colleges when I was there, far more than were in secular schools. Some were attending to prepare for a secular career, but not many Christian schools are yet catering to that audience. Most students go to prepare to be pastors and missionaries or—if they are girls—to marry a pastor or missionary.

Young people who decide to be missionaries encounter the

breadth of the Fundamentalist network firsthand. They usually affiliate with an independent mission agency that provides them with some benefits, such as insurance and retirement programs and job training and placement. The agency will not, however, provide compensation or travel expenses. That money must be raised through the process known as "deputation," putting together a package of contributing churches and individuals. Some churches may promise $1,000 or $2,000 a year, others $100 OR $200, and others only that they will pray and give "as the Lord leads." According to Pastor Thompson, it will probably take new missionaries two years, 90,000 miles, and $27,000 before they arrive on the mission field. That is the distinct disadvantage of the system. The advantage is that each church feels directly involved with the missionaries it supports and is likely to respond rather quickly to requests for prayer or emergency aid. The churches also perceive that they are thus able to be assured of the doctrinal purity of the missionary message they sponsor.[3]

Southside provides partial support for about twenty missionaries in places as diverse as Japan, Nigeria, Grenada, and a Navajo Indian reservation. Time is reserved one Wednesday night each month for missionaries who have returned from the field with their slides and stories or for new missionaries who want to present their case for support. Once a year, the church also sponsors a week-long Missions Conference, with nightly messages about missions, taped messages from missionaries still on the field, and an "international" dinner. The point of the week is to challenge people to make "faith promises" of money to support missions. After the Sunday morning sermon, members are asked to pray about how much they should give (over and above their regular giving to the church) and to write that amount on the Faith Promise Cards. These are then collected, tallied, and a report brought to the waiting congregation. In the fall of 1979, they pledged $52,000, up from $44,000 the previous year. The missions committee then had to decide whether to raise the church's support to the missionaries they already sponsored, to add new missionaries to their rolls, or both. If actual giving proved later to be over or under the projected amount, checks to the missionaries would be adjusted accordingly. Being a Fundamentalist missionary takes a great deal of faith. And being a Fundamentalist often means spending a good deal of time and money in supporting missions.

The brotherhood to which Southside's members belong is limited to those who have accepted the message they preach, but that brotherhood extends throughout the world. Because of the work of missionaries, believers can find people all over the world with whom they share a common faith, and, through the Christian mass media, those believers are increasingly sharing common ideas and experiences. The social structures that sustain the Fundamentalist world view are not limited to scattered local congregations.

The activities of each church provides an immediate framework for the believer's time, while its people nurture the believer in conversations that sustain the faith. Those who find a place in the fellowship often become highly committed, making large investments of time, money, and energy in the congregation. And their congregation, in turn, opens the door to a wide network of resources that enriches the lives Fundamentalists can lead.

CHAPTER SEVEN

The Shepherd and His Flock: Authority, Structure, and Ritual

Take heed therefore unto yourselves, and to all the flock, over the which the Holy Ghost hath made you overseers, to feed the church of God.
—Acts 20:28

THE SOCIAL structure in which the members of Southside live extends through time and space and relationships into every corner of their lives. It is significant for both its comprehensiveness and its distinctive character. Support for the Fundamentalist way of life comes from what they learn at church, the network of social institutions and relationships the church provides, and—more subtly—the way in which those ideas and relationships are structured. The way things are done at church provides the underlying structure for how believers expect the world to be. Believers are often admonished to remember whose they are, to take their first identity from the creator to whom they belong. But they also "belong" to the church.

For example, at church the most important activity is preaching. People come to "hear the Word." Structurally, that means that they expect to sit in pews facing a person who is recognized as an authority. He speaks to them, and they learn from what he says; he is their shepherd. He is, of course, male. None of them expects to have a close personal friendship with the pastor; rather, they expect to admire and imitate him.

The symbol of the preacher's office is the pulpit, and only an ordained man may stand behind it to preach. It is sometimes even referred to as a "sacred desk," and its space is guarded accordingly. Women may stand behind it to sing but not to speak. Men who are not ordained may speak only if an ordained man remains seated on the platform. Lay people may deliver a "message in song" by singing in the choir or other ensembles, but when the sermon is delivered, they take their places off the platform with the rest of the congregation. When the pastor gets up to preach, he stands alone before a congregation of waiting listeners. As long as he is behind the pulpit (as he always is on Sunday morning), people in the pews do not make verbal responses beyond an occasional "Amen." Only (as, for instance, on Wednesday night) when the speaker stands on audience level, using a lectern, is discussion expected. Although believers do not often realize it, this structure of the preaching situation permeates what they come to expect of themselves as Christians and of their church as an institution.

The Power of the Pastor

Above all, the preaching situation shapes and is shaped by the authority of the pastor. As the primary occupant of the pulpit and interpreter of scripture, the Fundamentalist pastor holds a position of enormous power. At Southside, Pastor Thompson teaches the largest adult Sunday School class, preaches twice on Sunday, and leads the Wednesday night service. A member goes to church to "hear the pastor," who almost exclusively leads in worship. And when people talk about receiving help in understanding the Bible, they point to the pastor. His preaching helps to shape what the congregation sees as important and true about the Bible. He explains what the Bible means and tells the people how the Bible says they should live. Although they are to seek God's will in prayer and Bible study, they understand what they find because the pastor has guided them.

The pastor's authority is also present in less obvious ways. He is likely to influence what members read in addition to the Bible. The pastor decides which periodicals will be used in Sunday School and which books will go into the church library or bookstore. He invites groups that sell books and magazines when they visit the church. He even mentions from the pulpit the books or television programs he finds especially good or bad. When members happen to read something that is out of keeping with the pastor's teachings, they are likely to recognize that fact and quit reading.

For the most part, people acknowledge the power the pastor has and celebrate it.[1] They recognize that a new believer can get lost when he or she starts to read the Bible. Joe Slavin claimed that the best advice to a new Christian is to "tell them to get a Bible right away, a King James Version, right off the bat. Tell them to start reading it, and come to church." Coming to church means hearing the pastor, and that is crucial to understanding the Bible. Jim Forester and Bonnie Towles talked about how it was when they were first saved.

> At first, I had a hard time reconciling how I was supposed to act, how I was supposed to talk, how I was supposed to just conduct myself as a Christian. But the influence of our pastor in Ohio helped me considerably in that area.

> Those first couple of years, you know, I quit wearing my slacks, threw them away. You know, that's it. Part of it was because people at Southside don't dress that way, and I had—my uppermost thought all the time was "What will pastor think?"

Learning to find God's will, to understand the rules and reasons in life, depends in large part on finding a trusted pastor.

The base for pastoral authority at Southside is at least partly charismatic (in the Weberian, not the pentecostal, sense). Pastor Thompson is a dynamic speaker, able to evoke strong emotional responses from his listeners. He is young and attractive and dresses well. He uses humor and story telling to give his audience a sense of intimacy with him. Yet actual intimate conversations between pastor and parishioners are rare. Most members see him only in his ritualized roles and maintain an idealized view of his character. One woman talked about how amazed she is that his sermons apply to ordinary, sinful people: "How would a man like him, who is, who is so, just so wonderful, how would he know the human traits that we people have that, that are like that? Because I'm sure he hasn't got them." Although most members know that the pastor is human and sinful, just as they are, they nevertheless see him as somewhat larger than life, a little above the messiness of the everyday world. That was especially true of Jim Forester: "I guess it's not really right to idolize someone or to want to be like someone, . . . but I look at our pastor and just the tremendous person he is. . . . I'm impressed with him very, very much. Sometimes I ask the Lord, 'If it's all right, I don't want to be Ronald Thompson, but you could give me some of his patience!'"

Even those who are less starry eyed come to equate the church with the pastor. He is the expert who answers their questions and the person whose messages restore their souls. Those who become committed to the church invariably do so in large part because they like the pastor. Because "preaching the Word" is central to the Fundamentalist identity, the person who preaches comes to embody the identity of the church. It is not out of character to hear believers say they belong to "Pastor Thompson's church."

Even if this pastor were personally unattractive and an uninspiring speaker, he would still be recognized as the final authority in the church. More important than charismatic authority is the power the pastor gains as a result of his "scriptural" mandate—what Weber (1968: 226ff.) would classify as "traditional authority."[2] The position of pastor carries with it the belief that as long as what the incumbent does is "scriptural," the church is obligated to follow his leadership. The formal justification for such pastoral power comes from the New Testament and the image of the pastor as shepherd. But the symbolic justification is more Old Testament in character. The model is Moses leading the Children of Israel across the desert to the Promised Land. If the people disobeyed, God (or at least the desert environment) would surely punish them. At least three times while I was there, the pastor told the story of a group of rebellious Israelites who challenged Moses, and "the earth opened her mouth, and swallowed them up" (Numbers 16:32). Challenging pastoral authority is definitely not part of God's will.

Both charisma and tradition combine to legitimate the authority of a Fundamentalist pastor. However, that authority is supported also by the bureaucratic structures of the congregation. The pastor's influence is not limited to spiritual matters alone. The social structure of the preaching situation shapes the power structure of the church. Because he speaks God's word from the pulpit, the pastor is also expected to know God's will in the committee room.

His influence over the business of the church begins with the fact that he appoints the nominating committee and works with it to fill all key positions. He also names the men who will become deacons and trustees. Through either direct appointment or direct influence, every church worker must meet his approval. The pastor is thus assisted by others who can also use their spiritual authority to persuade. In one business meeting, for instance, the trustees and building committee were recommending that the church have a banquet (at a cost of about $3,000) to kick off a fund-raising drive to eliminate the church's debt, all in preparation for building a new church building. All over the congregation there were objections to spending so much money and puzzlement over this strategy for eliminating debt. Before the discussion had gone far, Spence Schuster, one of the most respected deacons, got up, stood behind the lectern, and opened his Bible. He began to talk about the need for a "vision" and quoted a verse or two of scripture. He presented little in the way of specific argument, but when he sat down, the plan passed without a dissenting vote. Having assumed the "pastoral" role, modeled after the structure of the preaching situation, he had commanded agreement from the people.

Few lay people at Southside could have done what Schuster did. Rarely does anyone besides the pastor presume to instruct others in what the Bible says the church should do. Schuster occupies a key position of leadership as teacher of the soul-winning classes, leader of the visitation program, and moderator of the Sunday School class in which the pastor teaches. Although he probably has the power to create an independent following, he uses his power to support the pastor.[3] Most of the remainder of the men who hold positions of power in the church do not speak with their own spiritual authority but as surrogates of the pastor. They are less articulate, have less tenure in the church, and are seen as less mature Christians. They are part of the inner circle that manages the day-to-day affairs of the church and controls its $200,000 budget; but they are trusted not for their own spiritual stature but for the pastor's.

The pastor's authority is increased, then, by his ability to gather a group of loyal lay leaders and place them in positions of responsibility in the church. But his influence does not end when workers take office. Most of the church's business is handled in committees; and for the most important of them the pastor is likely to call the meeting, set the agenda, and even moderate. The church treasurer and trustees control all financial matters, but these hand-picked people never act without the pastor's approval. In one instance, it became apparent after some controversy that the pastor had approved the rental of a van (which subsequently had an expensive breakdown), perhaps had even issued the check, without consulting the trustees.

As in that case, when members of the congregation want details about how money is spent or decisions are made, information is not readily available. The trustees have discretionary control over nearly half the church budget. From that fund they pay staff salaries, but my best guess is that at least $30,000 is available for expenditures reported only as "trustees' fund." The information that appears on the financial reports each quarter is sketchy at best.

Nor are the rest of the proceedings at the quarterly church business meetings any more informative or influential. As a result, participation is low. At one meeting, they had to search the halls to bring in enough people to constitute the required 15 percent quorum. Committee reports are presented on an ad hoc basis. All recommendations come from either trustees or deacons and are usually adopted with little discussion. The chair of the deacons usually moderates, but the pastor is often called on to speak. When a special meeting was called to vote on recommendations from the building committee, the deacon chair was apparently not informed in advance that there would be a meeting, so the pastor presided. A few of the members wish they could have a greater say in the decision making, but most are content with leaving church business in the hands of the pastor and his men. Because he knows God's will so well, he should also know which piece of real estate the church should buy, which company should cater a banquet, and which activities should be scheduled when. Those who wish to influence the church's affairs must do so with spiritual authority, as "men of God," and the most powerful "man of God" in the congregation is the pastor.

To say that authority at Southside is in the hands of "men" of God is quite literally true. Women are so thoroughly outside the official power structure that an all-male committee can be described as a "cross-section of the congregation." Especially since the coming of Pastor Thompson, the church has taken nearly literally the biblical injunctions against women "speaking" in the church (I Corinthians 14:35). It takes those injunctions to mean that women should never have a major role in decision making, and they should not teach in any situation where their husbands might be students. Practically, that means that women do not serve on committees or boards, and they do not teach adult Bible classes. A woman who headed the work crew that painted and cleaned the Academy building apologized to the men present as she told them what to do. She said she could justify her role only because the pastor had asked her to do it, her husband was not serving under her, and it was work that women were supposed to do anyway.

Such comprehensive male authority does not go completely unchallenged. When the current pastor arrived, a beloved and respected elderly woman was teacher of the adult Sunday School class, as well as leader of numerous weekday Bible studies in homes. She had a strong personal following of people who were convinced that her knowledge of scripture and her spiritual stature were second to none. When the pastor tried to take over her class, he initially failed. He conceded that she could continue until she finished her study of the book of Hebrews. She managed to take two years. She finally finished only because she knew she was about to die (which she did, reportedly within one week). Meanwhile, however, the pastor started a rival class and simply waited her out.

Another challenge came from the leader of the youth group (wife of the dissident choir director). She was competent herself and thought little of the pastor's administrative ability. She had been heard to remark that the pastor "would be lost if his wife didn't carry his brains around in a basket for him." She mounted periodic campaigns to make the church's decision making more open and democratic; but she had no particular following or respect in the church and finally decided to give up the fight. She and her husband left to join another church.

The dominance of the pastor and his men in the life of the church is not without its pitfalls. For all those who join the church because they like the pastor, there are also some who leave because they do not. Almost everyone who has been part of a Fundamentalist church for long has been through a full-scale church split over a pastor. Southside has not been immune. The church began as a split, and most recently it experienced another split over differences between the former pastor and his associate. One member who stayed and supported the pastor described it this way: "Our church had a division about seven years ago—Thornton and Johns—and there was a lot of friction. But once the people left, after Johns left, then we got smaller, but stronger. It was just a case of finding the right preacher, which we did." Being able to decide on the right preacher, of course, was the issue over which the church could not agree.

At Southside Gospel Church, then, the pastor has enormous resources for shaping the life of the congregation. Occasionally he fails; but most often he is able to counter moves made by dissidents and finally encourage them to find another church.

Ritual Structures and Everyday Life

Although the pastor and his role are important for understanding the way Fundamentalists live, both inside and outside the church, that is not the whole story. In a number of other ways, the rituals and structures of the church provide reinforcement for the Fundamentalist world view.

Rituals of Authority

The preaching role does more than provide a model for the pastor's own far-reaching power. It also provides a model for the use of power by other believers, again both inside and outside the church. A delicate balance between clergy power and lay participation is maintained in churches like Southside, in part by borrowing some of the pastor's power for the laity. Witnessing is the most obvious instance of transferring the preaching structure to an everyday situation. Believers assume the role of preachers, declaring God's message to the lost and issuing an invitation. In turn, they expect their prospects to assume the role of the congregation—responding, respecting, and imitating. Likewise, those who hold positions as teachers and leaders in the church use the preaching situation as their model. And when husbands are told to be the spiritual leaders of their households, it is the preacher and his congregation they imitate.

Even within the church, the ability to "speak the Word" is a gift given by God to laity as well as to clergy. Despite emphasis on the sacredness of the pulpit and the importance of "preaching the Word," ordinary members of Southside expect to play an active role in every church service. They sing, follow scripture in their Bibles, and pray silently for the lost. Lay people also have ample opportunities to speak. Every member is expected to learn to deliver a spontaneous public prayer, and on Wednesday night nearly everyone prays aloud in a small group. During other church activities, various leading lay men may be called on to pray, although on Sunday morning that function is reserved for ordained clergy. Similarly, during informal meetings, both men and women are encouraged to testify about what God is doing for them. The ex-Catholics in the congregation find this balance between authority and participation just right. They like their new-found involvement in worshipping, witnessing, and learning; but they are also comfortable deferring to a pastor whose spiritual authority they respect.

The preaching situation thus provides the model for authority: A biblically legitimated expert provides unquestioned and respected leadership for those less able to care for themselves. Because this model of social relationships involves an unequal division of authority and status, believers come to see such a division as valued and right—both inside and outside the church. They come to expect groups to be divided between sheep and shepherds. The shepherds are entitled to deference and rewards, while the sheep are entitled to love and care. Just as their ideology is predicated on clear answers and on distinct boundaries between the saved and the damned, so the social structure reinforces the singleness of vision and clarity of boundaries by supporting both the idea and the substance of pastoral authority.

Rituals of Sacrifice

The rituals of a Fundamentalist church also support other aspects of the ideology. The routine of pledging, tithing, and sacrificial giving supports both individual commitment to the church and the church's connections to the larger Fundamentalist network. Because there is no centralized denomination to which the church gives a budgeted amount, a variety of organizations come to the church from time to time for support. In addition, anyone with a worthy cause can go before the church with an appeal. One Sunday morning, special offerings were taken for a Bible publishing agency that needed a new press, the medical expenses of a member's critically ill son, the Academy's scholarship fund, and the expenses of sending the church's deaf youth to camp. The church's regular expenses are met through the tithes of its members and friends, but many of those members also give regularly and generously to missions, to the building fund, and to special offerings for unbudgeted church expenses and special projects.

The pastor's sermons are important in encouraging the people to maintain such a high level of giving. Twice a year (once for the misssions conference and once for the building fund), he preaches a month-long Sunday morning series on "stewardship"; and at least once a month giving is a significant theme in his sermons about Christian living. Believers are always cautioned that God first wants their lives, but they are reminded that their pocketbooks are part of the package. They are told that God is indifferent to how much or how little money they have as long as they are willing to give as much as they can. If they are generous, they can expect tangible rewards in this life and in the one to come. The pastor often reminds his listeners that God supplies all their needs and even gave his Son to die for them: Knowing that, how can they keep from giving sacrificially to God through the church?

Sacrifice is, then, an important part of being a Fundamentalist, but it is not without reward. Many members would testify with Joe Slavin that giving is more than worth it: "I'm really glad that someone explained to me what tithing means right off the bat. Then I started praying about it, and right away we started tithing, and then all of our blessings came. The Lord gave me a new job. He just blessed us in so many ways through tithing." Believers give up their money, their time, and their relationships with outsiders. But in return they become part of an organization that offers them activities for every spare moment and friends with whom to share those activities. They become connected to a variety of institutions that offer alternatives to secular media, recreation, and services. They learn concretely that sacrifice brings rewards.

Rituals of Evangelism

The social structure of the church subtly molds the identity and behavior of Southside's members in other ways. Outsiders might be amazed that believers return Sunday after Sunday to hear sermons about how to be saved. Why should they be so insistent that the pastor preach evangelistic messages? The most obvious answer is that not everyone who attends on Sunday morning has already been saved. The people of Southside would be devastated at the thought of an unsaved person entering their church without hearing the message of salvation. Invitations are important at every church gathering, but on Sunday morning evangelism is the central theme.

A less obvious but just as important explanation for the emphasis on evangelism is that hearing about the need to be saved reminds believers over and over about how different they are from the world. They find great satisfaction in hearing the preacher condemn the evils of the unsaved world and laud the joys of salvation. Evangelistic messages reaffirm the believers' sense that being saved is indeed their most important status.

In addition, evangelistic sermons provide both a model for how to witness and an opportunity to confirm believers in that role. Members are often reminded that just coming to church is a witness to their unsaved neighbors, but when an invitation comes they feel even more directly involved. They can pray for the unsaved people in the audience and perhaps even speak to someone sitting near them. Best of all, when they have won someone to the Lord, they can publicly declare that fact by accompanying their convert down the aisle. Believers are always vicariously involved in giving the invitation, but for some it is a personal triumph. Both personally and corporately, response to an invitation provides affirmation of the ideas by which Fundamentalists live their lives.

Rituals of the Heart

It is also no accident that invitations involve the singing of a song. Music is extremely important in Fundamental churches. The fact that all the church's music is provided by the lay members helps to reinforce their sense of participation. On Wednesday night, the congregation even selects the hymns. In each Sunday service, they sing three songs besides the invitation; the choir sings a call to worship and an anthem; and there are specials by one small ensemble and one soloist. In addition, the instrumentalists (playing the piano or the organ) provide a prelude, an offertory, and a postlude. All this without a single paid musician on staff!

Sheer quantity aside, the style of Southside's music is also important. Rhythms, of course, must never be dominant because a strong beat appeals to fleshly desires. Every song must have words that are doctrinally sound, understandable, and convey a message about the way to salvation, the joys of the Christian life, or the hope of heaven. Believers do not listen to music simply to hear the beauty of the sound. But they do expect their music to sound a certain way. The music is frequently built around simple major triads, with melodies and harmonies that are easy to hear and sing.

Many of Southside's favorite songs were written in the late nineteenth century and reflect the popular styles of that day. That sometimes means that secular music of the same era is heard as "good" music. But it is also means that Southside's music creates an atmosphere of old-fashionedness that reinforces the sense of tradition and changelessness so important to believers. Members are singing the same songs today they sang as children and their parents sang before them. When people come to Southside, the music often reminds them of churches they attended as children and makes them feel as if they have "come home."

Southside's use of music points to another of the delicate balances they try to achieve—that between spontaneity and formality, between head and heart. This relationship between head and heart is a multifaceted one. Fundamentalists have always stood firmly with one foot on each side of the fence. When biblical scholars seek to apply "rational" methods to the study of the Bible, Fundamentalists argue for an understanding of scripture guided by the Holy Spirit alone. But when modern theologians speak of a "leap of faith," Fundamentalists are just as likely to respond that they need not "leap" anywhere; their faith is rationally proven by fulfilled promises, both in scripture and in everyday life. Likewise, against those who seek God in the experience of the Holy Spirit, they argue that those experiences must be tested against the principles found in scripture. Yet, against those who wish to worship by following a lectionary or book of common prayer, they argue that the Spirit must be free to work. They see themselves standing between the emotional Pentecostals on one side and the cold "ritualists" on the other.

Southside's response is a kind of controlled informality. Creeds are not recited and prayers are not read, but neither does anyone interrupt the printed order of service with anything more than an "Amen." Believers argue vehemently for a "religion of the heart," distrusting the rationality of modern science and theology. Yet they do not wish to abandon themselves to unthinking emotion, to turn either their lives or their worship over to "feelings." The compromise they achieve reflects again the central role of preaching, as well as the importance of music. The musicians' job is to create the right emotional climate for the hearing of the pastor's message. The people will then be ready to listen with "open hearts," allowing the preacher to direct both their thinking and their feeling. It is not that Fundamentalists refuse to allow emotion in their services—far from it. Rather, they allow the emotional content of the service to be directed from the pulpit, not from the pews.

Because of this emotional openness, powerful preachers can move whole audiences to respond to an invitation. Jim Forester talked about the way he sometimes feels: "I find that during special services, with particular preachers that come, you know, that God has a way of speaking to my heart about things." A young woman who had not yet joined the church talked about the way she felt on the first Sunday she attended: "Pastor Thompson made me think of—oh what's his name—Jim Jones. He made me think of him, and I just sat there in church for a while wondering if this was some kind of fake-out thing like he did." She and everyone else at Southside is convinced that Pastor Thompson is perfectly safe and sincere, but they also know how important he is to their spiritual and emotional well-being. They come to church to feel uplifted.

Rituals of the Word

It would be far from correct, however, to assume that messages at Southside have only emotional content. Believers expect not only to have their hearts warmed but also to gain in wisdom about living the Christian life; and wisdom comes from the Bible. Despite their assertions to the contrary, Fundamentalists do not differ from liberals in the quantity of scripture that is read in any given service. The difference is in how the scripture is presented. Liberals often read three or four extended lectionary passages, usually around a common theme. Fundamentalist preachers usually start by reading one brief passage or verse and then add dozens of other verses throughout the message to support the points they are making. Both preacher and listeners must keep Bible in hand, thus reinforcing the sense that the pastor's words are strictly biblical. No Fundamentalist preacher would ever dare enter the pulpit without an open Bible; it is an essential trapping of his authority. For a Fundamentalist congregation, the pastor's uplifted Bible is as ritually significant as is the elevated host for someone partaking of the eucharist. Pastor Thompson once declared that the Bible is more important than Jesus Christ, and although he might want to qualify the theology of that statement, symbolically and ritually he was right. The Bible is for Fundamentalists the very presence of God in their midst.

In addition to reinforcing the significance of the Bible to Fundamentalism, the messages at Southside also model for believers how to use scripture in their everyday lives. When the pastor uses one small word or phrase as the theme for his sermon, they learn that God can speak through any word they find. When he stops in mid-sermon to suggest that they search out what else the Bible has to say, they learn the techniques of Bible research. Members look up a word or idea in their concordance and check the center-column references to find all the places it is used in scripture. The pastor is always able to take such a "stream-of-consciousness" reading of verses and find God's message. His listeners learn to desire the same skill and "discernment."

The rituals at Southside, then, support the members' lifestyle and world view in both obvious and nonobvious ways. The relation-ships they form and the activities in which they participate create a world in which they can be comfortable. The words they hear give them specific direction in how to live the Christian life, and the social structure they experience gives shape to their interactions both inside and outside the church. The social structure of the preaching sit-uation comes to dominate all authority relations. The realities of sacrifice and reward are experienced both inside and outside the con-gregation. An emphasis on evangelism constantly highlights the lo-cation of their community's boundaries and reinforces their sense of advantage over the outside world. The emotional content of the ser-vices teaches them how to feel God's presence, and the scriptural content combines practical training with ritual reinforcement of their identity as the people who really believe the Bible. All these rit-uals are so full of tradition that they provide a point of stability in a world otherwise constantly changing. For the people of Southside, the church is a safe shelter in a stormy world.

CHAPTER EIGHT

Husbands and Wives

Wives, submit yourselves unto your own husbands, as unto the
Lord. For the husband is the head of the wife, even as Christ is the
head of the church. . . . Husbands, love your wives, even as Christ
also loved the church, and gave himself for it.
—Ephesians 5:22–23, 25

THE CHURCH is not the only safe harbor for believers. It is
not the only institution in which Fundamentalist rules can be
made to apply. Other social units can earn the name *Christian*
and can share with the church in the maintenance of the believer's
faith. Foremost among these is the home. It, too, is to be structured
according to Christian principles, demonstrating to the world that
God's way is best. Like the church, homes can reinforce and sustain
believers by creating an environment where the Fundamentalist way
of life is taken for granted. But in homes, more than in churches,
Fundamentalist rules come up against hard realities that sometimes
demand compromise. Both the rules and the compromises shape the
lives believers live.

The importance of Christian homes is a recurring theme at
Southside. Members are often reminded from the pulpit that the
world's families are falling apart, that there is a "50 percent divorce
rate," and that the problem of juvenile delinquency can be traced to
the lack of discipline in today's homes. In contrast, believers point to
evidence that Fundamentalist homes are much more successful than
others. The fact that their children are polite and honest is an important affirmation of the rightness of living by God's rules. The fact
that their marriages are surviving when divorce is so pervasive reas-
sures them that using God's plan for husbands and wives is indeed
the only right way to structure a marriage. Having a Christian home
is one of the ways believers distinguish themselves from the rest of
the world.

When they talk about how a Christian home is different from

any other, the theme of discipline is almost always present. Jim Forester explained, "You can see a stark contrast between our home life and our habits and our ideals and the way we run our household compared to some others." They see uncommitted, undisciplined families as the root cause of most social problems and believe they offer a distinct alternative.

It is not accidental that marriage and family are given so much attention at Southside. This is a congregation of young families; and singles and seniors are all the more left out because "Christian homes" (that is, households with two Christian parents and one or more children) are so important to the church's identity. Women married to unsaved men may say they have a "half-Christian" home; and Howard Otto talked as if he would no longer have a Christian family when his divorce was final, even though he would have custody of his children. The culture of the congregation establishes only one family structure as normative, and the dominant life experiences of the group reinforce that norm. This is a group where people learn to be successfully married, and where young children learn about God. Being a "member" requires sharing that group identity.

Because marriage is so important, believers take special care in the selection of a mate. Yet they do not face the task alone. Just as they are sure that God has a plan for their salvation, their church, and their vocation, they are sure that their mate has already been chosen for them by God. There is one perfect partner who is now (or eventually will be) a Christian. One young woman talked about the man she was seriously dating: "I have prayed for a long time that I would meet somebody that was, you know, different, somebody that knew the Lord. And I waited a long time, but it finally happened."

A clear answer, however, is not always so apparent. If she were to marry someone who was not a believer, they would be said to be "unequally yoked" (II Corinthians 6:14). That is most assuredly not God's will, but it does sometimes work out in the end. Jim Forester explained: "We were unequally yoked, but God did not—I'm sure God wasn't happy about it. That was God's permissive will. God let that happen to bring Doris and I together so that I would get saved and so that Liz, Donald, Jonathan, and Billy would have a Christian home." Even though it was not God's will in the beginning, there was still a reason; and the long-term good has outweighed the short-term problems. The norm of a God-chosen mate survives even when practical realities would seem to dictate otherwise. The idea that God has life under control is as important at home as it is at church.

Likewise, the idea of biblical authority pervades the homes of believers no less than it does their church. Their notion of proper family life is built on their reading of scripture. They are sure that the Bible prescribes the only correct way for husbands and wives to relate to each other and for parents to raise their children: "Everything revolves around the Word. What does God have to say about this? Because there is no other authority. That's why I feel so sorry for children in non-Christian homes." Bonnie Towles recalled that even in unhappy times the Bible still had rules that applied: "I remember one time coming home and screaming at my husband, opening the Bible and saying, 'See this? See this? That's why I'm here. Not because I want to be here, but I have to be here. The Bible says I have to be here. God says that I have to be here, and that's why I'm here.'" At home, as in the rest of life, the Bible's rules should not be broken.

The Bible decrees that husbands and wives stay together until death and that they relate to each other as Christ to the church. Southside members come to expect, then, that Christian homes will be headed by a saved man who takes responsibility for the physical, emotional, and spiritual needs of the household. By his side will be a saved woman who accepts her role as wife and mother in reverent submission. Ideally, she should spend full time maintaining their home and caring for their children. The imperative seems so clear to believers that they come to expect anyone who is saved to try to establish a family according to God's rules.

To say that the imperatives are clear, however, does not mean that everyday realities conform to the ideal.[1] Southside members live in the same economic world as do other Americans, and sometimes those economic realities overshadow Fundamentalist ideals. For instance, although the "ideal" Christian home has a full-time mother, not nearly all of Southside's mothers are outside the labor force. Of the mothers who currently have children under twenty-five, only about 15 percent have stayed out of the labor force entirely during their children's growing-up years. About 35 percent have worked at jobs that still allowed them to spend most of their time at home, but nearly half of all the mothers at Southside are employed full-time outside the home.

Despite this rather massive deviation from the norm, South-side's women continue to hold forth the idea of full-time mother-hood. Most of those who work have occupations rather than careers; and they still do the bulk of the work that must be done at home. They share with the rest of Southside's mothers the ideal of being the most important influence in their children's lives, of creating a warm and loving environment in which children grow to be happy, healthy, Christian people. Jim Forester described his wife (who does stay at home full-time) in just such glowing terms: "She works twenty hours a day. Today the housewife and mother seem to be looked down upon in many places. Without moms, without the right kind of mothers in this country, we wouldn't be where we are today. . . . I appreciate very much my wife and the tremendous effort that she puts forth just to give us a good, stable home life." Doris agreed that her primary source of fulfillment was creating a good home: "I never held a job outside the home, but I do work twenty hours a day. But I enjoy it. I don't feel right now like I've missed any-thing. Now probably when Billy is in school full-time, I'll just go bonkers and go outside the home and do something. But right now I enjoy being home and making a home for everyone."

Those who do not have the luxury of staying at home neverthe-less identify themselves first as wives and mothers. Ann Lazzaro works and goes to school, but she says, "My family does come first, and my husband approves of my going to school, so that is what makes a difference." Whatever Southside wives and mothers actually do, husbands must approve. Although most mothers may violate the letter of the rule about working, they by no means violate its spirit.

In the day-to-day lives of families, then, women shoulder the re-sponsibility of maintaining the home. If they are employed, they may persuade their husbands to help with a few chores; but cooking, cleaning, and child rearing are the God-given tasks of women. Major purchases and repairs are delegated to husbands, while the general physical and emotional condition of the home and family is the job of the mother. The father's primary job is to provide the resources, make the right decisions, and preside over the spiritual well-being of the family.

The husband's role as priest in the family is, however, no less ambiguous than the wife's role as full-time homemaker. Among other reasons, wives are often the first in a family to convert. When the husband is not saved, wives usually take over as spiritual leaders in the home. A woman whose husband is not saved described her arrangement this way: "He is head of the house in the sense that he's the head of the house, but not the head of the Christian house." Bonnie added, "I hope to see my husband saved and for us to have family devotions for all of us and not just me and the children." Out of necessity, these women learn to be priests to their families, but most, like Bonnie, long to relinquish that role.

Besides the fact that wives are often the first to convert, they often find themselves the more enthusiastic supporters of the church and of the Fundamentalist way of life. Another woman, who does have a Christian husband, was almost as dissatisfied as she would have been if her husband were unsaved. And she was, therefore, equally involved in leading her family: "I want my husband to be the head of the Christian home, not passive. I don't want to have to do it; I want him to, you know." These three women and dozens of others in the church are in fact the spiritual leaders in their homes. The norm of male authority is strong enough to make them dissatisfied and to shape the goals they hold up for their children; but this too is a norm that is not perfectly followed.

Among the father's responsibilities in the "ideal" Christian home is to lead his family in daily devotions. The church encourages every family to set aside a special time for Bible reading and prayer in which the whole family participates. In the rhetoric of Southside, missing "family altar" is almost as grave as missing Sunday services.

However, although gathering the whole family for father-led devotions is a model to which nearly every family refers, it is by no means the most prevalent actual behavior, even when everyone in the family is saved. Many, like Jim, have simply found it impractical: "Getting everybody together in the same room at the same time—it just didn't work out. So now I get up early in the morning, and I read the Bible and pray. First thing in the morning I have a time of prayer with the Lord. And the kids do the same thing; Liz reads the Bible. But as far as a formal family devotional time, I'm embarrassed to say that 'no, I don't.' It hasn't worked out." The norm is strong enough to make him feel embarrassed but not strong enough to survive the practical difficulties.

More often reading the Bible and praying are a constant but informal part of the everyday lives of Southside's families. The Danners, for instance, tried to have a special time for family devotions but often found themselves too busy. For them, mealtimes became a "family altar."

> So the table was a sharing time. That is one reason I could never sell our kitchen table. So much has happened around it. I have given it to our son. But it seemed like around the table we cried and shared and talked. And because Christ is a way of life with us, it does enter into our daily life. So he [Ray] does come home sharing who he is talking with, and I would come home doing the same thing. Then, of course, you would have to go look up a verse, and you would have to go to the Bible. We were doing a lot about evolution at one time. That seemed to be our area of sharing because the children were challenged with it in school.

Sharing in everyday life thus included witnessing, taking a stand against evolution, reading the Bible, and praying. This practice may not have precisely fit the recommended model for family devotions, but it even more effectively accomplished the same purpose.

Family altar is not the only ideal that must bend to the realities of everyday family life. In the relationship between Christian wives and husbands, a husband theoretically has all the authority. As one husband described it, "I believed that it was my position, whether I liked it or not, to be the head of the home, that my wife's religion came from me. As it says in Ephesians 5, that Christ is to the church as the husband is to the wife." Christian wives agree. Decision making is the husband's responsibility. When Rebecca Hughes talked about how the family might approach a major decision like moving, she said, "I'd like my husband to be the head of the house. I believe it's a decision that we both have to talk about, but I believe that in the end the husband decides." Although the husband decides, then, the couple should talk it over, presumably arriving at a consensus they believe to be God's will. The "ideal" of male domination is thus subtly accommodated to the reality of modern expectations for equality.

This question of female equality and power is a murky one at Southside. In a variety of ways, Christian wives are both powerful and powerless. Within their households, they have enormous powers of persuasion that are based in part on their intimate involvement with the everyday details of the family's life. They simply have more information, more emotional investment, and often more skill than their husbands. They may be able to run their homes so smoothly that their husbands rarely have any decisions to make, and they may discover ways to influence the decisions their husbands do make. As Janet Slavin put it, "Being submissive, the way I understand it, does leave me an active role and doesn't leave me in a quiet, nowhere role. I mean, I still can offer my opinion, which still leaves it with Joe to make the final decision. . . . If I honor his opinion after I've given him mine, and then if I go along with him, the Lord will make it right, and Joe will come around." Part of the lore that is passed from older wives to younger ones is how to keep a husband from making an unwise decision without appearing to usurp his rightful authority.

This delicate balance of submission and influence is even more difficult to maintain, however, when one party is not a believer. The conversion of one spouse, usually the wife, sets the stage for conflict. Often the other spouse will follow in fairly short time, but equally often a wife must resign herself to living with a man whose priorities and lifestyle she has chosen to reject but to whom she is tied for life. A few "unequally yoked" couples manage to build loving, tolerant, and healthy marriages despite the difficulties. But occasionally husbands take unfair advantage of their wives' unquestioning loyalty. Or wives subject their husbands to constant reminders that God is not pleased with their lives. And sometimes husbands cannot take the strain and leave.

A wife with an unsaved husband often finds herself in uncomfortable situations. Even if she has learned to live with his eternal damnation, she still must chafe at the temporal decisions he makes about their money, their friends, and their time. She wants to give substantial amounts of money to the church, but he objects.[2] She wants to go to church, but he would rather go fishing. And when he invites his friends for dinner or insists that she go along to a party, she finds herself in company she would otherwise choose to avoid: "All I've got really is Al's friends, and while I like them, they're—they all drink. I'm out with a crowd that drinks, and I don't drink. And they smoke, and I don't smoke. And sometimes they have friends—these three couples that we go with know that they can't tell dirty jokes when I'm there, but we occasionally meet friends of theirs who don't mind spitting all these dirty jokes out. I'd like to get lost." Another woman added, "I would like to be separated from the world. But it is hard to be separated with my husband because I certainly can't let him go off by himself with those people!" Although she may learn to become priest to the family, the Christian wife with an unsaved husband also learns to compromise. She knows she cannot always live by the biblical rules for families she would like to follow.

Unsaved men rarely object to a wife who converts and decides to be submissive. American husbands rarely expect their wives to dominate the marriage anyway. One husband who was saved after his wife remembered noticing that his usually "strong-willed" wife was suddenly letting him make all the decisions. Now he credits that change and his conversion with saving the marriage. If, however, in rare cases, the husband converts and decides unilaterally to assume a role as "head of the household," he is almost guaranteed to meet opposition. An unsaved wife has little incentive to submit. Even though Howard's wife is saved, she found the submissive role of wife less attractive than he did. His insistence on her submission brought an end to the marriage. Fundamentalist men do not have the power to impose their authority on women who do not choose to submit.

Most Southside wives do choose to submit, and, in doing so, they embrace both the rewards and the limitations of their role. Among the rewards is the joy of bearing and raising children. Here Southside women are encouraged to use their full creative powers (cf. DeJong 1965). Yet their role in even this process is limited by their submission to God and to their husbands. Almost every woman I talked to saw conception as something outside her control, despite the fact that birth control (other than abortion) is not openly condemned. Few members limit or plan their families. Neither do they seek help for infertility. Two women who had no children and one who had only one lamented that God had not provided the children they wanted, but none had sought any medical help. Those who had more children than they wanted also saw the situation as out of their hands. One whose third and fourth children were unplanned (and had put a serious strain on the marriage) has since had a fifth. Another who was expecting her fifth while I was there commented that "the Lord always gives you more than you ask for." Having and raising children are sources of status and power for women; but that power is limited by the fact that women do not control whether and when those children arrive.

To outsiders, such dependence on male authority may seem incomprehensible. Fundamentalist norms for structuring marriages are genuinely at odds with the norms in the larger society. The people at Southside argue that their way works, that they do not suffer from divorce and unhappy homes precisely because they abide by rules for a clear division of labor and authority. Each spouse knows what is expected. To support their success claims, Southside couples often point to their own marriages; there is, in fact, little divorce in the congregation. In addition, a remarkable number (20 percent of those currently married) claim that Fundamentalist beliefs have saved their marriages. Janet talked about their situation: "When we first got married, we both liked music and loved dancing and drink, and that was one of our common grounds. We both liked philosophy. But it seemed like a lot of our common ground was a terrible common ground. . . . We would have ended up with a divorce, not because we didn't love each other but because we didn't know how to be married." What she meant by knowing "how to be married" was that she and Joe were failing in their attempt to structure a marriage around two independent personalities, and they did not know any other model. Southside offered them an alternative. Learning to be a submissive wife was worth it to Janet if it meant saving her marriage.

For Joe and Janet, the effort was a joint one and came along rather smoothly. For others, however, the task is much more difficult. Another Southside wife described the years of agony that preceded her full acceptance of her proper role in the family.

> We had both very much been part of the world. I went back to school. I became very caught up in my own life. I had married young and had never really grown up before I had gotten married or really had a chance to be independent. And so I had two babies, and when they started nursery school, I started back to college. And I got very caught up in the modernism movement. I was influenced a lot by most of my professors who were divorced because they were out seeking their own identity. Consequently, I started picking up my own identity. And my husband needed a homebody-type wife for the type of person

that he is. And I was becoming more and more independent and growing further and further away. The marriage had been troubled before, but I was doing my best to wreck it, without even trying. . . . It resulted in a split, and there were some really bad years together, until we were saved. And even then, there were years of struggle. Consequently, I used to pray to God to make him a better husband and father. And finally, it dawned on me, you know, "Lord, change me! Make me the kind of wife that I should be!"

Her story is not unlike Bonnie's.

I would go to pastor in tears, expecting sympathy because of my miserable marriage and my miserable husband. . . . I'd go to pastor, and he would bring out the Word, and he would say, "Bonnie, read this." And, he would make me read it, and it would be, of course, God's plan for the wife. And I would go out of there so mad I couldn't see to drive home. . . . I used to say over and over again I hated my husband. I was so full of rebellion. But I began to see that it was me that needed to change too, because my prayer for those two years was "Change him, Lord, I can't stand him. Change him." Little by little, I began to see that my prayer needed to be "How can I change so that he will see Christ in me?" . . . The Lord has taught me how important my husband is and how important his feelings are. Until then, nothing was working. Nothing was working right.

In each case, women chose to give up their overt power in the marriage in exchange for avoiding divorce.

The norms against divorce are so strong, in fact, that some Southside marriages are preserved because no other option appears plausible. For believers divorce is never legitimate just because they cannot get along. Only if one partner commits adultery or abandons the family entirely can the remaining partner feel innocent. Even then, they may change churches to avoid facing their old friends.

Therefore, when Southside couples fight, they know that they must find a way to resolve their differences. Some, like Jim and Doris, credit God with keeping them together despite all their disagreements.

[If we were not Christians,] we wouldn't be married. We would have been divorced a long time ago. . . . I'm very, very thankful for many things, especially that the Lord has seen fit to keep us together. We could have quit. We could have given up. There were times in our marriage when it could have gone either way. It was nip and tuck, touch and go. But ultimately, after we went through all our plans, and the marriage counseling, and all this stuff, we finally went to God and asked him for help, and that's when things started to look up.

Others reflect similar sentiments.

> HUSBAND: We did get through our problems, many of them bumpy.
> WIFE: Without Christ we wouldn't be together, would we, Dad?
> HUSBAND: No, we wouldn't. That's right. We wouldn't have gotten through all those rough places.

> It's by the grace of God. I think everybody has a selfish nature, and sometimes little things—it's little things Satan works with—and I oftentimes wonder, if it wasn't for the Lord, if we'd be a family today.

Again, part of the pattern couples learn for keeping the peace in their homes is that in the end wives must give in rather than cause too much trouble. As Janet put it, she is learning to "keep my mouth shut when I don't want to." Abiding by Fundamentalist rules for marriage was cited by nearly half the couples in the Southside congregation as the way they keep the peace at home.

In most cases, then, Southside couples eventually find a comfortable accommodation to the biblical mandate for submission. Wives learn to give up the ideal of independence in exchange for the goal of living according to the plan of God and the reality of the influence they are able to have. Occasionally, however, the exchange simply does not work out as planned. The message of the church is that the Bible binds couples together for life, no matter how bad the marriage may seem. Some can live with that. A woman whose marriage is miserable said simply, "I've adjusted to my life, to the way things are between Bill and I."

Others cannot adjust to these demands; and when they fail to live up to the visible standards of the church, they often suffer enormously. When Mary Lou Otto filed for divorce, she also ended her relationship to the church. She knew she would not be accepted there, even if she wanted to participate. Even innocent partners in a divorce can be barred from positions of honor in the church. For some the resulting sense of isolation can have serious psychological consequences. Although Howard was maintaining his relationship with the church, he felt it becoming increasingly tenuous. He also had a tremendous load of anger and fear that was keeping him up at night and sending him to a variety of other sources of solace.

For some, these norms against divorce keep them in marriages long past the time when it is healthy for them to stay. One woman in the congregation had a major emotional breakdown before she finally concluded that divorce was in her best interests. Two other women were continuing to struggle with marriages that kept them in or near a state of depression.

The disjuncture between Fundamentalist norms and family realities is the primary cause of psychological disturbance in the Southside congregation. The number of people I found experiencing difficulties is not unlike what would be expected in a sample of urban people in the Northeast.[3] The content of their problems, however, bears the imprint of the religious community of which they are a part.

Besides divorce, other deviations from the Fundamentalist norm for families can cause problems. For women, child rearing is a special case. Three women in the church who had had major breakdowns dated the beginning of their problems to the birth of their first child.[4] Another woman had suffered the death of her favored child and was left with only the child whose emotional and behavioral problems made her feel totally inadequate as a Christian mother. Worse, this child did not like to go to church with her, while the child who died had been a star Sunday School pupil who had made her proud. Left with only an unsaved husband and a rebellious child, this woman was seeking psychological counseling; but the problem had distinctly religious dimensions.

Even for men, children can pose indirect difficulties. When faced with the injunction to be a provider and priest, some Christian fathers may feel like failures. Finding themselves totally responsible for a young family precipitated trouble for two of the men I interviewed.

Finally, failing to get married was the central problem for two other women. They had each reached an age where a lifetime of singleness was likely. "I'd really like a home of my own and family of my own to take care of. I like to take care of other people. . . . Some people think I want to escape into home, but that's the kind of life I, you know, was brought up with. I was brought up in an old-fashioned way. . . . I think I was born in the wrong century."

This woman indirectly put her finger on the common problem. She was not the only woman to complain that she was born in the wrong century. The values and expectations these women and men have acquired at home and at church have failed to equip them for the reality they must face in this century. Family problems often cause people distress, but they are intensified when a church like Southside defines one and only one family form as the Christian ideal. Those whose family lives are less than ideal are likely to suffer emotional and spiritual consequences. Some believers cannot conform, and others suffer silently rather than deviate. For some the strain is incapacitating, while others eventually find ways to cope.

All of Southside's husbands and wives must find ways to live with the tension between Fundamentalist norms for family structure and modern norms of individuality and equality. While adopting the ideal of priestly fathers, full-time mothers, and submission to male authority, each family works out its own compromises. Many men do not wish to be priests. Many women do not feel able to stay home full-time. Most families miss the ideal of daily devotional times. And most women learn to influence family decision making while still deferring to their husbands' authority. For a few, the model is oppressive and brings adverse psychological consequences. But for most of Southside's families, the ideals and the compromises offer a viable model, a model many claim has saved their marriages.

CHAPTER NINE

Bringing Them In: Recruiting
New Members

And the lord said unto the servant, Go out into the highways and
hedges, and compel them to come in that my house may be filled.
—Luke 14:23

B OTH FUNDAMENTALIST homes and Fundamentalist
churches exist in a world that lives by different
rules. Although the network of Fundamentalist institutions is
widespread, nowhere are Fundamentalists a cultural majority. Minority status, in fact, is part of their identity. As a result, Fundamentalist
churches cannot rely on a steady supply of members who come to
the church as a routine part of the culture. If they are to maintain
their institutional network and the view of the world it supports,
the members of Southside, like Fundamentalists everywhere, must
constantly be on the lookout for "prospects." A great deal of their
church's energy has to go toward recruiting new believers.

This institutional and social necessity gets strong theological
support at Southside. Fundamentalists sometimes claim that what
really distinguishes them from all other Christians is that they are the
only ones who take evangelism seriously. If evangelism is taken to
mean organized and intense efforts to obtain a "profession of faith"
from as many people as possible, then Southside Gospel Church
would certainly be justified in making that claim.

Methods of Evangelism

Witnessing to unsaved souls is among the activities most valued in
the congregation. In addition to the everyday encounters with nonbelievers that we have already explored, the church provides its
members with a variety of structured opportunities for proclaiming
the gospel.

Inviting the Lost to Church

The pastor often suggests from the pulpit that members witness by inviting unsaved people to church. At church people can hear the gospel in its most persuasive form, and at church sinners will be surrounded by a community where believing is the norm.

The church often plans events that are especially designed for recruiting the unsaved into the kingdom. Sometimes the events are overtly evangelistic—revivals, for instance. But sometimes they are overtly social, with evangelistic motives. Youth "socials" fall into this category. Unsaved teenagers are likely to accept an invitation to a church party; so skating parties or cookouts or summer camps provide useful ways for Southside's teens to witness to their friends. Inviting people to church social activities is a first step in turning schoolmates into Christian friends. Jim Forester talked about his oldest daughter's efforts in this regard: "Liz has the attitude that the Lord might be able to use her in that environment [a public school] to be a testimony. She's already asked them to come with her on a couple of the youth activities up at the church, a couple of kids from the school. So Liz feels that that might even be a little ministry for her down there." Inviting people to church is thus one way members witness about their faith. But it is especially functional for the church because being saved comes to be linked with being part of the church.

Such institutional motives, however, are not always dominant. When most members talk about witnessing, they talk about a host of other means before they mention the church. Just as the boundaries between saved and damned are not entirely coincidental with institutional memberships, so the path to salvation need not lead first through the institutional church. Members are eager that unsaved people eventually make it to church, but they know that going to church can sometimes come after a person has been persuaded, not before.

The church's efforts to encourage invitations to services do pay off. On any given Sunday morning, nearly one-third of the congregation are visitors who for a variety of reasons have decided to try out Southside Gospel Church. Some have been coming nearly every Sunday for months, without yet making a commitment to membership. Others have just arrived in the community, while still others have come in response to one of the church's many efforts at recruiting new members. Some will eventually stay, but vast numbers will visit once or twice, hear and even perhaps respond to the pastor's message, and drift away without making any lasting commitment to organized Fundamentalism.

Although the church's organized recruiting efforts cast a wide net into the community and snag many "fish," that net has many unrepaired holes. Often prospects are pursued without involving them either in activities beyond the Sunday morning preaching service or in relationships; they slip in and out each week without anyone to talk to. The words they hear never quite become a part of their everyday reality, and they eventually quit coming.

Broadcasting the Message

The radio ministry is among the evangelistic techniques that rarely brings an unsaved person to church and even less often into the fellowship. Broadcasts of the Sunday morning service and the pastor's daily devotional regularly provoke mail and phone calls (some irate) and occasionally stimulate a visit to the church's services. Several current members, in fact, reported that they had heard this pastor or the former one on radio or television before they joined. No one, however, reported that this was the primary factor in their coming. In each case, they were already looking for a church, or they had friends at Southside. The broadcasts were simply an easy way to try out a church without visiting.

Teaching the Young

Another branch of the church's recruiting efforts is aimed at reaching children and hoping that their parents will eventually come. The nursery school and, to a lesser extent, the Academy serve many families who are not believers; and aggressive efforts are aimed at their conversion. They are visited by teachers, their children bring home new ideas and habits, and parents are invited to special programs, one goal of which is evangelism. Rebecca Hughes talked about the nursery school's participation in an upcoming program: "We're having a patriotic program in March. It's gonna be something! We [the Nursery School] are included in it. And this way we'll get the unsaved parents . . . from nursery school in to see what the Academy's producing." She is hoping that what the daily activities of the nursery school have not already accomplished, the patriotic program will. She and others can, in fact, point to some successes. The ongoing relationship between parent and school sometimes does evolve into commitment to the church. At least a few current members have come to Southside by way of their children's enrollment in the Academy or nursery school. The fact that they found such schools congenial places for their children indicates a certain amount of ideological predisposition. Yet that predisposition would not have been translated into commitment if the organizational structure had not contributed. Because schools dominate children's lives, they inevitably have some impact on the parents as well.

Much less successful are the efforts to reach parents through children who are involved in at-church programs. When children merely come to Vacation Bible School, Sunday School, or AWANA, they are much less likely to involve their parents, and therefore much less likely to continue their own commitment. Attending once or even twice a week is simply not enough to overcome the influences of family, school, neighborhood, and friends. In American culture, parents often send their children to church, especially through the elementary years, hoping that the church will be a civilizing influence and arguing that such exposure provides the child with the opportunity to later choose whether and what to believe. A few such children find the people, ideas, and way of life at the church appealing enough that they make a lasting commitment. And a very few bring their parents along. Overwhelmingly, however, children at Southside are reached through parents, not the other way around.[1]

Busing Them in
The most interesting of Southside's failures at reaching adults through children is the bus ministry. Over the last twenty years, it has become apparent that many American parents are unwilling even to drop their children at the church door. If churches want to maintain contact with such families, they have to go get the children and take them home again—hence the advent of church buses.

However, buses are not just a supplement to the members' ability to transport extra children to church. Rather, they are an extension of the church into neighborhoods where no one would otherwise attend, and often those neighborhoods are predominantly poor and nonwhite. A small group of "bus workers" knocks on doors making known the service they offer. Mothers are often more than willing to have their children occupied with something worthwhile—away from home—for several hours on Sunday morning. The children attend for a few months, until they either move away or lose interest. No more than a handful of children have made lasting commitments in the years Southside has been recruiting by bus, and no adult members reported this as their first point of contact with the church.

The bus ministry fails for a variety of reasons, but all the reasons revolve around an inability to integrate the riders and their parents into the normal flow of church activities and relationships. To most church members, these children are known only as "bus kids," and bus kids neither belong nor act like they belong. Even the bus workers do not always know the names of all the children who appear on Sunday. Bus riders are ushered into Sunday School classes where teachers are likely to praise church members' children and reprimand bus kids. During the preaching service, younger bus children stay in Junior Church, where they will cause less trouble. Older bus children sit in an identifiable group in the service with the two or three teachers who care to try to corral them. Church members often complain that the bus kids do not know how to behave in church, but almost no one seeks to teach them or invites them to sit with families as the other children do. When they are at church, these children are thus kept marginal; and because the buses operate only on Sunday mornings, they are effectively excluded from the rest of the church's activities.

As a result, when children get off the buses on Sunday afternoon, they simply leave the world of church behind. Even those who are "won to the Lord" often do not tell their parents about that decision. No one in the church is likely to follow the child into his or her home world, explaining salvation to the parents and inviting the child to be baptized. Contacts between church adults and bus riders' parents are minimal. And because many bus families do not have private transportation, they would be unable to participate actively at church even if they took the initiative.

But the separation is more than practical. Vast distances in money, education, race, class, and lifestyle separate bus kids from the rest of the church. Their parents have probably never even seen the church's neighborhood, and it is unlikely that the bus family will be invited into the more comfortable homes of other church members.

Because these children and their parents do not belong to South-side's social world and because the bus ministry is not structured to change or overcome that fact, recruitment through busing is nearly a complete failure. The failure is hidden because new children keep coming, a few are saved from time to time, and, on any given Sunday, the buses are comfortably full.

Visiting Prospects

Another of the church's efforts at recruiting the lost into the fold is a structured visitation program. The names of people who have visited the church or about whom members are concerned are put in the visitation file; and on Tuesdays teams of "soul winners" are dispatched to call on them. Only a few of Southside's members participate in this program. It requires the kind of courage and aggressiveness characteristic of a door-to-door salesperson, and many members have not acquired such a measure of "spiritual boldness."

Those who do visit knock on the doors of strangers and announce that they are from Southside and would like to talk to them about Jesus. The members are not always warmly greeted. Some people will not let them in at all, while others allow barking dogs or blaring televisions to hamper the member's ability to witness. But believers are eager to report that God can turn such seeming defeats into victories by giving them another, more receptive, prospect or another chance to present their message. Indeed, a few of Southside's current members were brought to the church by the visitation program, but a visit alone is almost never enough. Even those who accept the member's message about salvation must still be "followed up," as Joe Slavin put it: "You can lead a person to Christ; that is very simple. I found a lot of people are hungry for the Word, and you can lead them to Christ just like that—trust Christ and become Christians. But the tough part is following up on them and teaching them later, disciplining them. . . . That is why a lot of people come and go out of the church." Unless there is a place in the church to serve, a friend to teach them—activities and relationships—people who are visited by strangers almost never follow those strangers to church.

The visitation program, like most of the church's recruitment effort, is built on the assumption that salvation is inherently a life-changing event and that the biblical "plan of salvation" can speak for itself. Believers are to be the messengers, and God will do the rest. Efforts are concentrated on telling as many people as possible the facts about salvation. The gospel is broadcast over the radio, delivered on buses, and proclaimed door to door. Yet all this effort flounders when the masses who hear the gospel do not also hear about and experience ways to become full participants in a church that can sustain their faith.

Walking the Aisle

The Sunday morning preaching service is typical of all the church's attempts to increase the population of God's kingdom. On most Sundays there are ample "lost" people in the congregation—there out of curiosity or courtesy, with friends and family or alone. Whether they know it or not, the service is aimed at them. Members have contacted them and brought them and now pray that they will not leave without being saved. Believers know that the pastor's message will be spellbinding in its use of stories and images portraying Christ's sacrifice and the need to accept that sacrifice in order to obtain salvation. There is almost always an emotional climax as the message ends, followed by an invitation to respond by walking down the aisle. As the pastor finishes, he asks the congregation to bow their heads and close their eyes while he probes for response from the audience.

> Perhaps you have not yet asked Jesus to come into your heart. You know today that you have not been saved. And you would like for me to pray for you today. Would you just raise your hand right now, right where you're sitting? If I don't see it, God will. Every head is bowed and every eye is closed. Christians are praying. If you know you need to accept Christ, just raise your hand right now. Dear Lord Jesus, we just pray that these who have raised their hands today will not leave this place without accepting you as their Lord and Savior. Continue to speak to their hearts now during this invitation time. In Jesus's name, Amen. As we stand and sing this hymn, won't you come now.

While the congregation stands to sing, the invitation continues.[2] Ushers and "personal workers" had been watching during the prayer time for people to raise their hands, and they now make their way to those people's side. As Janet Slavin described her experience,

"The invitation came, and I had tears in my eyes, and I had a tap on the shoulder. And a woman was there, and she said, 'Would you like to receive Christ?' 'Well, I have.' And she said, 'Would you like to make it public?' Well, with that question, I had no response. There was nothing I could say against making it public. I said, 'Of course I'll make it public.' So that meant walking the aisle." On any given Sunday, there is likely to be at least some response to the invitation. Institutionally, that is how churches and pastors measure their success.[3] And, for individuals, it is an emotionally and ritually significant moment. Many believers remember the moment they walked down the aisle as the moment of salvation: "Then when the invitation came, it felt like he was talking to me directly, as the Lord's tool. So I went forward and accepted the Lord." It is both very public and intensely personal.

Those who do walk the aisle are taken to a back room where the personal workers lead them through the plan of salvation. They pray the "sinner's prayer" and are given a packet of materials to take home. Included are an annotated Gospel of John, a schedule of church activities, and a booklet from the pastor entitled "Saved! What Now?" It contains a review of what salvation is and why we need it, plus explanations about baptism, Bible reading and prayer, church attendance, giving, and living a separated life. The personal worker records the convert's name and address for follow-up visits and rejoices that another soul has been added to the kingdom.

Even after such a public act, however, many of those who walk the aisle are rarely seen again. Their names enter the visitation file, but the person who visits is usually a stranger who never becomes more than that to the convert. In searching the visitation file, I could find the names and addresses of only twenty-five people who had gone forward during the preceding eight months, although I am sure more than that had responded to invitations. I called a random sample of eight of them and found that three were bus kids, one of whom had already dropped out. Neither of the other two had been visited or had increased their involvement in the church. Another of the converts was a neighborhood child whose mother was quite emphatic that her child would have no further involvement with "*that* church.*" One of the adults had a similar response. She attended one Sunday at the insistence of a member friend. Yes, she had responded to the invitation, but she certainly did not mean to imply that she was interested in joining *that* church. She is Catholic and means to stay that way. Another of the adults went forward mostly to please his son, who is a devoted member and a student at a Bible college. The father says he will still attend from time to time, but he has no plans to join or to change his life significantly. The other two adults were still attending with some regularity three and five months after responding to an invitation. Neither had yet been baptized or had officially joined, but there is a fair possibility that one or both will eventually become full-fledged members and committed believers. Although everyone who joins Southside Gospel Church begins by walking the aisle, not nearly everyone who walks the aisle will eventually join. For most it is but one moment in a life otherwise undisturbed. Simply hearing the message of salvation, then, is unlikely to produce the commitment Southside members hope it will.

The Converts

Although the net Southside uses has many holes, not every prospect is lost. About one-half of the current congregation were recruited into Fundamentalism as adults. And, of those, slightly over half have experienced a change in their lives that deserves the label *conversion*. Their lives today are significantly different from the lives they led before they were saved.[4]

The Most Likely Prospects

Describing who is most likely to convert is always difficult after the fact. Part of what it means to convert is to reinterpret one's past life, so descriptions from people who have already converted will be based, at least in part, on an acquired tendency to tell life stories in black and white (cf. Beckford 1978). In most instances, believers describe their former lives as miserable, but the behavioral changes they report lend credence to their claims. Many were in a chronic state of despair. They drank too much, fought with spouses, and were generally down on themselves and life. A young mother described her experience this way: "Things got bad again with our marriage. I used to have these terrible outbursts. It was just the old devil working in me, I don't know. But anyway, about two months later I finally broke down and said, 'That's it. I can't cope with this by myself.' And I really cried out to God and said, 'If you really exist, you show me; you help me.' And he did, because I got saved very soon after that." The message of salvation that she heard at Southside offered hope in a life that seemed otherwise hopeless, a way of coping with situations that had gotten out of her control.

Another common pattern among adult converts is to choose Fundamentalism when they are making other important changes in their lives. Both the Hughes and the Ottos came when they had young children. An older woman came after the death of her husband. Ray Danner's initial decision was even more dramatic. "During the war years I remember one time out on the ocean—it was a hostility area—I saw something happening, and I said, 'If I ever get out alive, I will do something for the Lord.'"

Usually the stress event is not so obvious. People simply change jobs or move or send their children off to college or experience a birth or death, and find themselves feeling disconnected. At a moment when the pieces of life seem to be slightly in disarray, Fundamentalism presents explanations that put everything back together again.

Before they discovered Fundamentalism, most of these converts had either given up on religion entirely or were experimenting with various marginal religious activities—yoga, eastern religions, and the like. Apparently, however, none had lost their openness to religious explanations for life. They were merely dissatisfied with the particular explanations they had found. Their tenuous ties to established religion made them more likely candidates for conversion than either those who were firmly committed to a religious community or those who had left religion entirely (see especially Beckford 1975).

Most of Southside's converts, then, experienced some sort of crisis or transition in their lives. Although they were only loosely connected to organized religion, they remained open to religious ideas. The message such people heard at Southside gave a name to the devil that plagued them, placed their private agony in a new scheme of things, and promised that God's power would rescue them from hell—present and future.

The Process of Conversion

For those who truly repent, the old life is often put aside with little regret, but first they must learn that they need to repent. Acknowledging that one is a sinner means taking on a whole new way of looking at oneself and the world. It means discovering that when measured against the radical holiness of God, human lives are woefully lacking.

> That was the first time that I knew that because of my sin I would have to pay for it and go to hell.

> I developed a consciousness of the things I was doing wrong, whereas before that I think I had so much sin in my life and so many things wrong that my conscience was seared. I had no conscience. I thought whatever you do is justified.

> He'd ruin more lunches for me, just reading the Bible to me and telling me I was a sinner! And I wasn't doing *anything*; I seldom even whistled at a girl. I was a good married man!

Even the best of husbands, the most conscientious of citizens, and the kindest of neighbors know that deep within their hearts lie thoughts too evil for words, impulses kept all too carefully in check. Pastor Thompson's message that "all have sinned" is not just aimed at the degenerate of the community. The standard against which behavior is measured is not merely human acceptability but the very righteousness of God. Not until potential believers experience the guilt of failing to meet that standard can they also experience the joy of salvation.

The process of coming to salvation also involves a fear of being shamed before this righteous God. The sense of guilt that comes from measuring one's deeds against God's standard is augmented by a sense of shame that those deficiencies are about to be revealed and punished.[5] Most basically, listeners are reminded that no one knows the hour when death will come. No one knows whether there will be a tomorrow to make things right. In addition, the doctrine of the Rapture, so pervasive at Southside, produces a sense of impending doom that invades the sinner's consciousness. When Christ comes again, spiritual accounts will be closed and tallied, forever sealing human fate. The analogy the pastor often uses is to the fear of nuclear war: If we fear the bomb, how much more we ought to fear God's judgment. Such a potent symbol of awesome destructive power forces sinners and saved alike to face their own vulnerability. In the nuclear age, people must face the constant threat of annihilation, unsure when it might happen, but sure that when it comes, life will end.

Hiding sin from God, then, is as futile as trying to hide from an atomic bomb. In an earlier age, Martin Luther, as quoted by Erikson, described the experience this way: "[People are] put to sin and shame before God. . . . This shame is now a thousand times greater, that a man must blush in the presence of God. For this means that there is no corner or hole in the whole of creation into which a man might creep, not even in hell, but he must let himself be exposed to the gaze of the whole creation, and stand in the open with all his shame" (1958:256). Luther and the people at Southside use theological terms to describe the sinner's predicament, but Erikson would point out that the same experience can be understood in developmental terms as well. Shame is also the fear of facing an angry parent. He describes sin thus: "Paradise was lost when man, not satisfied with an arrangement in which he could pluck from the trees all he needed for upkeep, wanted more, wanted to have and to know the forbidden. . . . He "knew" at the price of shame and gained independent initiative at the price of guilt. Next to primary peace, then, secondary appeasement is a great infantile source of religious affect and imagery" (1958:121).

As the people at Southside understand the arrangement, those who try to assert their own autonomous wills must face an angry God before whom they will be found guilty. And when this life ends with death or the Rapture, guilty sinners will stand naked before God, with no excuse to hide their shame. Learning to feel such shame and guilt is part of the process by which believers are converted.

Those who are saved are promised, however, that their guilt and shame can be taken away by Christ's death on the cross. Because Jesus "paid the price" for their sin, believers can stand before God without fear of being judged and condemned. They have been "washed in the blood of the Lamb."

This message of forgiveness can be good news indeed to people for whom guilt is a problem. Harry McLean, for instance, had been depressed enough to be getting psychiatric treatment when he finally understood what his brother kept telling him about salvation. He described the experience of admitting he was a sinner and asking for forgiveness as "just like a thousand pounds was taken off the top of my head." He rapidly left his medicine and therapy behind and successfully tackled the job of reconstructing his life and his mar-

TABLE 9.1. Religious Histories of Southside Congregation

Previous religious experience	Childhood believers	Adult "joiners"	Adult "converts"
Southside regular	10	0	0
Regular, other Fundamental	19	0	0
Regular, non-Fundamental	0	10	5
Dropout	0	6	10
Experimenter	0	0	5
Total	29	16	20

SOURCE: Data were gathered during interviews with randomly selected participants. Three nonmember, regular attenders are included, bringing the total to sixty-five individuals.

riage. For Elaine Young, the change came more slowly but no less decisively. She had grown up one of eight children in a home where one child would have been too many. She took on herself all the blame for her parents' misery and developed such a poor self-image that she would hardly talk. As she began to understand what had happened when she was saved, she said, "I finally accepted the fact that I was God's child, not just a saved, wretched woman." Having a new heavenly father meant that she could leave old burdens behind, feel good about herself, and talk so much that it has become a family joke. For believers like these the theological idea of grace has become a reality with tangible and joyous consequences.

The Other Recruits

Conversions like these, however, are not the norm. Even at Southside, not nearly everyone has been "converted" in so dramatic a fashion. Although all members can point to some moment when they personally admitted their inherent sinfulness and made a public commitment to believing in Christ, most of those members will also admit that their lives changed little after that experience.

Almost half the congregation experienced their "rebirth" as children or teens (see Table 9.1). About 15 percent of Southside's current members grew up in the church and have never moved.[6] For children raised in the church, Fundamentalism is the only plausible view of the world they know, at least for a while. As we will explore in Chapter 10, such recruitment is by no means foolproof, but it is efficient. Children learn the Fundamentalist way of thinking along with everything else, so that it becomes second nature.

As a result, they would be hard pressed to name specific sins for which they needed to repent. Although they claim to be "born again," they are more accurately described as "once born," in the sense that James (1935:199) uses that term. These believers are not "divided selves" who must repudiate part of themselves or part of the past. If they experienced a time of adolescent rebellion and crisis, they resolved their doubts in favor of the course on which they had already embarked.

Joiners

Even in the half of the congregation that has chosen Fundamentalism as adults, there are many for whom *conversion* stretches the meaning of the word. Many were regular churchgoers in other faiths and felt little need for change in their lives. For almost half those who join as adults, the decision to "make a profession of faith" was largely a choice to follow in the steps of some significant other person. They have "joined" rather than "converted." They have now learned to look back at the experience as a watershed; but, at the time, it was an adoption of an additional set of explanations rather than of a new and exclusive explanation, an evolutionary change rather than a revolutionary one.[7] Jim Forester described his experience this way: "I wanted to make sure [my family] had a good church. I attended occasionally, but I was still going to Catholic church. I was serving Mass and everything, and reading the missal. . . . I really didn't grow much in the Lord. I still went back and forth [between churches] for quite a while, for a couple more years." Such conversions are preceded by no sense of crisis and are followed by no life-changing catharsis. As the convert comes within the orbit of a church like Southside, changes in belief and lifestyle begin to make the conversion look increasingly important. Still, many of those who have joined Southside as adults have done so primarily because someone they loved joined first.

Sheep from Other Flocks

A final mode of entry into the congregation is from another Fundamentalist church. About one-third of the Southside congregation found this church through the informal institutional network of

Fundamentalism. Because there are no official labels of organizations to identify member churches, believers have to use less obvious means for finding a "good Bible-believing church." Often they find one by looking for cues that usually signal an evangelistic church, such as radio broadcasts and church buses. They also look for a church whose calendar of activities and style of preaching meet their standards. Ray Danner recalled how they chose Southside: "The reason we came to Southside was the man that led us to the Lord tried to help us find a church in the area. So we looked for billboards that said Wednesday evening services, which our friend told us meant that the church was alive and did some praying and meeting during the week, other than socially. . . . Of course, it was in Stanleyville at the time, but that is why we tried it, even though we had to come quite a distance." When the Foresters moved from the Midwest, their church shopping was complicated: "Before our move . . . one of my concerns was to find a good church, and Pastor Tyndale had given us some names. But, in the meantime, I had also located Midtown Baptist, here in Westfield, and Grace Baptist. And the pastor at Grace Baptist told me about John Williams. I told him I was looking for a good fundamental, you know, Bible-believing church, and he recommended Midtown." But, after sampling the programs and preachers in several congregations, the Foresters went against everybody's advice and chose Southside as the best match for their family.

When for any reason a believer severs ties with one Fundamental church, there are numerous ways to find another: "My cousin had already gone to another church, a Baptist church—First Baptist —and they had a marvelous choir, and I liked to sing, so I went to the choir. But I never got anything out of the man [the preacher]. After a couple of years of that I switched and went to Southside." Within each geographical area, members of various churches are connected through their own grapevine of family and friends, and shopping or switching is always a possibility. Not nearly all those who come from other Fundamental churches come because they have changed residences.

Keeping Them in

What brings recruits firmly into the fellowship is precisely the social and organizational ties of which commitment is made—the development of relationships that can guard the believer against the on-slaught of competing ideas and lifestyles. Overwhelmingly new members are brought first not by impersonal means like buses or radio but by someone they already know. Nine out of ten converts (and a similar number of joiners) come to church first with a friend or family member.[8]

Of the new converts I interviewed, for instance, the one most likely to continue his involvement is Darrell, a man of about thirty, with a wife who has also been saved and a young daughter he is eager to teach about God. He had done a variety of religious experimenting before a factory co-worker introduced him to Fundamentalism and to Southside. Every day Darrell had heard this believer talking about his faith, and finally Darrell was convinced. When he started going to church, his co-worker provided him with introductions and with a tie between the world of work and the ideas he heard at church. But when I talked to Darrell, he and his family had not been to church for about a month. Their car had broken down, and no one had offered them transportation. Social ties were crucial in bringing Darrell into the faith, but they would also be crucial in determining whether he remained there.[9]

Sometimes a friend or family member spends months or years cultivating a prospect before that person ever enters the church doors. Other times a member issues a casual invitation to someone who happens to be ready to come. That is what happened to Frances Bright, a widow who is about seventy and who had just joined the church when I talked to her. She met a long-time Southside member at a community senior center: "He said, 'Would you like to go up to Valley View with me to a senior meeting, up in my church?' Well, I didn't know what I might be getting into, you know. I was at the point I would do most anything to meet people. So I said, 'Yes, as long as it is a church meeting.'" The member not only invited her but provided transportation. She started going with him to the Southside Senior Fellowship, and Frances found the group and their meetings a delight: "So I went with him, and honestly I just fell with a plop into that group of people as if I'd always belonged there." From there, her friend began to introduce her to the rest of the church, its activities, and ideas: "So then he took me upstairs and showed me the sanctuary. . . . He knew every inch of that church. He took me all around, and I could see how much people thought of him up there, and how well he was respected. And he taught me an awful lot about the Bible that I didn't know." Her friend also picked her up for church every Sunday, and soon she found herself responding to an invitation.. "So I just started going, and first thing I knew I held up my hand one Sunday. My hand went up, and I joined the church."

Holding up her hand during an invitation came to stand for the entire membership process in Mrs. Bright's mind, but that decision was by no means merely a response to an evangelistic message. By the time she raised her hand, she had in effect already joined the church. She had become a part of a circle of friends with whom she played and studied and worshipped. She had grown up in a conservative Protestant church but had been in other churches for all her adult life. Now the ideas sounded familiar enough not to be disturbing, and the fellowship was just what she had been seeking. To join officially, she would have to sign a doctrinal statement and give her testimony before the deacons, but the part she remembers most is the official welcome.

> The night that I was taken into the church, it was on a Sunday night, and there was about eight of us, I guess. And we went up front and got our little papers. It was at the end of the service, I guess, when the minister said for people to come up and welcome us. Every single soul in that church filed by and shook hands, and the women kissed me. The little kids kissed me. It was the nicest thing. I filled all up and choked so I couldn't even say "Thank you," you know, when they'd say "Welcome." They really meant it. They were sincere.

For Frances Bright, the transition into Fundamentalism was a rather smooth one. Because she was older, a less-modern view of the world felt comfortable, and her religious background provided her with the traditional ideas on which Fundamentalism is built.

Other converts have more difficulty. Younger people have grown up in a world that takes nothing traditional for granted. Charlie Vitelli is such a person. At the time I talked with him, he had been attending Southside for about a year, had been saved, but had not yet officially joined. He too had first come to Southside when he was open to a change in his life. For him, the inviter was his wife, who in turn had been brought by her sister, who—in turn—had followed her husband into the faith. As Charlie describes it, the impact was rather immediate: "My life wasn't very pleasant, as far as I was concerned, with my experience up until now. When Rose started going, I really, you know, was thinking it was a joke. Finally, I went just to shut her up. And when I heard the Word—after the service I was saying, 'You know there is a lot more to this! . . . There was like something in the back of my mind that kept telling me that, you know, this is the only way.'"

In the months that followed, Charlie's life and ideas began to change dramatically: "I used to be quite a drinker. I don't have that urge any more. Some other nasty habits I had, you know, are gone. . . . I don't curse any more. . . . I try to witness to some of the guys at work. . . . I used to be just really all for women's rights—they should have their right. And now I just can't. If I'm going to read the word of God, I can't abide by abortion any more."

While his life had been changing, so had his friends. Besides the relatives that first brought him, he has made friends with another church family. Sometimes he feels left out because of the distance between home and church (thirty minutes) and because he works nights and can get to church only on Sunday morning. But Charlie has been trying to study the Bible on his own, and he has a friend at work who can help him interpret what he reads. The pastor's sermons also help: "When I first started I guess Pastor Thompson had just begun the Beatitudes, week by week; and that's what did it for me, hearing the Beatitudes. I was really impressed because my interpretation of 'The meek shall inherit the earth' wasn't what the biblical translation turned out to be. I was really, really impressed with that. As a matter of fact, I want to get the tapes. He's got the whole series on tape." Reading the Bible, going to church, listening to tapes, and having people at home and at work who are encouraging him have made it possible for Charlie to exchange an old life he describes as miserable for a new one that seems comforting and full of promise.

Not all the ideas are coming easily however. Charlie often skips parts of the Bible that he finds incomprehensible, hoping that eventually they will make sense. Other ideas are not so much incomprehensible as just contradictory to what he has always believed to be true: "You know, what I've had a hard time with is the fact that our life here on earth is, according to the Bible, approximately 5,000 years old. Because up until just the last few months I've been indoctrinated into believing life has existed here on earth for millions and millions of years. . . . It's much easier for me to grasp hold of Jesus's teachings and the miracles he performed than it is for me to all of a sudden say things aren't what I thought."

To "say things aren't what I thought" is particularly hard for younger people who have learned modern scientific ideas about the history of life on earth. To accept on faith that all the scientific evidence is erroneous requires a strong commitment to the rest of the ideas of Fundamentalism. If the issue of evolution arises too early in the process of integration into the fellowship, it can destroy the plausibility of the rest of the world view. In the outside world, discarding evolution is seen as ridiculous. Only when a convert is firmly on the inside do the arguments against evolution make sense. In the early weeks and months, new members may have to put that issue aside, concentrating instead on the ideas and life changes they find acceptable. As Charlie put it, "As my faith gets stronger and stronger, I think it's probably just going to be a natural process." Another man, much older in the faith, reflected on how that had happened in his life: "I just did what I had to do. And it was a short time after that that I realized what they were talking about and started relating it to me, and later on, in fact, what it does mean to me." As converts devote more and more time and energy to religious activities and adopt Fundamentalists as their primary reference group, even ideas that are difficult to apprehend become plausible.

Another part of this process is learning and accepting a new language in which to express those new ideas. Before people convert, they go through at least some time on the boundaries, noticing how strange insiders sound. Janet Slavin admitted how she used to hate hearing people talk about "getting saved." But by the time she decided to convert, both the logic and the language had begun to make sense, and socialization into full membership could begin. Sermons and Sunday School lessons provided a model for how believers talk about life. She expanded her biblical knowledge and language in daily Bible reading and through Christian magazines, books, and radio. In conversation with Christian friends, she began practicing new ideas, words, and categories, leaving behind the swear words of days gone by. "Getting saved" soon became an important part of her own identity and vocabulary. Such a convert-now-member is like an emigrant who writes home in the language of her adopted country, completely forgetting that those she left behind speak in a different tongue.

Commitment and relationships, then, are the key to bringing new converts into the church and keeping them there. Buses and radio programs and door-to-door visits may bring in the masses; but work to do in the church and friends to share it with are the stuff of which lasting commitments are made. Activities occupy the believer's time, and friends surround the convert with encouragement and support. A new convert needs such a reference group. The most effective group is that in which the convert participates and where he or she learns new ways of thinking and acting. But it is also common for new converts to find someone in the church to look up to, even if they do not know that person well. They watch everything the other Christian does, listen to his or her testimonies, and try to imitate what they see and hear. The admired person is often the pastor, but it may also be a Sunday School teacher or just a more mature Christian. People already mature in the faith provide models for how to live when outsiders challenge the new ideas that are just taking hold.

It is nearly impossible for a new believer to survive without some link between the faith as it is preached on Sunday and the faith that faces the world during the week. The task of bringing new members into the fold stops neither when the prospect comes to church nor when the convert walks the aisle. Only when people are surrounded by believing friends, family, and people they admire; only when they are quickly integrated into the church's round of activities; and only when they finally begin to think and speak and witness like a Fundamentalist is the conversion complete.

CHAPTER TEN

The Nurture and Admonition of the Lord: Raising Children

Train up a child in the way he should go; and when he is old, he will not depart from it.
—Proverbs 22:6

Children, obey your parents in the Lord, for this is right. . . . And, ye fathers, provoke not your children to wrath, but bring them up in the nurture and admonition of the Lord.
—Ephesians 6:1, 4

THE OTHER major source of recruits for Fundamentalism is the children of believers. Southside members not only want to reach the lost in their community but also want to make sure that the lost in their own homes come to salvation. Although Christian homes may exist in part to extend the shelter of the church into everyday life, their most important function in the minds of believers is bringing children into the world and raising them "in the nurture and admonition of the Lord." While providing a shelter for adult believers, Christian homes also provide the primary means for introducing young believers to Fundamentalism. Parents who take the task seriously find that the goals that guide their nurturing are shaped by the Fundamentalist world of which they are a part. As Bonnie Towles put it, "I hope to see my children grow up to surrender their lives to the Lord."

The Nuture of the Church

In part, children learn about "surrendering their lives to the Lord" by participating with their families in the church. Adults find that church offers activities and relationships that replace the attractions of the world, and they are eager for their children to have the same opportunities. From the time they are dedicated as babies, the children of Southside's faithful members become "church kids." As one mother put it, "These kids, all they've ever known is church!" The people of the church become a kind of extended family, with relationships that carry over into weekday activities. Church kids become best friends with each other and help each other to learn the ways of the faith. They go to church together on Sunday, to AWANA on Wednesday night, to Vacation Bible School in the summer, and to any other activity the church plans. And, like their parents, Southside's children do "church work" at home, memorizing next Sunday's Bible verse, inviting a friend to church, and the like.

One of the most important things church kids learn from all this activity is that the Bible is a part of everything. They begin to memorize its verses before they can read, and they know the names and order of all sixty-six books about as soon as they know their home address. Both at church and at home, they hear Bible stories instead of fairy tales and learn more about Mary and Joseph than about Dick and Jane. By the time they are six or seven, they are as likely to have a favorite Bible verse as to have a favorite color, to be able to tell a Bible story as to be able to recite a nursery rhyme, to be able to sing a hymn as any other song. The people and places of the Bible simply become a part of the everyday world of Southside's children.

Church kids also learn about faith in subtle ways. They learn to think about life as a battle by singing about being in "the Lord's army" and by constantly engaging in competition. From Sunday School to Junior Church to AWANA, Southside's kids learn to be adept at fighting hard to win, and they learn to expect rewards for their actions. Prizes and trophies and ribbons are tangible reminders of the everlasting rewards God's children can expect in heaven when they do their best for him. The also learn that one of the surest ways to be rewarded is to be obedient. There are rules to be obeyed at home and at church and authorities in each place to enforce those rules.

Church kids learn too that what a person is allowed to do depends on who that person is: Members are not pastors; children are not parents; and girls are not boys. God made each with a special and different plan for how to live. For instance, from the earliest ages, there are separate activities, different styles of dress, and divergent expectations for boys and girls, building and reinforcing the idea that God made the sexes to be different.

Southside also introduces its children to the world of Fundamentalism by offering them an alternative set of heroes. For church kids, foreign missionaries are as heroic as Luke Skywalker or Mr. T may be to other children. They begin to learn about missionaries as soon as they are old enough to understand what is happening at church. They see slides of exotic lands and hear stories of terrible evil being overcome by the gospel. They write letters to missionaries in Sunday School and send them gifts at Christmas. They may even make their own faith promise and have a missions piggy bank. Southside's kids know that preachers and missionaries have "surrendered their lives to the Lord" and that no other vocational choice would make their parents prouder of them. Church kids dream of being missionaries no less than other children dream of being Olympic athletes or "president of the world." Sometimes youthful dreams come true but always they shape the present and the future.

Once church kids reach their teens, the task of providing alternative dreams and plausible explanations becomes more difficult. The church realizes that teens are especially susceptible to the influences of worldly friends and activities, and it counterattacks with a vigorous youth program. The church hopes to keep its teens so busy that they have little time for outside friends or activities.[1] To keep youngsters away from secular social activities, they plan an event of their own, for instance, at the same time youth might otherwise attend a school dance. Because the youth group is fairly large, there are plenty of available friends and potential dates. When they need a sympathetic adult ear, Southside's youth minister is there to be a positive role model and confidant.

In addition, the church invests its youth with the adult responsibility of witnessing to their unsaved peers. Trying to convince a friend can be an experiment in owning the Fundamentalist identity. Those who learn well the lessons of witnessing and separation are able to establish for themselves an identity that includes both being Christians and being in the world. The church also encourages its youth to try on identities as teachers, preachers, and missionaries (cf. Garrison 1976). Among the activities sponsored by Word of Life Bible Clubs is Teens Involved, in which youth try their hands at preaching (for boys) and story telling (for girls and boys). When teens are older, they may even have an opportunity to spend a summer working with a foreign missionary on the field. Southside works hard to make the Fundamentalist way of life attractive to its youth and to give them opportunities to establish their identities within its boundaries.

The activities and relationships, ideals and goals that the church provides mold the lives and thinking of children even more than of adults. They simply have fewer alternatives to compare with what Southside offers them, especially if they are from a home where both parents are believers. As we saw with bus kids, the church cannot succeed alone. It is most influential as an extension of the home. Children with unsaved parents must balance the church's ideas against everything else they experience. But church kids with saved parents receive consistent information about how life is to be lived, consistent models of what is good.

The Nurture of the Home

Church kids with church parents rarely step outside the sheltering canopy of the faith. Competing ideas and ways of life are as foreiqn to them as the native customs they see in missionary slides. Southside's parents see the church's responsibility as an extension of theirs, neither effort being complete without the other. Mary Danner, for instance, reflected on raising her children.

> When you have a little one, you think, "How do I want to raise her?" So she was raised in the church. The church became her second home. She loved Sunday School. We worshiped together. I remember when we first started, we used a little folder of verses. Then we had family devotions, time to pray together. For our children, church was always a place they wanted to be. . . . Children have a way of knowing something that is real and right with you, something you really believe in and are not just saying.

The church and its families work together to make sure that children know that Fundamentalism is what is "real and right."

The homes in which Southside members raise their children are guided by the ideas and expectations of their religious world. Above all, they are characterized by discipline, respect, and obedience. Southside's children learn about rules both at home and at church. We have already heard parents talk about discipline and about not watching television; but most church kids also have rules about how they can dress, where they can go, and, most importantly, with whom they can play. The mother of a five-year-old said that her son is always required to be within her sight and is not allowed to play at other neighborhood homes because the other families are not Christians. Ann Lazzaro has teenaged children, but they have similar restrictions: "We always know where they are; they are with Christians. If they do go with someone who is unsaved, it is either in our home or with their parents. But our boys are told, they know to lead their friends to the Lord, and we are thankful. Well, Stanleyville is quite a town. We never have to tell them; they know from reading God's word that they are to be separate."

As Ann pointed out, her sons know not only the rules but the reasons for the rules. Another parent observed that his neighbors are always amazed when they see his teenaged children going to church, even when he and his wife are away. The children who grow up in Southside's fold are likely to emerge from adolescence firmly entrenched in a Fundamentalist world. Their development has been shaped by Fundamentalist norms no less than the development of a child in any other culture is shaped by its norms. As Erikson (for example, 1963, 1982) so thoroughly documents, each of the predictable stages of childhood is encountered in ways that prepare the child for full participation in his or her particular adult society.

In the early stages of childhood, for instance, church kids learn about initiative and guilt: "Occasionally I would have one that when you went to wake them up didn't want to go today. And I never hollered at them or pushed them. I just simply said, 'Well, you know the Lord has been very good to us.' And I reminded them of all the answers to our prayers and the things he had done, and then I would just walk out. . . . They always got up and went." Guilt and obligation are recurring themes at Southside, but what is interesting here is that as young children go through the natural process of acquiring a conscience, their religious culture is supplying them the substance over which they are to feel guilty: not going to church, forgetting to read the Bible, disobeying, or playing with an unsaved child. Sometimes they are spanked when they step out of line, but external control is soon replaced by firm internal discipline.

All children come to internalize their parent's demands, but at Southside that process is made all the more dramatic by the constant presence of a heavenly father in addition to the earthly one (cf. Freud 1927). The idea that sin inevitably produces suffering takes root first in the punishment children receive from their earthly fathers. The more sure and swift the punishment—or reward—the more firmly children become convinced that neither sin nor righteousness will be overlooked by their heavenly father. At church, as well as at home, children learn that God is like a father, and they come to expect him to be a tangible presence in their lives. One four-year-old was so sure that Jesus was "in his heart" that he was afraid Jesus might get dizzy from all his jumping around. The boy might not yet quite understand, but he is already learning that Jesus sees everything he does. Good deeds please Jesus, and bad deeds make Jesus sad. By the same process that a conscience is formed, an omniscient (potentially punitive) God becomes the overseer of the conscience. Long after they become adults, these children will still explain their misfortunes as God "disciplining" them, punishing them for stepping out of line.

As the conscience takes shape and the child's desires become internally regulated, attention can be turned to substantive matters. Each culture must teach its offspring necessary skills, and Southside is no exception. Among the most important skills to be learned are the use of the Bible, how to be separated, and how to witness. We have already noted that the church and the home work together to teach children about the Bible. As they participate in all the Bible activities of the church and family, they learn more about scripture than many seminary students know. If church kids also go to the Academy, they have additional Bible lessons every day. As they learn to locate and memorize scripture, they come to understand that the Bible can provide answers for whatever questions they might have.

One of the most important reasons to learn about the Bible is to be able to use it in witnessing. Southside's children not only come to accept the faith at an early age but also learn that witnessing is the most important activity for even a young Christian. By the time they are teens, church kids are expected to be fully responsible for spreading the gospel among their peers, but they often start to practice much earlier. The mother of a first-grader proudly told about her daughter's efforts.

> Stephanie went over on Sunday—it was so cute—and she sat them all down, the three kids. She said, "If you don't do this, you're going to hell." And she said, "If you want to come to

heaven and see me up there. . . ." And then she said, "I'll start a prayer, and you just say what I say." She got the three kids to say the prayer after her. . . . She was real excited, and she said, "I think I'm a missionary, Mom!"

Bonnie gave a similar account of her second-grade daughter's activities: "That little girl that is with Sarah now is Jewish. Sarah led her to the Lord, but her family, of course, won't let her come to church or anything." By witnessing to their playmates, Southside's children become firmly committed to a Fundamentalist identity and practice the skills necessary to sustain that commitment (cf. Festinger et al. 1959).

Children at Southside also establish their skills and identity by learning to abide by the rules of separation and to explain those rules to nonbelievers. Some of the rules are common to believing and nonbelieving families alike: Don't hit other children. Don't steal. Be polite. Don't use curse words. Other rules are unique to a Fundamentalist household: Turn off bad programs and bad commercials on television. Don't go to the movies. Don't dance. These are rules that must be explained to even the best of nonbelieving parents. Southside parents know that when their children are with outsiders, the children are not always able to resist the temptation of living by the outsiders' more lenient rules. Nevertheless, parents work hard to teach their children what to expect and how to "take a stand." Bonnie has taught her children well and was especially proud when they could even explain why they would not participate in a camp square dance: "We walked up, and all the other kids were out on the dance floor, and my two were sitting in chairs. And my cousin came over to me, and she said, 'Sarah told me she can't dance because she's a Christian. Is that true?' And I said, 'Yeah, that's true.'" In the midst of learning the other necessary skills for adult survival, Southside children are also learning that they have special rules "because they are Christians."

One of the rules they learn, both overtly and subtly, is that families are supposed to divide their labor by sex. They learn the ideal standards for Christian families—priestly fathers, full-time mothers, and daily family devotions—and they watch as their parents work toward that goal. They probably also learn, though, that their mothers do far more than anyone admits. They know that mother provides part of the family's resources, subtly guides the family's decision making, and is likely to be the more enthusiastic teacher of religious values. Sometimes children thus learn at home how to make practical compromises between the Bible and the modern world. Even when ideals do not quite match reality, however, Southside children learn at home to experience and justify a Fundamentalist way of life.

The Nurture of the School

If Southside children also attend the Academy, they learn the lessons of the Fundamentalist life even more thoroughly. They are able to spend all their youthful energy learning the ways of the faith and are protected from almost every conceivable evil influence.

Learning the rules and skills of Fundamentalist culture at an academy is a relatively new phenomenon. Until recently, it was enough for Fundamentalist children to learn their religious skills at church and at home, leaving it to the public schools to provide general knowledge. For a variety of reasons, that arrangement has become unsatisfactory, and "Christian academies" are being started all over the country. These schools emphasize basic verbal and mathematical skills, as well as preparing children for using the Bible, witnessing, and living a separated life. At an academy, children learn about biblical rules and a disciplined life at the same time they are learning their multiplication tables.

Southside Christian Academy was founded in 1974, soon after the present pastor arrived. It began with six grades and gradually added junior and senior high. The pastor's dream is to build a complete new church complex, including a sanctuary and buildings for the school. The people of the church are busy raising money toward that goal; but in the meanwhile the elementary school occupies the lower two floors and the high school the upper floor of an old elementary school building that is owned by the town of Valley View. The nursery school meets in the church building, about two miles away. There are about fifty nursery schoolers, one hundred elementary pupils, and seventy secondary students. About two-thirds of these are children of church members, while the rest come from the community. During the 1979–1980 school year, there was one class for kindergarten and first grade, one for second and third grade, another for advanced third graders and fourth grade, and one each for fifth and sixth grades. Classes averaged about twenty pupils.

All the elementary teachers are women and are described as "committed, born-again Christians" who are also well qualified to teach. Many on the school staff are also members of the church staff. The pastor serves as superintendent and leads chapel every day, while his wife teaches English, French, and speech in the secondary school. The youth minister helps with choir, Bible, and physical education; and his wife teaches the kindergarten/first-grade class. The second-grade teacher doubles as elementary supervisor, and the headmaster and high school principal each also teach in the secondary school. There are ten full-time and three part-time staff members in the combined elementary and secondary schools. Despite the small staff, however, the school is approved by the state board of education, so that credits can be transferred to the public school system.

Financially, the Academy requires sacrifice from everyone. Its teachers work at low salaries. Parents must pay tuition and are called on for additional gifts and for labor. In addition, the church has provided underwriting funds in nearly every year of the school's operation. When the Academy has a need, parents and other church members give their time, energy, and money. For most the sacrifice is worth it. They are eager to maintain the Academy as a part of the ministry of the church and of the proper upbringing of their children.

The new headmaster at the Academy uses the idea of a triangle to talk about what children need. His school is one side of the triangle, the other sides being the church and home. Each is equally important and depends on the others. His idea is echoed by other Southside members. Bonnie sees the Academy as especially important because her children's father is not saved: "I think the main thing I wanted for them—because Sam isn't saved—I wanted them to have a complete circle, a complete picture, as far as—I don't know how to explain it. In other words, I didn't want them to think that salvation and the love of the Lord and living a Christian life was just my opinion. I wanted Sunday School and home and school. I wanted them to see as many Christians living a Christian life as they could. I wanted as much influence in their life as possible." Similarly, Janet Slavin sees the Academy as a way of choosing the influences in her daughter's life: "I think she is going to have less options thrown at her in a Christian school than if she was in a public school, where there might be a few more things that she might have to choose about. I would rather control her environment as much as possible while she is young, until she is old enough to be let go."

Almost everyone who supports the Academy sees it as a place with a "good Christian atmosphere," the sort of environment parents can trust. There children encounter ideas and behavior that are consistent with the Fundamentalist world view they experience at home and at church. Children are educated within the bounds of the world they call Christian.

In part, schools like Southside's have been started in response to perceived deterioration in the public schools. Even Southside parents who do not send their children to the Academy agree that schools are pretty bad these days. That is one of the things most often cited as evidence of the world's deplorable condition. At the most basic level, parents fear for their children's safety in schools they see as lawless. They also think their children are not getting a good education and that there are no good models for teaching children how to learn and how to behave. As Howard Otto said, "Linda doesn't really have a clear idea of what would be happening or what she would be doing if she weren't at Southside. But as far as I'm concerned, from seeing some of it, the public system is so bad . . . that I can't conceive of placing my daughters on the altar of sacrifice to offer them up to the public school system. They're treasures, God-given treasures."

Parents also worry that their children will pick up the bad habits of public school children. One mother, who works part-time in a public school, talked about how glad she is that her own daughter is at the Academy: "She has that whole atmosphere, you know, good Christians. You don't have to be worried that the kids are going to start swearing; and believe me, during the lunch program, they think nothing of saying it to the adults. I don't have to worry about all that."

That woman's sister touched on an even more important advantage of the Academy: "I think it is something that we missed out on. We always felt like we were different." When Southside children maintain their standards in the midst of a public school, they risk feeling different, having no real friends. At the Academy, they can feel normal and make friends with others who think and act just as they do.

Feeling that the public schools are a bad environment for Christian children is at least in small part a result of racial tensions. Not many say it openly, but the common assumption is that the students most likely to cause trouble in school are black. One mother mentioned that black and minority girls had been a problem for her daughter in junior high, and a father gave this account of his sons' enrollment in another Christian academy.

> We moved to this area from Meadowbrook because the Negroes in those days were getting so strong that they were making noise so that the teacher could not be heard in the class if you wanted to learn. And so we moved up here, looking at first for the school. Not long after we moved up here, in a few years, problems began to erupt in this school. We heard a group of people from Dorchester Christian Academy come and sing. We had two of them in our home, and their manners were so lovely that I said I'd like to get my boys out of the environment here, get them into that Christian academy.

Very few Southside people would have so openly tied the problem to race. These believers are not ideologically committed to segregation. They are, however, committed to separation; and much that is assumed to be typical of black and minority subcultures is viewed as sinful by the members of Southside. Although they are willing to admit pupils to the Academy without regard to "race, color, nationality, or ethnic origin," they also believe that many black students are simply unwilling or unable to live by Southside's standards. As a result, the Academy enrolls only about half a dozen blacks out of a total of 170; and blacks are among the most likely to be asked to leave for academic or disciplinary reasons.

For whatever reason, then, public schools are seen as undisciplined environments and potentially bad influences for Christian children. Equally important, the public schools are seen as repositories of knowledge that is contrary to Fundamentalist ways of thinking. Believers have long known that they could not trust secular colleges, but now they do not trust elementary and secondary schools either. They see public school children being taught false ideas not only about biology but also about government, economics, history, geology, astronomy, physics, and other sciences. About the only safe things to be learned are reading, writing, and arithmetic; and most schools do not seem to be doing a good job of that.

The changes believers perceive are not entirely imaginary. As recently as the early 1960s, evolution had barely entered the classroom, but religious observances were fairly common. Now the case is reversed. Since 1963, schools have become careful about supporting religious activities; and since Sputnik science education has been restructured and now includes evolution as an overarching theoretical framework. Evolution does, in fact, permeate virtually all the physical and social sciences. Schools assume that everything can be explained by human reason and can be changed for the better by human initiative. This is the "secular humanism" against which Fundamentalists rail. Its prevalence has prompted both their efforts to again ban the teaching of evolution (or at least to give creationism equal time) and their decision simply to give up and start their own schools.[2]

The establishment of separate schools implies that the public schools were equipping Fundamentalist children with a set of skills unsuited to the culture of their parents. This is a familiar problem for minority cultures, but it is a problem not often resolved in favor of the minority. Public schools have historically served the purpose of assimilation. Parents may have grieved that their children were losing the ability to speak in the native tongue, but they rejoiced that those offspring would be able to function in the new land. Even Catholic and Hebrew schools have not sought to challenge the basic assumptions of the larger society about the kind of knowledge that is necessary. Perhaps the schools closest to Fundamentalist schools are those supported by the Amish (cf. Nordin and Turner 1980). Academies are not just teaching religion in addition to other knowledge, not just teaching in a strict, well-mannered environment. They are seeking to make all knowledge conform to their understanding of the Bible. The Bible is to be the "hub of the educational wheel" (Academy *Handbook*, p. 9). The members of Southside correctly perceive that other schools are not willing to entertain Fundamentalist views as plausible, and they have responded by enlarging their own territory to include the social function of education.

Ironically, at the same time that believers are protecting their children from the ideas and behavior of decadent public schools, they may be depriving those children of the skills necessary for living outside the boundaries of Fundamentalist institutions. Many of Southside's members worry about that possibility. They are afraid that Academy graduates will be trained only "for the Lord's work." They fear that those who emerge to face the secular world of work will be totally unable to handle the challenge: "I am realistic. I mean we are different in that we have this personal commitment and beliefs, but we still have to coexist side by side with those in the world, and if you don't know what is out there, it is a pretty wild jungle, if you are seventeen or eighteen and start facing it. It can throw you."

Some parents speak to the problems out of their own successful experience in sending children to public schools: "In the Christian school, kids are not exposed to negative things of life. They are more protected. In public school, they are more exposed, but I think that if they have a good basis in the home, it shouldn't shatter them. It didn't my children. . . . They have an opportunity to prove themselves, to share what they have received." Mary reflected similar ideas: "It's hard never to be in your community. It's through our children that we made many contacts for witness."

A few Southside members also worry about other ways in which the Academy narrows the experience of its students. The Academy has no room for exceptional students of any kind. Everyone must conform to one set of standards. Emotionally disturbed children, those with physical or mental handicaps, and those who have had academic or behavior problems in other schools are not permitted to enroll at the Academy "if their condition were to hold back the progress of the entire class" (*Handbook*, p. 11). Ann lamented that her son, who is a slow learner, was not able to make it at the Academy: "I wish he could be there, but it is just too limited over there, it is just too small. They don't have the facilities to offer all of the subjects." The problem is largely one of size and facilities, but it is also one of protecting the Christian environment. As a result, everyone is the same: well behaved, moderately bright, physically normal, middle class, and white.

Southside Christian Academy, then, creates an enviornment where Fundamentalist ideas and behavior are normal. The *Handbook* says that "the school will endavor to provide an atmosphere that is conducive to the best Christian living" (p. 9). When that theoretical goal hits the practical reality of the classroom, it finds concrete form in rules, emphasis on traditional skills, and the presence of Bible study in all the subjects. This biblical, traditional, regulated structure is the everyday world in which the consciousness of Southside's youth is shaped.

The first thing everybody mentions about the Academy—pro or con—is that it has strict rules; and they are right. Rules against lying, cheating, stealing, swearing, and the use of alcohol or drugs would be expected at any school. At the Academy, the rules go far beyond such obvious offenses. Students are expected to be respectful, to have a good attitude, not to "gripe," and to be courteous. They are also expected to maintain Christian standards when they are away from school because their behavior might "harm the testimony of the school" (*Handbook*, p. 14). If they disobey or act in any way unbecoming a Christian, they are subject to detention, suspension, or expulsion. They may be spanked by teachers or administrators, or their parents may be called in for a conference. The Academy strives toward self-discipline in its students, but adults emphasize that those who do not exhibit self-discipline will be disciplined (that is, punished) by others.

Southside Academy also has rules about how Christians should dress and groom themselves. Girls of all ages must always wear dresses, although culottes are allowed for physical education, and slacks may be worn under a dress in cold weather. Make-up, hair styles, stockings, blouses, and everything else about their appearance must be modest and "becoming to a Christian girl" (*Handbook*, p. 16). Little girls are allowed to wear short skirts, but by the time they reach junior high, their skirts must touch the floor when they are kneeling. For boys, the rule of thumb is "neat and conservative." Jeans are not allowed, belts are required, and shirts must be buttoned and tucked in. T-shirts, sandals, and facial hair are forbidden. And, in all cases, the "judgment of the Administration will be final" (p. 17).

As with all the rules of the Fundamentalist life, these dress rules can be defended from the Bible. For instance, the Academy *Handbook* states, "Hair (for boys) should be clean and groomed at least two fingers' width above the brows. It must not come down over the ears or shirt collar" (p. 16). This rule is enforced with periodic hair checks for all junior and senior high boys. One day, nearly half the boys failed the check and were told that they could not go to the

Friday basketball game if they did not get haircuts. There was considerably grumbling, and one of the boys summoned the courage to ask why long hair was so bad. The teacher pointed them to I Corinthians 11:14, which asserts that it is a shame for a man to have long hair. When someone else complained that his hair was not really long, the teacher went back to the seventh verse of that same chapter, which says that a man should not "cover his head." The teacher explained that if the ears and forehead are covered, a boy is on his way toward a "covered head." Finally another student made what he thought would be a winning argument: "But, didn't Jesus have long hair?" The teacher was indignant and cautioned the students that the pictures they see of Jesus are just representations painted by sinful men. The Bible teaches that long hair is a sin and also teaches that Jesus never sinned; Jesus, therefore, could not have had long hair. Case closed.

This group of teenagers had just learned a rather complicated explanation for a minor rule. More importantly, they had been reminded again that the Bible is their ultimate authority, the source for all their explanations. Yet it is also possible that for some of them the seeds of doubt were sown. They may have heard that Fundamentalist explanations do not always make sense of the world as they see it.

Not surprisingly, Southside Christian Academy also worries about "proper Christian conduct with the opposite sex" (*Handbook*, p. 14). It does not so much discourage the formation of relationships (hoping, after all, that its children will marry Christians), but it seeks to prevent those relationships from becoming either serious or actively sexual. It discourages steady dating out of a feeling that teens are too young to be ready to marry. It seeks to protect the "purity" of those future marriages by prohibiting any physical contact at school and forbidding couples to arrive or leave alone in a car. Pairs may sit together at school, and they may ride in cars with a set of parents, but they are strictly forbidden any public display of their affection or any opportunity for the private expression of it.

All these rules have little overtly to do with education, but the same structure of rules and discipline shapes what is learned in the classroom. Students learn not only what to wear and how to behave but also where to put their names on a paper and how many sharpened pencils to have on their desks. In the elementary school, students have a carefully structured routine. They know when they must line up, stand beside their seats, or sit quietly. Each subject and activity comes in a predictable order, and whenever they have extra time, there are "seat-work" assignments on the board. Students who fail to do their homework or to bring required equipment to class are given demerits as quickly as they would be for being disrespectful or wearing inappropriate clothing.

How well the rule keeping is integrated into the learning process varies greatly from class to class. Some teachers seem to be able to maintain an acceptable level of discipline with only occasional reminders, while others spend a good deal of time supervising the details of their pupils' behavior. In each classroom, however, students are expected to do their schoolwork with the same kind of self-discipline that governs the rest of their behavior. They are expected to work hard and do well. As the sign in the second-grade classroom says, "It is a sin to do less than your best."

This emphasis on hard work and discipline is the traditional Protestant work ethic, which has historically dominated American society and education. It is part of what the people at Southside mean when they say that they want their children to have a good, old-fashioned education. They also mean that they want the Bible and the flag to be honored in every classroom. We have already seen that the Bible is very present at the Academy, with daily Bible classes and chapel. Biblical ideas are also likely to appear on spelling tests, in biology lessons, and in government or history classes. History, in fact, is called American Christian History. Each detail of the past is understood in light of this nation's special calling to spread the gospel.

The United States, by this telling of the story, is meant to be a Christian nation, and, at Southside Academy, capitalism and democracy are as essential to that identity as is conservative religion. Government and Economics is taught as one subject and consists of learning how to defend the American way. J. Edgar Hoover's *Masters of Deceit* (1957) is one of the texts. Students in Rudiments, another high school requirement, are taught to develop a self-disciplined, loyal, patriotic character. Although as good Christians these students would never subvert duly elected authorities, they do not support their country "right or wrong." Rather, they are taught to work toward keeping the United States the kind of Christian nation God established it to be. As one parent described the ideal nation, "It would be Fundamental, just the way the whole country was built —with Fundamental, Bible-believing Christians, like when America was really great."

Besides teaching a work ethic, emphasizing patriotism, and requiring study of the Bible, the Academy is traditional in subtle ways. The learning process reflects Fundamentalists' Baconian view of the universe. For them, knowledge is a fixed body of facts, all of which have their origin with God and can be found in one form or another in the Bible. The learner's task is to uncover the facts and to appropriate them. Students at the Academy, therefore, spend a great deal of their time copying, memorizing, and reciting. They faithfully reproduce in their notebooks what the teacher has written on the board. They are tested on what they can remember and recite. Even in the high school, there is no attempt to move toward creative, critical, or integrative thinking. Biology students memorize the parts of plants and animals—not to discover relationships among various species or to understand the adaptive features of some plant or animal but to add to their store of knowledge about God's unique creations. When speech students learn how to conduct a debate or discussion, they learn a list of rules. It is not the place of human beings to criticize or to create new knowledge. The way in which these students learn equips them for a world where tradition is more valued than change.

The education Southside's pupils receive, then, is both structurally and substantively different from that offered in the public schools. At the elementary level, the skills that are emphasized enable Academy students to do as well as or better than public school students their age.[3] They are, for instance, required to read regularly with and to their parents. Their school and home environment emphasizes the value of learning basic skills and the unacceptability of failure or sloppiness. Although the school does not have the material resources of books, machines, and highly paid staff that have come to be equated with a quality education, it does have a solid elementary program. Students emerge with a vast knowledge of the Bible and with good basic language and number skills.

At the high school level, the lack of equipment and personnel becomes more of a problem. The entire staff of the junior and senior high is four full-time teachers, part-time help from the headmaster, pastor, and youth minister, plus a study-hall aide. Science equipment consists of one microscope. Typing classes have two ancient machines. There is no facility for teaching home economics or shop or instrumental music. As a result, students have almost no choice of electives or of which course to take to fulfill a requirement or of teachers. There is only one government course, one chemistry course, and one English course, and one teacher for each. With only twenty-six junior high and forty-three senior high students, even the range of available friends is limited. Many parents would echo one of Jim Forester's reasons for withdrawing his daughter: "I don't think the education she was getting was worth the sacrifice and the turmoil it was causing." Even Academy administrators admit that the high school does not offer everything it should.

If one of the primary tasks of adolescence is "trying on" available roles and settling on a comfortable identity, Southside Academy's teens face a far less bewildering time than their secular peers. They have few roles from which to choose, a limited number of models to observe, and a narrow range of knowledge about the world with which to make their choices. If they remain at the Academy through graduation, these adolescents are likely to commit themselves to identities firmly within Fundamentalist boundaries, in part because their present and future alternatives have been so effectively controlled.

Where Nurture Fails

Not every Fundamentalist child grows up to be a Fundamentalist. The best available national data[4] hint that "sectarians" are less likely to keep their children in the fold than any other denominational group (Hadaway 1978; Roof and Hadaway 1977). Although few people who grow up as sectarians drop out of religion entirely, at least 40 percent switch to other denominations by adulthood. Of the thirty-three families I interviewed who had teenaged or adult children, fifteen had at least one child who was raised in the church but about whose salvation the families were now worried. Of the parents who responded to the Sunday morning survey, 15 percent of those with teens reported that their children do not attend with them. One mother, who has two grown children in the church and two who are not, talked about her feelings of helplessness: "It is very frustrating to have your children grown and to know that they are not Christian. Pastor is always saying 'Get your house in order,' and there is nothing that we would like better, but it doesn't work that way. . . . [Our son] is too far away and too old." Many of Southside's youth drop out of church when they are old enough to say "no" to their parents. Some eventually return to another church or denomination, but many leave organized religion entirely.

What happens? With a system of socialization as all-encompassing as Southside's, how do so many children escape? Because I do not have systematic data on these dropouts, my conclusions must be tentative. I wish, however, to suggest a possible explanation. Just as relationships and activities inside the church's fellowship support the ideas of believers, so strong attachments outside the church may make Fundamentalist ideas implausible even (or perhaps especially) for those who have never known anything else.

The teen years are a time when most children experiment, and Southside's youth are no exception. If they have an opportunity to choose, they may select friends of whom their parents do not approve or participate in activities their parents would condemn. Sometimes youthful experiments turn into adult careers; other times they are but passing fancies. The difference has a good deal to do with the strength and nature of the relationships that are formed along the way.

When theorists explain juvenile delinquency, for instance, they ask about the relationships in which a young person is involved and the behavior that is considered normative within those groups (for example, Sutherland and Cressey 1978). For Fundamentalist youth, leaving the church may be analogous to juvenile delinquency. It may be possible to explain who leaves by asking similar questions. Those who leave may be those who spend more time, more often, with doubters, and less time, of poorer quality, with those who believe. Dropouts either develop close relationships with outsiders or have deteriorating relationships with insiders or both.

Sometimes the influence of the outside world comes from inside the home: Nearly one-third of the families I interviewed who had "wayward" children were families where the father was not saved. In such homes, the ways of the world are always present as an alternative. Just as often, the outsider is a friend from the neighborhood or from school. The mother we heard earlier mentioned that her son had had a "friend who was strongly antireligious," and she suspected that had something to do with her son's disaffection.

By the time children reach their teens, it becomes difficult to isolate them from friends and romances that can draw them away from Fundamentalism.

That same young man also had "some teachers at church that turned him off." Sometimes the reason for leaving is more push than pull. Some youth come to dislike and rebel against specific people in the church, including their parents. In Dudley's (1978) study of students in Seventh Day Adventist academies, the strongest predictor of rebellion was poor relationships with parents and school officials. Sorting out the causal direction is difficult after the fact. Some children may turn away from Fundamentalism because they are angry with their parents, and others may develop poor relationships with their parents because of their irreligious ideas and activities. In either case, without strong, positive bonds with people inside Fundamentalism, Southside's teens are likely to drift away. If they have the opportunity, they may well choose another religion or no religion at all.

Southside's nurture of its children is designed to make the Fundamentalist identity the only plausible choice. But ironically the very thoroughness of their efforts at socialization may sometimes backfire. Sometimes the problem is that once outside the sheltering canopy, young adults have no internal controls to guide them back to the fold. That is a possibility about which one woman voiced concern: "Sometimes there are kids that are brought up in Christian schools, Christian homes, Christian this and that, and sometimes they learn to act like a Christian before they actually really accept Christ. They even know how to get up and pray, but sometimes they don't have a personal relationship with Christ at all. They just know how to act." She would have said such youth needed to be converted, but the only true "conversion" possible for someone brought up in Fundamentalism is to leave. Indeed, upon achieving some distance from the all-encompassing faith of their childhoods, many Fundamentalist youth find it inadequate to meet the demands of the world they now live in. Rather than leaving religion entirely, many "convert" to other denominations and become among the most committed leaders of the same liberal churches they grew up disparaging.[5]

In many cases, the church's efforts are simply not enough to counter the definitions of reality and standards of behavior that exist outside of Fundamentalism. As Fundamentalist ideas and lifestyles diverge increasingly from those in the larger culture, it is becoming more necessary for parents to limit their children's opportunities to choose, to isolate them from the people and activities of the world. As we have seen, it used to be sufficient to keep youth out of secular colleges; now they must be kept from public elementary and secondary schools as well. Some parents are able to counter successfully the influences of a secular education, but few children can pass through twelve years of public schooling without modifying the beliefs with which they have been raised. Some children are able to maintain their conviction that everything outside Fundamentalism is inherently evil, but others begin to encounter people, ideas, and activities they simply cannot bring themselves to condemn. In neighborhoods and in school, children are likely to find the outside world not nearly so offensive as they had been warned it was. If parents, in cooperation with the church and the Academy, are able to isolate their children from such positive experiences with the world, those children are less likely to stray. But the opportunities for failure are legion.

CHAPTER ELEVEN

Fundamentalists in the Modern World

For the preaching of the cross is to them that perish foolishness; but unto us which are saved it is the power of God.
—I Corinthians 1:18

W E BEGAN this exploration with the simple goal of describing a group in which the ideas and institutions of Fundamentalism are a lived reality. We traced Fundamentalism from the intellectual and social revolutions of the late nineteenth century to its emergence as an identifiable movement with the goal of resisting "modernism." Into this movement believers carried both traditional conservative doctrines and recent ideas such as dispensational premillennialism and aggressive revivalism. When these believers failed to win back the main-line Protestant denominations in the 1920s, they withdrew to form a crazy quilt of independent churches, colleges, and agencies. By the end of the 1940s one segment of this movement had begun to seek ways to accommodate modernity without compromising basic conservative doctrines. They came to identify themselves as *Evangelicals*, leaving the name *Fundamentalist* to those who still sought to resist modernity in all its forms.

The world Fundamentalists have constructed is by definition, then, a world in opposition. Because they see the outside world as chaotic, their world is full of order. They believe that God has a plan for every detail of life and find meaning for their lives in trying to follow God's plan. God knows who will be saved and when and which church that saved person should join. God also knows whom they should marry, which jobs they should take, and how they should make each decision. Believers are sure that within God's plan they can know what they should do and why. They are also sure that God knows what will happen in the world tomorrow and when everything will come to an end. No matter what happens, they can be sure that God is in control. The "sacred cosmos" of Fundamentalism is constructed in defense against the terrible chaos believers perceive in the modern world outside.

Living in such an orderly world requires of believers both individual and corporate discipline. Because these people refuse to admit that rules might be variable, they declare the literal words of scripture to be the only reliable path to truth. They pledge their willingness to accept whatever rules are defined as biblical by those who claim to speak for God. Believers memorize verses of scripture, listen to the pastor's sermons, and watch the lives of respected church members to discover how God wants them to behave. In the world Southside members construct, tradition and authority are honored; change and individualized private morality are banned.

Just which rules are truly biblical could be hotly debated. The rules these Fundamentalists choose, however, are shaped in part by their need to set themselves apart from the rest of the world. If outsiders enjoy drinking, dancing, and movies, Fundamentalists can identify themselves by avoiding those pleasures. If liberals have formal worship services and engage in social action, then Fundamentalists can recognize each other by their informality and exclusive attention to evangelism. Both the strict doctrine and the strict rules of Fundamentalism serve as badges of identity. They are also the practical expression of the idea that God's truth is unchanging and universal.

Living a life of discipline, order, and obedience is not, however, simply a matter of settling one's eternal destiny and reading the Bible. As we have seen, it is also a matter of participation in a temporal community that creates and sustains a Fundamentalist view of the world. For most of the members of Southside, the church is the dominating institution in their lives. It gives them work to do and supplies friendships with like-minded people. Other activities and relationships simply become unimportant compared with the sense of purpose they find with fellow believers. Like an ethnic neighborhood, the religious community provides a place where familiar customs and language are honored, a place where one can truly belong.

We have also seen that the task of supporting a Fundamentalist view of the world is not that of the church alone. Believers look to their homes and marriages as a place of refuge from a world where they and their ideas are disvalued. Homes are run with the same strictness that guides the believer's spiritual life. Here, too, tradition and authority are respected. In a Christian home, Fundamentalist ideas about the world can be assumed to be true. Homes both sustain adult believers and provide an ideal environment for raising believing children.

In addition, the members of Southside have undertaken the task of providing their children with a Christian education. They have rejected the secular public schools as operating on principles they cannot accept. It is not just evolution or sex education or the lack of discipline that Fundamentalists hold against public schools. It is the assumption that all problems can be solved by human effort and that variations in lifestyle should be respected. Such humanist and pluralist ideas are not allowed in Southside's Academy. There, the Bible is the ultimate textbook, and everyone must obey the same rules. Parents can choose the Academy and know that they are protecting their children from the ways of the world. Whether such isolation will result in a net gain for Fundamentalism, however, is still an open question.

Choosing and maintaining a life in opposition to the world is a difficult business for children and adults. Living by biblical rules requires both inner discipline and support from a community where others live by those same rules. Finding explanations for life's events requires not only prayer and Bible study but conversations with others who construct explanations according to the same principles of order and divine control. Sometimes believers feel alienated, alone against a hostile outside world, but they have no desire to return to a life where they could see no order, no purpose, no rules. Sometimes they seek to change their immediate social environment by witnessing to their peers. At other times, they may venture into the outside world to try to change it by their influence or even through political activity. But for most believers the predictable world inside the fellowship draws them in and keeps them beneath its shelter. There they find a "brotherhood" that is distinct in belief, language, and lifestyle from the unsaved world outside.

The Effects and Causes of Membership

Until now, I have avoided asking the broad questions that are raised by a group like this. That aversion has been deliberate. Having studied only one congregation, I have no assurance that the phenomena observed represent Fundamentalism as a whole (although we may have a strong suspicion that they do). Likewise, because my goal was to get as close as possible to the everyday reality in which Fundamentalism is lived, I set aside theoretical frameworks that might have imposed an alien order on that reality. Having now completed a description of Fundamentalism, however, I can step back and take a longer view.

Skeptical observers of Fundamentalism almost always wonder whether Fundamentalism can possibly be "good" for its adherents. Are they better off, individually, for either having been brought up in this tradition or having adopted it as adults? The answer depends on one's definition of *good*. And, as we have seen, the answer may also vary depending on the particular life history and psychology of the individual believer. This is not a psychological study, but it is possible to discern certain regularities in the stories we have heard. For at least some, Fundamentalism provides comfort in the midst of otherwise intolerable situations; it offers resolution of their own inner conflicts. If, as happens at Southside, a church places a great deal of emphasis on the absolute trustworthiness of God, it may meet the special needs of people who never learned such basic trust as children. Likewise, religious rituals can provide opportunities for reliving early crises of guilt or shame or dependency. In each ritual act the worshipper can experience reassurance that forgiveness and confidence and independence can be had. In the case of Fundamentalism, the crises of early childhood seem to be recurring themes, never far from the surface of the group's experience. For people who especially need forgiveness, Fundamentalism may provide a path to personal autonomy and confidence.

Constructing causal arguments from such regularities in experience is, however, precarious. With so many members having never existed outside Fundamentalism, it would be ludicrous to say that they sought Fundamentalism out of some inherent psychological need. Especially for the lifelong members, we would have to argue that the church shaped their experience, not that their experience led them to the church. Even for converts, we cannot be sure that their perceived needs preceded their conversion. We are forced to settle for the explanation that individual experience and group life come to mirror each other, each pushing the other in compatible directions. Yet, we are also left with the distinct possibility that, at least in part,

Fundamentalism provides a coping strategy for those who find themselves adrift in the world that seems untrustworthy and unforgiving.

There are, in addition, social dimensions to these psychological needs. The world seems far more untrustworthy when it is changing than when it remains stable. In an age when mobility and divorce have contributed to a feeling that many relationships are impermanent, when rapid technological change exceeds our ability to respond, feelings of lostness are to be expected. At such times, growth in Fundamentalism can also be expected. Fundamentalism has its greatest appeal in times and places where values and ways of life are changing. Those who are relatively new to the middle class, for instance, may find it disconcerting to see the rules by which they achieved their status declared no longer operative. Having been hard working and respectable, they are especially unhappy to see the rules bent for others (cf. Skerry 1982). Likewise, those who grew up in small towns or on farms but have moved to the city know firsthand the chaos that characterizes the transition to modernity. And, for the college-educated, home-owning sons and daughters of immigrant laborers, change is a personal reality. They belong neither to their parents' world nor fully to the postindustrial middle class. For people like these, caught between two worlds, Fundamentalism provides an attractive alternative.

These observations suggest that membership in a church like Southside is the result of a complex combination of social and psychological factors. It is not merely a response to some inner conflict nor a simple product of social forces. As we have seen, those forces are not effective until given direction by a group of believers actively seeking others who need to be saved. Although cultural forces set the stage and psychic forces perhaps provide the individual motivation, no individual comes to Fundamentalism without concrete institutional contacts. When the networks are strong enough, little other explanation may be needed.

Most especially unneeded are the old explanations that emphasized the role of status in producing Fundamentalism. Fortunately, these are increasingly falling by the wayside. The people of Southside certainly do not fit any neat economic categories. And status (taken as income, occupation, or some combination of the two) is consistently proving a poor predictor of attitudes supportive of the

New Christian Right. Also, when "status discontent" is taken to mean some discrepancy between earned and actual status or between childhood and adult status, there is still no relationship with socio-moral issues. In study after study "cultural" attitudes, moral values, region, religiosity, and the like are far better predictors of identification with the New Christian Right than are any demographic characteristics. Fundamentalists are not defending declining prestige or economic position but a culturally coherent way of life.[1]

Powerlessness and Power among Believers

One of the reasons sociologists have always paid attention to status is that it is presumed to have something to do with power. Another way to ask the question of Fundamentalism's value to the person is to ask whether it empowers or alienates, whether it is an "inspiration or an opiate"—to put the question in Gary Marx's (1967) terms. To what extent do these believers perceive that they have the ability to participate in the construction of the social world in which they live? Do they have the power to create ideas and organizations and ways of living? Power understood in this sense is not just the ability to impose one's will on others by force or influence but is the building block of social action.[2] If any religion has effects on social life, its most basic effect will be in determining people's perception of their own power. Do they understand the social arrangements of this world to have been prescribed by God and therefore to be either unchangeable or irrelevant? Or do they see this world as God's workshop and themselves as God's agents?

Karl Marx argued that religion served the interests of the ruling classes by convincing both them and their workers that this world was as it should be, that good and evil would be rewarded in a world to come. His description of religion as the "opium of the people" was among the kinder things he had to say. He goes on to posit that the abolition of religion will be possible when people no longer need illusions. Religion stands alongside philosophy as an interpretive scheme that gets in the way of human beings' perceiving that they have the power to change their circumstances (Marx 1844). For Marx, the only possible effect of other-worldly beliefs is alienation—the perception that humans do not have the power to act creatively in this world.

A similar but more sophisticated argument about religion and alienation is made by Berger (1969). He too defines alienation as perceiving the social world as totally outside oneself, separate and apart, impermeable to human efforts at change. People who are alienated are powerless because they believe themselves to be so, because they accept the state of the world as a given. Religion contributes to this picture by positing explanations that come from a sacred realm that is by definition "totally other," existing above and apart from us. Such religious legitimation of existing social structures makes them remote from the potential actions of mere mortals.

According to Berger, though, it is not just religious legitimation that creates alienation. The very ordering of the universe provided by religion creates a comforting "sacred canopy" that believers are loath to abandon. To acknowledge the social world as "merely human" would be to give up a measure of order and predictability for each measure of freedom and power that is gained.

On the other side of the theoretical fence, Weber would emphatically deny that religious explanations of this world necessarily deprive people of their power to produce change. For Weber, a religiously legitimated social order can empower as easily as it can alienate. As he saw it, the religious ideas of Calvinism, for instance, provided the impetus for a dramatic social revolution: "The ascetic derives renewed assurances of his state of grace from his awareness that his possession of the central religious salvation gives him the power to act and his awareness that through his actions he serves God" (1922:169). Although Weber admitted that mystical or otherworldly religion could create believers as passive as Marx might have thought, he recognized the potential of religion for encouraging powerful action in this world.

Most recently, we have seen such powerful, religiously motivated action in the civil-rights movement and other movements of liberation. And, as Weber would have expected, black believers who placed their hopes on another world were unlikely to support civil-rights activism, while black believers who held a this-worldly ethic supported the movement (G. T. Marx 1967). They sought change because they perceived that God cares how we live in this world.

On the surface, at least, the members of Southside would appear far more likely to be passive and other-worldly (to "gather at the river") than to take up "the sword of the Lord" for an invasion of "the citadels of sin," to put the dichotomy in Cox's (1984:48) terms. They seem to be as "alienated" as any social theorist would expect. They live according to strict moral rules that they perceive as unchangeable, and they spend a good deal of energy longing for the end of the present evil world. They say that the only important human activity is spreading the message of salvation. And they are quite sure that the best way to live is to turn everything over to God, to let God make their choices for them.

> I know that I am going to have a lot more problems, and what else is there to draw strength on?

> I don't know what I would have done if I didn't have the Lord right by my side.

Human powerlessness is suggested also when Southside's believers talk about the world. They are convinced that there is nothing they could do to make things better.

> It's a sorry world, and there's nothing you can do to change it except to be as faithful a witness as you can.

> I don't think that men as such can do anything. . . . I don't think it can get better by anything we do.

> You're not going to change human nature. . . . Nothing's going to happen. Period.

In sermons and in everyday conversations, these believers are likely to claim that God has all the power while they have none.

The passive side of Fundamentalism is also apparent in the rules and authorities believers recognize in every aspect of life. And the source for those rules is an unchanging Bible. If an idea or practice is seen as biblical, no amount of human initiative can change it. Individual freedom is limited by tradition, authority, and scripture.

Ironically, no member of Southside would perceive rules and authority as a limitation or a liability. For them, rules provide a way to understand the world and to order their lives, and the benefits they receive from knowing and obeying God's plan far outweigh any costs a social scientist may tell them about. For believers, some things are better left outside the range of possibility. They do not envy the seeming freedom of outsiders.

There are no lines, I guess, there. You are totally free. And now I realize that lines are definitely better.

I love the absolutes. . . . I don't have responsibility. [God] gives us all the answers. He makes the decisions for me, and that is great!

You hear preachers say a lot, "The Lord is still on his throne, and everything's gonna be all right, and God's gonna take care of us." Just accepting that has given me a lot of peace in my heart I didn't have for a long time. . . . God is in control of our lives; God is in complete control.

Despite—or perhaps because of—the limitations imposed by traditions and rules, these believers experience a new sense of powerfulness. Bird (1979) has noted a similar phenomenon in several of the new religions. He writes, "By acknowledging these [religious] authorities, they gain thereby a kind of license, a derived sense of personal authority, which authorizes them to ignore or to count as of only relative importance the claims made by various other secular authorities."

Such a conversion of powerlessness into power is just the beginning of the subtle ways in which Fundamentalist claims about human power mask a different reality. Although human power is worthless in this Fundamentalist economy, God's power can accomplish anything. When Southside's preacher speaks, he assures his listeners that nothing in this world can defeat God. Both his tone and his message leave the people with a diffuse feeling that they can attempt anything: "I started to become more conscious of God's power in the world. You could feel the power even the first day that we went there. I had tears in my eyes at the end of the service. The preaching was so powerful."

Not only do believers feel empowered, but they also experience power in practical ways. They are given important work to do in the church, and the support they receive helps them to believe that they have the necessary resources for doing that work. They appropriate God's power for earthly activities, especially the work of the church. There are Sunday School classes to be taught, songs to be sung, testimonies to be given, and special events to be planned. In most instances, the people who do these things for the church have had little previous training or experience in leadership. Few have practice in public speaking or organizational management. Like sectarian groups before, Southside offers its members opportunities to practice skills for which the larger society gives them neither credit nor opportunity. The larger society judges these people as incapable, but in God's society power is available to do what needs to be done.

Even more important than the work of staffing a church program is the task of witnessing to unsaved people. In many ways witnessing is the prototype for the availability of God's power. Nearly everyone admits that talking to friends or strangers about the faith is a thoroughly frightening prospect. Believers are terrified that they will be humiliated, will not be able to answer questions, will be branded as religious fanatics, or will just plain fail. And actual experience often confirms all those fears. Yet somehow they manage to continue. They find the courage to bring up an unpopular subject and confront people with the idea that they ought to be saved. Members who are most courageous at witnessing are recognized as having the most of God's power. The more they witness, the more power they have. Harry McLean said that the power he feels when he witnesses is even more exciting than the power he derives from being a police officer. Without God's help, he could never do it; but with God he can talk to anyone—truck driver or professor.

One of the keys to this power is the knowledge believers have that, as one of the saved, they automatically outrank anyone who is unsaved. No matter what outsider they are with, believers have the higher status. Their standing before God makes any earthly standing irrelevant. What they know about God's plan for the world is far more important than any other kind of knowledge, and the life they experience inside Fundamentalism makes any apparent pleasures of the modern world pale in comparison. As long as the social situation can be constructed as one in which the believer can witness, he or she can be in control, control enhanced by a sense of spiritual superiority.

Witnessing can also have more long-lasting implications. If believers are successful, they stand to gain the ability to restructure their environment around biblical rules. As the number of believers grows in any given setting, they are increasingly able to establish Fundamentalist rules as the rules that will apply. One young man at Southside went to work in a small machine shop as the only believer.

Within a couple of years, four others had been converted, leaving the nonbelievers in the minority. Now that shop is a "Christian" place to work.

This appropriation of divine power in the service of proselytizing and church work has also been noted in other religious groups. Barker (1978) writes of the Unificationists she observed that the perceived urgency of their task often brought out skills that no outsider would ever have expected such people to possess. Sectarian religious organizations may often benefit from the practical social skills their members gain when they believe that God's power is available to help them.

Power for What?

Although it is interesting that believers discover hidden talents that they put to the use of the church, even more interesting is the degree to which God's power is taken out of the church into the rest of social life. Although they are "ascetics" in Weber's (1922) terms, the strains of both the inner-worldly and the other-worldly are here. Fundamentalists have never been quite sure what to do with this world. Their perception of their own power has always been limited by what they think God is interested in accomplishing here. But what they do think God is interested in accomplishing is seen as easily within human reach. The important question, then, is not whether this religion empowers or alienates but where these people draw the line between what can and cannot be done.

For the people at Southside, the social arenas in which God is presumed to be active can be identified by listening for the adjective *Christian*. Churches deserve that description, and so do homes. Marriage and child rearing are not for them simple matters of emotional support or civil obligation. Rather, it is their God-given responsibility to establish Christian homes. In turn, God gives them the ability to find the right partner and ways to be happy and to get along with each other once they do. They are confident that they can avoid divorce and raise a house full of loving, obedient children. Although the entire secular world may conspire against them, believers claim the power to construct and maintain a happy home.

God is also seen as concerned about the education of believers' children. Southside members are convinced that no public schools can convey a proper understanding of the world to their children and that they have the sacred duty of establishing institutions in which their children can get a "Christian" education. They have, therefore, taken on the rather formidable task of beginning a school. They have found a suitable building to rent, recruited teachers from their own congregation and from various Bible colleges, located textbooks and equipment, and otherwise performed tasks usually reserved for professional school administrators. Today they do everything necessary—from painting the walls to keeping grade records—to maintain a Christian academy for students from kindergarten through twelfth grade.[3] Because God is interested in Christian education, these believers claim powers they might never have thought they possessed.

Christian homes and Christian schools are arenas in which God is active and in which believers therefore have power. At Southside, the other social entity that is often labeled "Christian" is the United States. The Fundamentalist reading of the nation's role in divine history is a peculiar blending of Puritan theocracy and Jeffersonian religious liberty. Fundamentalists see the Puritan experiment as a model to be emulated. The Puritan notion of being a "light on a hill" blends, for them, with the later role of the United States as a missionary nation. The country, they say, must return to her roots, restore the "Christian principles" on which she was founded. God has commissioned Americans to use their religious heritage and vast national resources to spread the gospel throughout the world. The United States is no less a chosen nation than was Israel.

Because they take the role of the United States so seriously, they worry a good deal about our collective standing before God. They fear that this nation may be so thoroughly losing its moral fiber that it can never again serve as a "light to the world," a base from which missionaries can go out with the gospel. The range of acceptable behavior in the United States has expanded so dramatically in the last generation that Fundamentalists can no longer hold their peace. The distance between the strict rules they uphold and the norms portrayed on television is enormous, as is the distance between the sexual exclusivity they practice and the permissiveness seemingly condoned under the labels *pro-choice* and *gay rights*. Citing Sodom and Gomorrah or the fall of Rome as precedents, they are sure that such license can lead only to destruction. They feel compelled to sound the warning, to do what they can to halt the erosion of morality in a nation called to be an example to the world.

Fundamentalists have thus come to claim for themselves the role of prophet, calling the nation back to morality. They have always played that role in calling individuals to repentance, but they are now willing to use their political power to force morality on otherwise unrepentant sinners. Anything that would take the United States away from a "godly" way of life is taken as seriously as heresy would be in the church. Believers see themselves, then, as having the God-given responsibility of calling the United States to repentance and preserving the nation's righteousness. Sometimes that responsibility takes the form of preaching, but it may also take the form of political action. As one of Southside's members put it, "If someone, if God's people, who are the only ones that can, if God's people don't get together and start reversing the trend—. It's going to be up to the Lord's people to do that."

Their strategy for change differs from that of liberal or secular political reformers. It begins with seeking spiritual change in individuals. But they firmly believe that spiritual change will produce changes in social institutions. They are convinced of that fact by the differences they see between their churches, homes, and schools and those of people who are not saved. A call for national revival is integral to the Fundamentalist political platform. Only after first seeking this spiritual change do Fundamentalists proceed with seeking to change the rules by which society is structured.

They are, however, willing to seek changes in those rules. As they see things, for any institution to be Christian it must satisfy one of two criteria: Either all its members must be saved, or it must run by biblical rules. In the case of the American nation, believers may preach the need for revival, but they have no illusion about everyone being saved. Their theology does not lead them to expect God's kingdom on this earth. There will always be unbelievers, but unbelievers can still obey biblical rules.

The Christian nation Southside's members envision would be a place where God's plan was followed, requiring that those in power recognize divine authority and that a majority of the citizens agree on which rules were prescribed by scripture. It would not, then, be so tolerant of pluralism as the United States has historically been. Nor would church and state be so clearly differentiated as they have become. These Fundamentalists do not accept the idea that public places must be kept free of religious activities and ideas. They do not see having a moment of prayer in the classroom or presenting creationism alongside evolution as a violation of the rights of nonbelievers. Rather, they see such activities as those of a godly state affirming its godliness and offering its citizens the free opportunity to participate. Fundamentalists believe that honoring God should not be an embarrassment in a "Christian nation." Nor should it be too much to ask that government protect, rather than harrass, the Christian institutions within its borders.

On the domestic scene, then, Fundamentalists are interested both in strenghtening the American "moral fiber" and in protecitng the other institutions they see as potentially "Christian." God has entrusted churches, homes, and schools to their care, and they are willing to enter politics if necessary to protect that social territory.[4] Outsiders often miss the profound sense of threat felt by Fundamentalists to their freedom of religion. On all sides they see themselves under siege. They see churches being asked to apply for licenses for fundraising. They see social workers trying to decide whether fathers may use physical punishment in disciplining their children. They see the Equal Rights Amendment (ERA) as threatening the ability of Christian women to practice their calling as homemakers and mothers. They see towns that refuse to let them put a nativity scene on the town green. They see courts declaring that church agencies cannot regulate the beliefs and lifestyles of their employees. And they see schools that will not allow their children to sing Christmas carols or meet for Bible study after school—never mind being able to pray in the classroom. To them, their right to practice their religious beliefs is being seriously threatened by a government so intent on enforcing separation between church and state that it is actually enforcing secularity as the only appropriate public belief.

Much of the political activity at Southside, in fact, is aimed at defending Fundamentalists' ability to establish and run Christian institutions as they see fit. The pastor and school staff are active in the American Association of Christian Schools, an organization that seeks to protect the rights of schools like the Southside Academy. Leaders and members alike oppose the ERA, abortion, and gay rights because all those measures seem to threaten their ability to structure Christian homes as they wish (see also Neitz 1981). They also oppose the Domestic Violence Act because they fear it would lead to government interference with their duty to use physical punishment when necessary in disciplining their children. When any government action seems to threaten a church, a Christian home, or a Christian school, the members of Southside are willing to mobilize. They begin to pray that God will intervene, and they begin to act in God's behalf with letters, phone calls, petitions, and special offerings for legal expenses.

In a similar manner, on the international scene, the issues that concern these people have to do with defending their ability to spread the gospel. They want this nation to have an image abroad that will enhance, rather than hurt, their missionaries' efforts. And they are willing for the U.S. government to intervene whenever a revolution might threaten their ability to continue missionizing. If socialism inevitably leads to communism, and communism is built on atheism, the United States must resist socialism at all costs. Here, too, Southside's believers are beginning to see that God's power might be available for maintaining by political means the Christian nation they love.

This use of political power by believers is a relatively new phenomenon. There has always been a certain affinity between conservative religion and conservative politics, but Fundamentalists were relatively invisible between 1925 and 1975.[5] Many proclaimed that politics was one of those "worldly" activities from which believers should remain separate. After all, if the world is doomed and believers are assured of escape in the Rapture, political action seems hardly necessary. But, as we have noted before, premillennialism can also encourage believers to take up the sword of the Lord, especially when the world seems ready. And, as Wuthnow (1983) has pointed out, the changing cultural climate in the mid-1970s produced a perception that "lifestyle" concerns were important political issues and that Evangelicals had a contribution to make (see also Lorentzen 1980). If national magazines were going to do cover stories on being born again, then believers were going to make sure that people knew what that meant.

But it took much more to mobilize these believers than mere national attention to the role of religion in politics; religion had, after all, been important in the civil-rights movement, and Fundamentalists had studiously avoided that political arena. Fundamentalists did not become politicized until they perceived that the issues with which they were concerned had become political issues. Their sense of God's concern had to be wedded to a political agenda, and the agenda of the 1980s lent itself perfectly to that cause. Once politicized, however, they were able to mobilize the considerable resources they already had. They would not have become so visible if they had not already been so strong. Marsden summarizes the situation this way: "These circumstances—a deeply rooted ideological-spiritual heritage, vigorous institutions, skills in promotion, and an era when people were open to spiritual answers to national and personal crises—combined for the evangelical resurgence of the 1970s" (1983:157). Believers had both ideas and skills to meet the demands of the times.

Fundamentalists such as those at Southside have begun to seek change through politics. They hope to use their influence to enact and enforce the biblical rules that would make this a truly "Christian" nation. They recognize that their task is monumental and that it is complicated by the continuing presence of hosts of unbelievers. Yet at least some Fundamentalists are convinced that such changes are worth pursuing. That fact is significant. Just as God gives them the power to create and maintain Christian churches, homes, and schools, God gives them the power to influence their nation. At the least they are contributing to an enriched mix of voices being heard in American politics.

The Limits of Fundamentalist Power

Despite the fact that the times seem to be ripe for Fundamentalist political activity and despite the fact that some believers are willing to use God's power to try to change the rules of American public life, important obstacles block their path. There are clear differences between the goals toward which Fundamentalists claim to be working and the practical reality of their participation in American politics. Those differences, in fact, pose major problems within the Fundamentalist movement. Ironically, in the very act of making claims of singular moral authority, Fundamentalists must be heard in the pluralistic arena of American politics. Their ideas about the nature of public morality must compete with other ideas, mostly in the forum of mass media. Although they may assert that there is only one right way to live, the individual who hears that message receives it along with dozens of other messages about what is best for people or for the nation. In the midst of campaigning to change the rules, Fundamentalists are forced to play by those rules, to live with a pluralism that they dislike (cf. Lechner 1985).

There is also an irony for Fundamentalists in the nature of political activity. Politics, it is said, is the art of compromise; and that is an art unknown in the Fundamentalist world. A corollary is that politics is the art of building coalitions—another art foreign to a people who thrive on their separateness. For these reasons Jerry Falwell often makes enemies of his Fundamentalist friends. What he is doing is nothing short of revolutionary by Fundamentalist standards. To build alliances with Catholics who oppose abortion, with Mormons who oppose the ERA, with feminists who oppose pornography is unheard of in the history of a movement that would disown Billy Graham for allowing Lutherans and Episcopalians to cooperate in his crusades. A large portion of those who have historically claimed the label *Fundamentalist* are not yet ready for that kind of political activity, even in an attempt to restore this nation to "morality." Fundamentalist use of God's power in the political arena may be limited by their inability to find a middle ground with the forces that oppose them or even with the outsiders who might join them in various causes.[6]

In addition Fundamentalist political power is limited by the fact that only a small proportion of believers are involved. Good evidence indicates that the actual level of mobilization achieved by groups such as the Moral Majority is far less than an alarmed press might have us believe.[7] That is certainly the case at Southside. Perhaps half a dozen members routinely do more than vote. There are no ongoing political-action groups. The congregation is sporadically mobilized more broadly than usual when the pastor (or another respected member) alerts them to an issue of concern. Fundamentalist political power, then, may be only as good as the information available to pastors and their willingness to use their authority to encourage otherwise inactive members to become involved. That power, however, should not be underestimated.[8]

Fundamentalists' ability to claim God's power in the political arena is limited, then, by the plural realities of American social life and by their own inability to engage those realities. In other areas of the social world, however, the idea that God's power is potentially available does not often occur to believers. Not all of social life falls within the territory that might be claimed as "Christian." The line between God's kingdom and the rest of the world can also be seen in the activities assumed not to be God's concern. That line coincides with the division between what believers think they can and cannot do.

Nowhere is their sense of powerlessness more apparent than in conversations about work. Many feel trapped in their work, unable to control what they do and how they do it. Listen to them describe their situations. First the successful owner of a small business.

> After you are fifty in this country, you don't leave any position you are in anyway because you will never get a job.

Next, the wife of a man with a secure job as a machinist:

> He doesn't like his work, honestly, but we had no choice. We had a family.

The same woman about her own job:

> I am working as a nurse's aide in the hospital, but I like and enjoy it. Of course, I have my times when I was depressed about it, because I had a lot of experience in the ER [emergency room] and you name it [before coming to this country]. But here you come, and you do just the scum work. It is not pleasure, believe me. . . . I either had the choice to start from scratch or go just be happy with what I had.

A widow about the job she has had for many years in a large insurance company:

> Well, of course, I like my job, and I feel that I can't just up and leave because I'd have no one to fall back on. . . . I feel at times I'm taken advantage of because they feel, well, Sarah will do it, you know, just let her do it. And that's it; I have to do it because I have no one else to fall back on.

And finally an industrial sales representative:

> I think the frustration with the job is created by the policies of the company more than anything else . . . so it's frustrating. There are many frustrations, but you have to accept it.

These are not people at the bottom of the economic order. For the most part, they have jobs that are secure and provide them a comfortable living. Yet they feel powerless either to change the conditions of their work or to find new jobs. They see their jobs as hedged in by "company policy" and their mobility limited by their age, their sex, or their lack of proper credentials. The world of work is for them dominated by rules and organizations over which they have little control.

Such feelings of worker alienation are not at all unusual in American society. Assembly-line workers are not the only ones who feel unable to make important choices about how and where they work. From skilled workers in the "rust bowl" to women and minorities excluded from decision making to middle managers who must produce but cannot complain—at nearly every level, in every economic sector, people work for organizations that hand them a rule book and expect them to comply (cf. Kanter 1977). The members of Southside are not unusual in sensing that the organizations where they work are too big and powerful to be changed by "mere mortals." But their church does not attempt to overcome their powerlessness. Believers respond to their work situations with a sense of resignation. They do the best job they can, and they respect the boss's authority. They join the union if they have to, but if there is a strike, they may ask God's help in crossing the picket lines. It would be unthinkable to ask God's help in taking over the plant. When believers voice their alienation, they do not hear contrary arguments about God being active in the structuring of economic activity.

They do hear that the power of God can offer them the ability to do a good job. This is power vested in the individual, power to achieve within the system.[9] Ray Danner and Joe Slavin—who both have good jobs—are confident that God helps them every day.

> I do enjoy the challenge of my job. And I enjoy walking with the Lord daily because I am not of that caliber that I can handle this type of position without his guidance.

> I thought I could never do a job like that. Now the Lord has given me real wisdom to do a good job. I can write reports now; I can go to meetings and talk in front of people. They have given me responsibility to do a lot of things, and I think the more pressure there is, the more excited I am.

For these two men, the demands of the job are not greater than the resources available from God. Yet in neither case do they envision God helping them to change the demands of the job.

Even those who feel good about their labor do not describe theirs as "Christian vocations" or "callings." They accept the division of the world into sacred and secular, private and public. The structures of the economy are not expected to run by God's rules, although individual workers and owners are supposed to obey God (something Southside members do not think they see much of). Believers are as cynical about today's big business as are their neighbors. When profit comes first, ahead of God, corruption and dishonesty are only to be expected.

The economic world operates by rules that are not seen as changeable by the actions of Southside's believers. They not only are resigned to the conditions of their labor but also are willing to adapt the church's demands to the demands of the marketplace. This willingness is especially apparent in the fact that so many Southside mothers work outside the home, usually to be able to buy a house. Such a decision represents a significant compromise of belief—a compromise imposed by high interest rates and exorbitant housing costs. It also reflects the enormous value placed on home ownership in American society. To own a house, preferably in the suburbs, is a badge of participation in the "American way of life" (cf. Perin 1977). One can prove that one is worthy of the kingdom by succeeding in the American system, at least enough to be able to buy a modest, well-kept house in a clean, if unassuming, neighborhood. Although the form is attenuated (and the supporting beliefs are not even Calvinist), the Protestant ethic may still be alive in this segment of American society. But, as Weber (1905) foresaw, it has indeed turned into something of an "iron cage." The very means by which these believers seek to demonstrate their membership in the elect (home ownership) disconnects them from the basic principles by which they believe a Christian family ought to live. The economic necessities of capitalism are outside the territory in which God's rules are expected to prevail.

And again Southside Gospel Church does not challenge its members' concessions to the world of work. The pastor preaches about the value of full-time motherhood, but he does not explicitly condemn those who decide they must work. He and his members do not presume to challenge the power of the market with God's power. In fact, Fundamentalists embrace the power of the market, even adopting a laissez-faire system of organizational structure for themselves. And this is perhaps the greatest irony of Fundamentalism: By failing to challenge the market forces that created the modern world, Fundamentalism falls prey to its mortal enemy.

Despite their unwillingness to challenge the economic sphere however, Fundamentalists are not economic determinists; they do not believe that profit is an inherently evil influence. Rather, as laissez-faire capitalists, they believe that honesty and hard work should come before money in the values of both workers and owners. A Christian entrepreneur can be honest, humble, and a good steward of his (or even her) money. There are rich Fundamentalists, and they (along with their businesses) serve as examples of what "Christian" businesses might look like. Even the Christian Yellow Pages is a recognition that ordinary economic activity can be pursued according to biblical rules by believing people.

Although most of Southside's people do not think about either their labor or their consumption in religious terms, the verdict is not yet in. Their ideology contains categories that could easily be translated into "Christian" economic activity. Here, too, God's power might be available. But for Southside's members today, work is one of the parts of life that is simply taken for granted and ordinary. It is not part of the social territory in which they expect God to be active. God may help individuals to get along, but the rules of the game are set by others.

Whether it is economic activity or another part of life, some portion of the social world will always be relegated by believers to an outside status. It is part of the Fundamentalist ethos to divide the world between good and evil, between redeemed and condemned. The believer inhabits the part of the world in which God is active, but there will always also be an outside world in which believers are quite willing to admit that they have no power. That is the realm from which they are "separate." There the devil reigns, at least until his eventual defeat and final judgment. The outside world is doomed, so there is no reason to try to change it or to expect God to take an active part in it beyond rescuing a few souls. The social arenas believers identify as "the world" are, in the fullest sense, alien. The premillennial insistence that this world will never be completely restored means that some social territory will always be so defined.

God's kingdom, as Fundamentalists see it, will never triumph in this world. It will always be limited by the active presence of evil. The practical consequence is that groups of people and areas of life can be placed outside the believer's sphere of responsibility. Unlike Weber's inner-worldly ascetics, Fundamentalists do not see all of life as God's concern. But unlike the alienated people Marx or Berger might have expected to find, they seem quite capable of taking charge whenever they do perceive God to be concerned. They have constructed for themselves a religious world in which there are rewards and power. And they recognize a clear boundary between that world and an outside world that they do not expect to be able to change.

The Future of Fundamentalism

The situation for Fundamentalists like those at Southside is full of ironies. One such irony is the nature of the power these people possess. While claiming that all power belongs to God, they actively appropriate some of that power as their own. While claiming that believers must submit to religious authorities rather than acting on their own, they receive the blessing of those authorities for doing work they might otherwise have thought impossible. And while claiming that life must be lived by unchanging rules, the rules themselves often provide opportunities for adaptation and change. The very act of marking off boundaries between themselves and the rest of the world allows a vastly increased sense of efficacy within the social territory they claim as their own.

The ideology, then, is a flexible one. It neither dooms believers to passive waiting for another world nor gives them unconditional power in this world. The necessary question to ask, then, is where to locate the boundaries between God's kingdom and the rest of the world, between "Christian" institutions and those assumed to be unredeemable. Likewise, it becomes important to note that the perceived boundaries of God's kingdom can change with time and circumstances. A few years ago, this same group might not have claimed either education or politics as issues with which Christians needed to be concerned. But the world in which they live has changed, and their perceptions of where God's power is available have changed as well.

The fact of the matter is that believers are realistic about the limits of God's power or at least about their ability to appropriate it. Because an institution can be Christian only if all its participants are believers or if it is governed by biblical rules, believers make daily assessments of the likelihood that either of those eventualities will occur. They eagerly claim churches and homes as potential Christian institutions. They have also come to see that they can create separate educational institutions and govern them so as to keep them Christian. Recently, despite the presence of multitudes of unbelievers, they have been encouraged to hope that the American nation might be redeemed by "returning" its government to the "Christian" principles on which it was founded. They are even willing to admit that business could be a Christian enterprise, but they do not expect the organizations in which they themselves work to run by biblical rules. But in none of these areas are they guaranteed success. Churches can be lost to heresy; homes are often only "half-Christian"; schools can fall to creeping humanism. In the economy and politics, they face even more formidable foes.

Since its beginning, Fundamentalism's primary foe has been "modernism." And in this century, the modern world has become more and more greedy for allegiance. Modernity has moved from the periphery of society to its core. As Fundamentalism has attempted to stave off this encroachment, it has had two basic alternatives: fight or retreat. In the battles against the denominations in the 1920s, continuing opposition to evolution, and current forays into politics, Fundamentalists have taken the sword of the Lord in hand to face off against the modern world. They have not often enjoyed much success in their efforts. Until recently, modernity has reigned with little challenge. But that is no longer the case; modernity is no longer an unquestioned good.

Whether believers will be able to translate discontent with modernity into their particular version of a nonmodern world depends both on the nature of the surrounding culture and on the ways in which this particular religious ideology adapts to that culture. That the culture is in a time of transition, seeking new rules, seems clear. The culture is ready, but it is not at all clear that Fundamentalism can provide a way to the future. Hadden (1985) argues that if Fundamentalism is to become a truly potent cultural force, it will have to shed its premillennial ideology in favor of postmillennialism. His point is that premillennialism does not leave this world open to human activity and renders its believers powerless. However, as we have seen, Southside's members have been quite able to envision battles and victories in this world, despite looking for the Rapture at any moment. In a variety of ways, premillennialism can adapt itself to the demands and possibilities of the hour. Believers need only remind themselves of the necessity of fighting Satan's influence so as to maximize the possibilities for souls to be saved.

A far more serious obstacle for Fundamentalism than its ideology is, I suspect, its inability to deal with pluralism. As Cox (1984) points out, the postmodern world may share Fundamentalism's refusal to differentiate knowledge and institutions according to function. The postmodern world, however, is unlikely to be one in which people of like mind and culture can live in blissful isolation from others with whom they disagree. Nor is it likely to be one in which everyone agrees. To fight against modernity and win, Fundamentalism would have to become something it is not, namely tolerant of pluralism.

Likewise, at the individual level, Fundamentalism would have to learn to accommodate doubt. And here the irony of the dilemma is most clear. The very firmness of belief that makes Fundamentalism attractive to so many also prevents it from changing to accommodate the changing needs of its members and their worlds. When walls cannot bend, they can only break. The Fundamentalist exclusion of doubt may prove comforting to some, but it dooms others to leaving the fold entirely when the preordained answers cannot satisfy their needs. Although Fundamentalism may continue to exist as an institution as long as there is modernity against which to define itself, individual commitment to Fundamentalism is often impermanent, unable to survive throughout lifetimes and across generations. What for some people in some moments is a haven against modernity can become for others at other times in their lives a prison. Fundamentalism's strength, then, may also be its most significant weakness.

However, direct fights with modernity are not the only strategy Fundamentalism has employed. Whenever Fundamentalists have lost a battle, they have responded by withdrawing to establish their own alternative institutions. Fundamentalist social inventions have largely kept pace with the challenges posed by "secular humanism." Believers have, in fact, taken back from modernity a social territory in which to live. Today, a significant segment of an otherwise "mod-

212 / Chapter Eleven

ernized" nation can find in Fundamentalist churches, schools, businesses, and political organizations a satisfying alternative to the secular world. Rather than trying to change the world that surrounds them, they establish alternative institutions within which they can live by the rules they have chosen.

Building such institutions is no less a creative social act than the political activity chosen by some of their fellow believers. It is simply a different, and complementary, response to the same dilemma. As we have seen, the people of Southside have created a world of home and church and school that supports and confirms their ideas about life. Many withdraw from the outside world almost entirely, while others learn to manage their encounters with outsiders so as to minimize psychic and social conflict. The establishment of such an alternative social world has come as Fundamentalists have encountered modernity and found it wanting. As modernity has refused to yield ground to the onslaughts of Fundamentalists, they have responded by creating a territory of their own, existing alongside and in continuing reaction to the institutions and assumptions of modernity.

As long as there is a modern world characterized by seeming chaos, there will be believers who react to that world by refusing to grant it legitimacy. Although some may do so in solitary reflection, most will seek out social structures in which certainty can take the place of doubt, in which clear rules and authority can take the place of subjectivity, and in which truth is truth without compromise. Churches like Southside provide such modern wanderers a home. They provide an all-encompassing sacred canopy in which belief is possible.

Notes

Chapter One

1. Commentators have become increasingly aware of the evolutionary bias that has influenced scholarly interpretation of conservative movements. Warner (1979) points out that much study of religion has assumed that once religious people are educated, urbanized, and modernized, their beliefs will disappear. Such an interpretation of Fundamentalism was most apparent in the earliest analyses, such as Niebuhr's (1929) and Cole's (1931), but the same assumptions influence more recent writers, especially Moberg (1962), Hofstadter (1964), Johnson (1971), and Clabaugh (1974).

2. Douglas's (1983) essay is a masterly exploration of this myth, its roots, and its consequences. Berger (1983), in the same volume, writes a eulogy for secularity, noting its often dogmatic nature. Coleman's (1978) excellent overview of secularization theory makes clear that the theory has never been unified in its claims only in some underlying suspicion that religion might be dying.

3. The two pillars of this argument come primarily from Herberg's *Protestant Catholic Jew* (1960) and from Berger's (1961) argument that the function of religion in American society is to be irrelevant, to teach coping skills, and to stay safely away from the world of public decision making.

4. The series of studies by Glock and Stark in the 1960s (especially 1965 and Stark and Glock 1968) found that Americans knew little of the content of their religious systems and that religion had few consequences in the way they led their lives. Americans might believe in God and pray to God in times of crisis, but they saw those activities as primarily private.

5. This argument is made most clearly by Luckmann (1967), but it was implied much earlier in the writings of Durkheim on the "cult of man" (1898, 1925). Berger (1969) likewise views modern religion as essentially privatized, having lost its cultural base. Parsons (1963) turns this argument on its head to say that culture is not thus more secular but more Christian, having been so thoroughly permeated with the values of Christianity that the institutional supports are no longer needed. If Parsons is arguing for the triumph of the Protestant Ethic, Bellah and associates (1985) seem to counter that it is Weber's "iron cage" that has won—that is, that religion (along with almost

everything else that matters) has been relegated to the private sphere and there dominated by "expressive individualism."

6. Many researchers have included categories for this "inner-directed" religiosity, some assuming more institutional support than others. Allport (1966) found intrinsically religious people as well as extrinsically religious ones. Roof (1978) found "cosmopolitans" whose religious identity was tied not to the local institution but to larger humanitarian concerns. Hoge (1976) found "public" Protestants along with the "private" ones, people who could envision religious responses that went beyond the walls of the institutional church and the limits of their middle-class positions. Even observers inside the church, like Dudley (1979), have noted that many of those who have left institutional religion are not at all irreligious—a fact with which Stark and Bainbridge (1985) and Martin (1969) would readily agree.

7. Another way to understand the distinctions between differentiated and individualized religion is to see them in light of the traditional categories of *church, sect, mysticism,* and *denomination.* The differentiated response is essentially the response of American denominationalism (Niebuhr 1929, Martin 1962). The individualized response is analogous to the mysticism that Troeltsch (1931) describes and that Bellah and associates (1985) relate to the American scene. Fundamentalism fits the traditional category of sect in ways we will explore throughout the book.

8. Here I agree with Cox (1984) and Lechner (1985) that Fundamentalism can be interpreted as an essentially antimodern movement.

9. As we will see in Chapter 11, it is precisely this refusal to cooperate with outsiders that causes Falwell so much trouble with his Fundamentalist brothers (and sisters). Falwell's program of coalition building is nothing short of revolutionary by Fundamentalist standards.

10. Several small denominations can also reliably be called Fundamentalist, among them the Baptist Bible Fellowship and the General Association of Regular Baptists. Dollar (1973:213ff.) lists the groups he considers true to the faith. Although organized as denominations, these groups still maintain a high degree of local autonomy.

11. On these characteristics of conservative Protestants, I concur with both Warner (1979) and Hunter (1981).

12. A study of the Ohio Moral Majority (Wilcox, 1986) nicely demonstrates the differences between self-identified Evangelicals and Fundamentalists. It is not clear, however, whether a sample of Moral Majority members should be taken as representative; they are probably among the people most aware of ideological differences.

13. These criteria are drawn from the work of historians and theologians more than from earlier sociological work. Sandeen (1970) builds his history of the movement on the gradual wedding of millenarianism to literalism. Dollar (1973) puts literalism and separation at the top of his list, but he also includes premillennialism as essential. Quebedeaux (1974) identifies iner-

rancy, separatism, and premillennialism as the marks of "separatist Fundamentalists." Carpenter (1980) includes all three of those characteristics but insists that evangelism is the heart and soul of the movement. Marsden (1980) also touts the importance of evangelism and premillennialism. He, however, also notes the ties of early Fundamentalists to the holiness movement, a late-nineteenth-century variation on Methodism that stressed the achievement of perfection in this life through the power of the Holy Spirit and strict separation from worldly things.

Until recently, sociologists have typically ignored most of these characteristics and have lumped all non-mainline Protestants into variously designated categories of conservatism. Among the many studies of "Fundamentalists" that must be interpreted cautiously because of their lack of precise definition are Johnson (1962, 1964), Feagin (1965), Stark and Glock (1968), Maranell (1974), Brady and Tedin (1976), Dudley (1978), Peek and associates (1979), and Johnson and Tamney (1982). Others must be treated with some caution because the groups they studied are probably atypical (for example, DeJong and Ford 1965, and Richardson and associates 1979). Most recently, the problem has been distinguishing between Fundamentalists and other Evangelicals (see Ammerman 1982b, Hunter 1982, and Smidt 1983) and distinguishing Fundamentalism, the movement, from fundamentalism, the perspective (a problem for Ethridge and Feagin 1979). Good critical reviews of the literature can be found in Hunter (1981), Ethridge and Feagin (1979), and Warner (1979).

14. Interestingly, although these factors are obviously correlated, Gallup never controls for one when presenting data on the other. Hunter (1983) uses these same data and implies that there is an interaction effect between nonurban residence and region; that is, Evangelicals are concentrated in the rural and small-town South. I will argue later that this southern overrepresentation biases many of the other demographic statistics on Evangelicals in the direction of less education, less urbanization, and a larger percentage of blacks than is typical of Evangelicals outside the South. Johnson and Shibley (1985) have produced convincing evidence that mixing southern and nonsouthern Evangelicals, especially in political behavior, is "an exercise in obfuscation."

15. As is customary, the names of people and places have been changed to protect the anonymity of those who so graciously allowed me to share in their lives. For further details on my role in the congregation, see Ammerman (1982a).

Chapter Two

1. "Landmarkism" can be traced to the writings of J. R. Graves (for example, 1855), a Tennessee Baptist. Bryan (1973) examines its continuing influence in Baptist life.

2. This unsettling of religion is seen by Berger (1969), Luckmann (1967), and many others as crucial to understanding the modern world. Nearly every historian of Fundamentalism points to these secularizing trends as an important ingredient in producing the movement.

3. I am keenly aware that using gender-specific pronouns to refer to God is not appropriate. I shall avoid it where I am speaking in my own voice; but because my subjects think of God as male, I shall use male pronouns when describing their ideas.

4. Sandeen (1970) most thoroughly explores the links between the early millenarians and the Fundamentalists who would follow. Marsden (1971) vigorously argues that Sandeen has overstated his case and that not all early Fundamentalists were premillennialists. It seems to me that Sandeen is right, that millenarianism was necessary for Fundamentalism's growth, but that Marsden is right in emphasizing that it was not a sufficient cause.

5. This account of the organizational and ideological sources of Fundamentalism is drawn from several sources. Ahlstrom (1975) provides an overview of the movement and details its relationship to the rest of American religion. Sandeen (1970) and Marsden (1980) provide the most thorough investigations of the ideas and structures that formed the movement. Cole (1931) and Furniss (1954) offer special insights into the denominational battles of the 1920s. And Dollar (1973) paints a picture of the entire history of the movement from an insider's point of view.

6. Marsden (1980) points out that holiness conferences thrived alongside the Bible and prophecy conferences; and in those early years, there was a good deal of overlap in purpose and attendance (cf. Ahlstrom 1975:II: 275FF.). The more direct descendant of the holiness movement, however, is Pentecostalism.

7. For many years, those who studied Fundamentalism were told, on the basis of Cole (1931), that the 1895 Niagara Conference adopted a statement of "Five Fundamentals," which became a kind of creed for the movement. Sandeen (1970) documents that no such statement was ever adopted.

8. The seeming exception to this rule was the antievolution crusade. Antievolution laws were proposed in states throughout the North and South beginning in 1920; but in only a few southern states did they succeed. And it was in the South that the most famous battle of the 1920s pitted Clarence Darrow against William Jennings Bryan. Marsden (1980) argues that this larger crusade to ban evolution from the schools was a result of a variety of cultural forces as much as of any specifically religious impulse. Nevertheless, it made allies of northern Fundamentalists and the southerners who shared their revulsion against modernism (cf. Ahlstrom 1975:II:181).

9. Norris shot a man in a dispute over money. Norris claimed it was self-defense, and the jury agreed. Shields finally resigned as president of Des Moines University after hints of a liaison with his secretary and rioting by the students.

10. Historians like Furniss (1954) and Hofstadter (1964) were simply mistaken in assuming that religious Fundamentalism had faded away after the great battles of the 1920s. Carpenter (1980), Marty (1976), and Dollar (1973) document the organizational growth that continued despite the absence of national attention.

Chapter Four

1. As Marsden (1980) points out, these two different ways of knowing about the world correspond roughly to the Kantian and Baconian traditions in science. For the Baconian, orderliness was inherent in the nature of things and would be apparent to any rational person who might systematically seek it. The object of science was to discover the "laws" of nature as nature is in itself. For the Kantian, our human perception intervenes between the object as it is in itself and our knowledge of that object. We humans can never directly apprehend any unchanging, objective truth concerning objects as they are in themselves but can know objects only in the forms in which they are perceived by us. Marsden claims that Fundamentalists are the last of the Baconians, clinging to a view of science that was once almost universally accepted but now has almost universally been left behind. Barr (1978:272) makes a similar point. He describes the Fundamentalist philosophical base as "a pre-Kantian eighteenth-century empirical rationalism."

2. Tipton (1982) describes the "Living Word Fellowship" he studied as having an "authoritative ethic" combined with the expressivism of Pentecostalism. As at Southside, the emphasis is on obeying God's commands; but, unlike Southside, the Living Word Fellowship also emphasizes "getting high on Jesus" as the experiential basis for authority.

3. Such a belief is not altogether unusual. The 1980 *Christianity Today*/Gallup poll found that 42 percent of all Americans and 48 percent of Protestants believe the Bible to be "the word of God and never mistaken" (Elwell 1980:23). Similarly, a 1976 Gallup poll found that 46 percent of Protestants believe the Bible is to "be taken literally, word for word" (Woodward et al. 1976:68).

4. On the other side of the theological fence, someone like H. Richard Niebuhr can describe such a view of the Bible as "an error, a denial of the content of the scriptures themselves. To give final devotion to the book is to deny the final claim of God" (1956:43).

5. This emphasis on the authority of church leaders is also present in other nonepiscopal groups such as the Mormons (see O'Dea 1957) and Jehovah's Witnesses (see Beckford 1975). In each case, the group combines an emphasis on scriptural and ecclesiastical authority, rules, and obedience, with an emphasis on participation by the laity and the importance of lay mission work. This issue is explored further in Chapter 7.

6. It should not be assumed from this reverence for authority that the members of Southside are likely to have "authoritarian personalities." Theirs is at least as much a cultural trait as a personal one. The ideology of this group is one of norm maintenance (Loye 1977). Although it is likely that many members would score high on an F-scale (Adorno et al. 1950:255) or on Rokeach's dogmatism scale (1960), it is impossible to judge whether such scores represent underlying personality traits (that may or may not be traceable to childhood experiences) or whether they represent acceptance of the dominant ideas and patterns of behavior in the congregation.

When Milgram concluded his famous series of experiments, he asserted that "it is not so much the kind of person a man is as the kind of situation in which he finds himself that determines how he will act" (1974:205). He may have overstated the case, but his work served to place the issue of authoritarianism in its social context. More recently, Sennett (1980) has asserted that authority seeking is a social process in which all persons at all stages in the life cycle participate. Although relationships to authority may become either socially or psychologically unhealthy, they remain a basic part of human life. The members of Southside have a particular cultural authority pattern that should be viewed as a variation on this universal theme rather than as a symptom of the personality traits of those who join.

7. Swidler (1986) points out that most of culture is carried in these habits of everyday life and in the "strategies of action" our circumstances and experiences make available to us. Most decisions, then, are not coherently governed by ideology or explicit values. That so much of life at Southside has come under the sway of ideology marks this as a culture arising from "unsettled lives."

8. Geertz's (1966) treatment of theodicy nicely captures the manner in which Southside members operate. He asserts that religion can create as many problems relative to suffering as it does solutions. The world is not sensible. What matters most is not having a sensible explanation but knowing and being ritually connected to the one who is presumed ultimately to order the universe.

9. Berger (1981) argues that ideas that help people get through their lives ought to be respected. Moral ideas, in his view, are "tools and instruments, *culture*—like shovels, rakes, and chain saws—to help people get through their days, and in helping them through, providing some pride, even ennoblement, for having got through safely (and, indeed, some comfort and succour for injuries and defeats in the process)" (p. 185, emphasis in original).

Chapter Five

1. This distinction between an involvement that is all-encompassing and one that is more narrow corresponds to the classic distinction between

church and sect (for example, Troeltsch 1931, Niebuhr 1929). In this case, it might be argued that "churchlike" religiosity has accommodated itself to the modern world. It fits the "individualized" or "differentiated" patterns outlined in Chapter 1. "Sectlike" religiosity, in this case, does not accept the modern relegation of religion to the periphery.

2. Rokeach and Mezei (1966) and Byrne and Ervin (1969) reached similar conclusions about the relative strength of shared beliefs, as opposed to prejudice, in determining behavior. At least in part, these findings contradict the long tradition of research that has sought to prove a link between religious orthodoxy and prejudice (for example, Allport 1966, Glock and Stark 1966, Rokeach 1970). Over the years, the link has been shown to be mediated by the manner in which members are committed to a church (Allport and Ross 1967), the larger culture in which members and church exist (Hoge and Carroll 1973), and what members learn and practice at church (Strickland and Weddell 1972). Some research supports the possibility that individuals with a narrow, localistic, dogmatic, or intolerant (depending on the measure being used) way of understanding the world are likely to be both very religious and very prejudiced (for example, Hoge and Carroll 1973, Roof 1974). Whether people in the Southside congregation are disproportionately prone to such closed ways of thinking is impossible to tell from the data at hand. The ideas they adopt are clearly dogmatic, but the lines they draw between themselves and the damned do not necessarily coincide with racial lines. For a discussion of the ways in which those two lines do coincide, see the discussion in Chapter 10 of integration at the Academy.

3. Christian television is a potentially powerful tool for unifying and mobilizing believers. Stories, sermons, and issues experienced electronically can shape the way believers understand and talk about their world. It is at least possible that electronic preachers will provide for this generation a new, unifying set of categories, analogous to those provided formerly by the Scofield Reference Bible.

But none of that is happening at Southside simply because the available "Christian" programing is so scarce. It does not seem to meet the viewing needs of most church families. Some watch Oral Roberts and Jerry Falwell and Billy Graham on independent stations, but other acceptable programing is minimal. The Christian station's signal, finances, and scheduling are spotty at best. The most faithful members also recall that many "Christian entertainers" (including those who appear on popular Christian television shows such as the "700 Club" or the "PTL Club") have been condemned by Pastor Thompson as not good examples of the separated life. As a result, Christian television is not nearly so strong an influence as we might expect. This church, unfortunately, cannot serve as a test of the apparently growing influence of televangelists.

4. Social psychologists (following Festinger and Carlsmith 1959) have

demonstrated that people try to minimize the dissonance that results when one part of experience does not match some other part—when we perform an odious task for which we are not rewarded or when we like a person with whom we seriously disagree. We can bring the two dissonant parts into greater harmony by convincing ourselves that the task was not unpleasant after all or that the person is not as attractive as we thought.

Chapter Six

1. The sample I drew (from a population of 167 households) consisted of fifty-nine randomly selected households in which there was at least one adult member. Therefore, the number of highly committed adults in the sample (38; see Table 6.2) should be about 35 percent of the number in the population (110).

2. The church claims 350 members. I could find only 281 names, and 30 percent of the sample drawn from that list (about 84 members, if projected to the total) either could not be contacted locally or no longer considered themselves a part of the congregation. In other words, only about 197 of the church's 350 "members" are actually part of the church.

3. This Fundamentalist organizational and fund-raising network is not unlike the structure that existed in most of Protestantism a century ago. As Primer (1979) points out, the bureaucratic structures that now exist in most denominations developed in the fifty years surrounding the turn of this century, which parallels the development of Fundamentalism. If the main-line denominations were centralizing and bureaucratizing, it is not surprising that Fundamentalists chose to remain decentralized and loosely organized. Some denominations kept an ideology of local autonomy, while in fact adopting bureaucratic structures. Harrison (1959) and Takayama (1975) describe the tensions created by that incongruity.

Chapter Seven

1. Monaghan's (1967) study of Fundamentalist churches revealed "three faces" of "true believers." One was being an "authority seeker," but not everyone fit that category; there were also "comfort seekers" and "social participators."

2. Fundamentalist pastors are not "traditional" in their authority base in that they do not usually inherit their jobs. However, the pastoral search process is highly infused with the rhetoric of divine call. After having used "rational" processes to find the best pastor/church fit, all parties concerned describe the process as divinely guided.

3. About two years after I left Southside, Pastor Thompson resigned to go to a large church in Ohio. In the search for a new pastor, Schuster was

able to dictate who would be considered. Another deacon, my informant, sought to offer some alternatives and to keep the process open, but Schuster's desires carried the day. The new pastor has come to the church clearly indebted to Schuster. Therefore, just who will influence whom is unclear.

Chapter Eight

1. Richardson and his associates (1979) and Tipton (1982, chap. 2) offer similar descriptions of Fundamentalist norms of family life. Rose (1985) and McNamara (1985) provide additional strong ethnographic accounts and also describe the subtle ways in which rhetoric and reality do not match.

2. Interestingly, all those whose spouses do not attend reported giving less than 10 percent of their income to the church (see Table 6.3) in stark contrast to the patterns in other kinds of families.

3. A 1969 community survey conducted in New Haven found that 14 percent of the people interviewed reported moderate numbers of depressive symptoms. A 1975 survey provided an estimate of about 7 percent of the population that might be considered clinically depressed, while only one percent had ever been hospitalized (Weissman and Myers 1978). My data do not include a formal measure of depression, but many of the people I interviewed spontaneously reported information about their emotional and functional states. Those who mentioned three or more of the symptoms contained in the Weissman and Myers checklist are those I classified as distressed. As in their study, exactly 14 percent of my sample could be so classified. In addition, 5 percent of those at Southside were seriously enough depressed to have been so diagnosed, and 4 percent had at some point been hospitalized.

4. Rose (1985) documents a similar pattern of breakdowns among women in another Fundamentalist congregation. Women far outnumber men among the troubled people at Southside. This finding is in line with those of most mental-health surveys; see Gove (1978) for a review. That their illness is related to constraints on available roles for women is consistent with the findings of Gove and Tudor (1973) and with the observations of many others, including Bernard (1972).

Chapter Nine

1. Several early studies indicated that adults with children are more interested in religion than other adults (see Lenski 1953, Nash 1968). Hoge and Carroll (1978) also give this idea some support. That the presence of children tends to make adults more interested in religion does not, however, seem to translate into recruiting adults by way of those children.

2. This technique is classically "revivalist" in structure, and the conversions that result would be so classified by Lofland and Skonovd (1981). An

invitation at Southside is similar to an invitation at a Billy Graham crusade, with similar results (see Lang and Lang 1960, Altheide and Johnson 1977).

3. Frankl (1985) points to Charles G. Finney, the nineteenth-century revivalist, as the originator of the idea that ministers were to be measured by the number of souls saved. His work and his writing began the process of "rationalizing" revival techniques and quantifying their results.

4. Insisting on a strict definition of conversion is in line with other writing in sociology of religion. Lofland and Stark (1965), in fact, constructed their model of the conversion process around joining a deviant "cult," which by definition entails a radical life change. If, however, the group being joined is not so new or radical, the new member may be either a convert or a "joiner," who comes into the group in less dramatic ways.

5. The sense of shame being discussed here is an internalized fear, not the social rituals anthropologists usually mean when they identify shame (for example, Benedict 1946, Leighton and Kluckhohn 1947). Walking the aisle and praying the sinner's prayer can be seen as shaming rituals, but shame at Southside is much more than these external rites. Piers and Singer (1971) argue that shame and guilt can take both internal and external forms, with the differences lying in childhood experiences. Although the origins are unimportant for our purposes, it is important that guilt and shame be distinguished here on the basis of the content of the emotion rather than on the presence or absence of internalized sanctions.

6. This figure is similar to the 17 percent that Bibby and Brinkerhoff (1973, 1982) report as the proportion who join conservative churches by "birth/conversion." The percentage of "reaffiliates" (that is, people whose previous membership was in a similar church) at Southside is considerably lower than the 70 percent they report, and the percentage of "proselytes" (that is, people for whom Fundamentalism is new) is therefore higher than their 13 percent.

7. Travisano (1970) would describe this as "alternating" rather than "converting."

8. Data were gathered in the survey distributed on May 25, 1979, to the Sunday morning congregation. Questions were asked about the respondents' religious histories and their first contacts with Southside.

9. Social networks are among the most potent explanations for affiliation with all religious groups; see Stark and Bainbridge (1980) for a review of the evidence. Stark and Roberts (1982) demonstrate that recruitment through existing networks can have positive effects on church growth.

Chapter Ten

1. Fowler's (1981) ideas about "stages" of faith are helpful in analyzing what happens to Southside youth. During childhood, a "mythic-literal"

faith, emphasizing stories and rules, is quite typical. This kind of faith matches the child's ability to reason, both cognitively and morally. In adolescence, the focus changes from objective rules to the expectations of peers in a "synthetic-conventional" stage of faith. In both these stages, Southside's program nicely matches the needs and abilities of youth with programs and stories about the faith.

2. Some parents are also willing to sue to get their position heard. The Tennessee parents who sued their local school board in 1986 over reading texts described those texts as "anti-Christian." They were able to enlist expert testimony that the picture of believers presented in the books was analogous to the picture of blacks in pre-civil-rights history books: If religion was present at all, it was not shown in a favorable light. Although their arguments may stretch the limits of credibility on other points, the parents were able to demonstrate that believing the Bible (especially as they understand it) is not valued in the public school classroom.

3. This is according to Academy administrators' reports and should be evaluated in light of the Academy's exclusion of "problem" pupils whose scores may lower the averages public schools report.

4. These data come from the General Social Survey, with its less-than-ideal definition of *sectarian* (see note to Table 3.5). Although there is enormous variety among the groups counted in that category, they include mostly those who see themselves as different from society in one way or another. In that way, they provide an adequate comparison.

5. This observation emerged in personal communication with Barbara Hargrove. It is also supported by the data Hadaway (1978) presents. To recall Fowler's (1981) "stages," it is possible that young adults brought up in Fundamentalism leave behind their dependence on peers and on authorities in order to develop an "individuative-reflective" faith, for which there is no room in a Fundamental church.

Chapter Eleven

1. On the inadequacy of economic status as a predictor, see Shupe and Stacy (1983), Johnson and Tamney (1982), Yinger and Cutler (1984), and Johnson and Shibley (1985). On "status discontent" see Simpson (1983) and Wood and Hughes (1984). On the role of various "cultural" variables, see Harper and Leicht (1984), Lorentzen (1980), and Moore and Whitt (1985).

2. This definition of power grows out of Kanter's definition of power in organizations as the "ability to get things done" (1977:166). It also, however, takes a Marxian notion of alienation (cf. 1844) as its counterreferent. As in Fromm (1955) and May (1972), the emphasis here is on the ability to influence the content of one's social world, not just on the ability to impose one's will on another. However, the perceived ability to influence one's world ob-

viously rests on the "structure of domination" (Simmel 1950), and that is as much a matter of legitimacy as of force; see Weber (1968) and Clegg (1975). Participation in the "social construction of reality" is distributed quite unequally.

3. Their power to run the school is still circumscribed by the power of government to set standards however.

4. These concerns with family and church affairs are reflected in the issues that have given rise to the New Christian Right: opposition to the ERA and to abortion; see Brady and Tedin (1976) and Neitz (1981).

5. 1980 was not the first time conservative Protestants adopted conservative politics (or vice versa). During the early twentieth century, liberalism and social reform became identified together as "modernist." Fundamentalists took their identity from opposing everything modernists stood for (cf. Marsden 1980, Moberg 1972, Pierard 1970). The result has been a continuing affinity between religious and political conservatism that has occasionally been mobilized into political activity. Among the many who have written about previous manifestations of this right-wing alliance are Clabaugh (1974), Stellway (1973), Jorstad (1970), Lipset and Raab (1970), Orum (1970), Parenti (1967), Rohter (1967), Quinney (1964), Bell (1963), and Johnson (1962, 1964). Johnson's 1985 work (with Shibley) demonstrates that "a tradition of political conservatism has existed for many years among a segment of the evangelical laity" (p. 18).

6. Research by Kellstedt (1985) reveals that supporters of the Moral Majority are also likely to express anti-Catholic sentiments. He speculates that this anti-Catholicism may prevent alliances with Catholics on issues of joint concern. Early in the Moral Majority's history it appeared that cooperation with outsiders would be a major problem, a perhaps wishful point made by Marty (1982). Outsiders seemed no more willing to join than Fundamentalists were eager to have them (cf. Guth 1982, Zwier 1984, and Dionne 1980). Somewhat contrary evidence is reviewed by White (1986) in the case of a possible alliance with the Mormons. He concludes that the strength of the agreement on issues by Mormons and conservative Protestants (and evidence of some existing cooperative organizational structure) is sufficient to overcome their doctrinal disagreements. Likewise, the Moral Majority members and sympathizers among Guth's (1985) Southern Baptist clergy agreed by a substantial majority that "clergymen of different faiths need to cooperate more in politics, even if they can't agree in theology."

7. See, for example, Fitzgerald (1981), Latus (1983), Johnson and Tamney (1982), Pierard and Wright (1984), and Zwier (1984). Johnson and Shibley (1985) note that only in the South has there been a trend toward increased political conservativism among Evangelicals that exceeds the movement toward conservativism in the country at large. And, in the South, it was Jimmy Carter's candidacy that increased voter turnout, not that of the pro–Moral

Majority Ronald Reagan. However, Simpson (1985) argues that the politicization of moral issues by the New Christian Right contributed (even if not decisively) to Reagan's success.

8. Kellstedt's study (1985) confirms that pastoral activism is still relatively rare but that it does have an impact on lay political participation among Evangelicals. Likewise, Johnson and Tamney (1985) report that perceived church support for the Moral Majority contributed positively to individual support. If that is the case, and if Guth's data on Southern Baptist clergy (1985) are indicative, we may look for significantly increased levels of activism, at least among southern Fundamentalists. These pastors were more likely to approve of the Moral Majority in 1984 than they were in 1980, and they are even more active now than before, much more active than their more "moderate" counterparts in the Southern Baptist Convention.

9. Johnson (1960) claimed that the skills and values learned in certain holiness/Pentecostal congregations contributed to the upward mobility of their members. Schwartz (1970) noted a similar process among the Seventh Day Adventists he studied, but not among the Pentecostals. Anderson (1979) argues that Pentecostalism is inherently pessimistic and escapist and does not lend itself to upward mobility, while Fundamentalism offers more hope to believers. Whether a given group offers incentives and skills for mobility seems to depend more on the particular local constituency and what happens in the group (opportunities for leadership, emphasis on practical success) than on the group's belief that Christ will return again soon.

Bibliography

Adorno, T. W., E. Frenkel-Brunswick, D. J. Levinson, and R. N. Sanford
1950   *The Authoritarian Personality.* New York: Harper and Row.
Ahlstrom, S. E.
1975   *A Religious History of the American People.* 2 vols. Garden City, N.Y.: Doubleday, Image Books.
Allport, G. W.
1966   "The religious context of prejudice." *Journal for the Scientific Study of Religion* 5:447–457.
Allport, G. W., and J. M. Ross
1967   "Personal religious orientation and prejudice." *Journal of Personality and Social Psychology* 5:432–443.
Altheide, D., and J. Johnson
1977   "Counting souls." *Pacific Sociological Review* 20:323–348.
Ammerman, N. T.
1982a   "Dilemmas in establishing a research identity." *The New England Sociologist* 4:21–27.
1982b   "Operationalizing Evangelicalism: An amendment." *Sociological Analysis* 43:170–171.
Anderson, R. M.
1979   *Vision of the Disinherited.* New York: Oxford University Press.
Barker, E.
1978   "Living the Divine Principle." *Archives de Sciences Sociales de Religions* 45(1):75–93.
Barr, J.
1978   *Fundamentalism.* Philadelphia: Westminster.
Beckford, J.
1975   *The Trumpet of Prophecy.* Oxford: Basil Blackwell.
1978   "Accounting for conversion." *British Journal of Sociology* 29:249–262.
Bell, D., ed.
1963   *The Radical Right.* Garden City, N.Y.: Doubleday.
Bellah, R. N.
1967   "Civil religion in America." *Daedalus* 96:1–21.
1970   "Christianity and symbolic realism." *Journal for the Scientific Study of Religion* 9:89–96.

Bellah, R. N., R. Madsen, W. Sullivan, A. Swidler, and S. Tipton
1985   *Habits of the Heart.* Berkeley: University of California Press.
Benedict, R.
1946   *The Chrysanthemum and the Sword.* Boston: Houghton Mifflin.
Berger, B. M.
1981   *The Survival of a Counterculture.* Berkeley: University of California Press.
Berger, P. L.
1961   *The Noise of Solemn Assemblies.* Garden City, N.Y.: Doubleday.
1969   *The Sacred Canopy.* Garden City, N.Y.: Doubleday, Anchor Books.
1982   "Secular branches, religious roots." *Society* 20(1):64–66.
1983   "From the crisis of religion to the crisis of secularity." Pp. 14–24 in M. Douglas and S. Tipton (eds.), *Religion and America.* Boston: Beacon Press.
Berger, P. L., and T. Luckmann
1966   *The Social Construction of Reality.* Garden City, N.Y.: Doubleday, Anchor Books.
Bernard, J.
1972   *The Future of Marriage.* New York: Bantam.
Bibby, R. W., and M. B. Brinkerhoff
1973   "The circulation of the saints: A study of people who join conservative churches." *Journal for the Scientific Study of Religion* 12:273–283.
1982   "The circulation of the saints revisited." Paper presented to the Society for the Scientific Study of Religion, Providence.
Bird, F.
1979   "The pursuit of innocence: New religious movements and moral accountability." *Sociological Analysis* 40:335–346.
Blasi, A. J., and A. J. Weigert
1976   "Towards a sociology of religion: An interpretive sociology approach." *Sociological Analysis* 37:189–204.
Brady, D. W., and K. L. Tedin
1976   "Ladies in pink: Religion and political ideology in the anti-ERA movement." *Social Science Quarterly* 56(4):564–575.
Bryan, P. R.
1973   "An analysis of the ecclesiology of Associational Baptists, 1900–1950." Ph.D. diss., Baylor University.
Byrne, D., and C. R. Ervin
1969   "Attraction toward a Negro stranger as a function of prejudice, attitude similarity, and the stranger's evaluation of the subject." *Human Religions* 22(5):397–404.

Carpenter, J. A.
1980   "Fundamentalist institutions and the rise of Evangelical Protestantism, 1929–42." *Church History* 49:62–75.
Clabaugh, G. K.
1974   *Thunder on the Right.* Chicago: Nelson-Hall.
Clegg, S.
1975   *Power, Rule, and Domination.* London: Routledge and Kegan Paul.
Cole, S. G.
1931   *The History of Fundamentalism.* New York: Smith.
Coleman, J. A.
1978   "The situation for modern faith." *Theological Studies* 39:601–632.
Cox, H.
1984   *Religion and the Secular City.* New York: Simon and Schuster.
Davis, J. A.
1984   *General Social Survey, 1972–1984*: Cumulative Codebook. Ann Arbor, Mich.: National Opinion Research Center.
DeJong, G. F.
1965   "Religious Fundamentalism, socio-economic status, and fertility attitudes in the southern Appalachians." *Demography* 2:540–548.
DeJong, G. F., and T. R. Ford
1965   "Religious Fundamentalism and denominational preference in the southern Appalachian region." *Journal for the Scientific Study of Religion* 5:24–33.
Dionne, E. J.
1980   "Poll finds Evangelicals aren't united voting bloc." *New York Times*, September 7, 1980, p. 34.
Dollar, G. W.
1973   *A History of Fundamentalism in America.* Greenville, S.C.: Bob Jones University Press.
Douglas, M.
1983   "The effects of modernization on religious change." Pp. 25–43 in M. Douglas and S. Tipton (eds.), *Religion and America.* Boston: Beacon Press.
Dudley, C. S.
1979   *Where Have All Our People Gone?* New York: Pilgrim.
Dudley, R. L.
1978   "Alienation from religion in adolescents from Fundamentalist religious homes." *Journal for the Scientific Study of Religion* 17:389–398.

Durkheim, E.
1895   *The Rules of the Sociological Method.* Trans. S. A. Solovay and J. H. Mueler; ed. G. E. G. Catlin. New York: Free Press (1964).
1898   "Individualism and the intellectuals." Trans. S. and J. Lukes. Pp. 59–73 in W. S. F. Pickering (ed.), *Durkheim on Religion.* London: Routledge and Kegan Paul (1975).
1925   "Moral education." Trans. E. K. Wilson and H. Schnurer. Pp. 190–201 in W. S. F. Pickering (ed.), *Durkheim on Religion.* London: Routledge and Kegan Paul (1975).
Elwell, W. A.
1980   "Belief and the Bible: A crisis of authority?" *Christianity Today,* March 21, pp. 20–23.
Erikson, E. H.
1958   *Young Man Luther.* New York: Norton.
1963   *Childhood and Society.* New York: Norton.
1982   *The Life Cycle Completed.* New York: Norton.
Erikson, K. T.
1966   *Wayward Puritans.* New York: Wiley.
Ethridge, F. M., and J. R. Feagin
1979   "Varieties of 'Fundamentalism': A conceptual and empirical analysis of two Protestant denominations." *Sociological Quarterly* 20:37–48.
Falwell, J.
1980   *Listen America.* Garden City, N.Y.: Doubleday.
Falwell, J. (with E. Dobson and E. Hindson)
1981   *The Fundamentalist Phenomenon.* Garden City, N.Y.: Doubleday.
Feagin, J. R.
1965   "Prejudice and religious types." *Journal for the Scientific Study of Religion* 4:3–13.
Festinger, L., and J. M. Carlsmith
1959   "Cognitive consequences of forced compliance." *Journal of Abnormal and Social Psychology* 58:203–210.
Festinger, L., H. Riecken, and S. Schachter
1959   *When Prophecy Fails.* Minneapolis: University of Minnesota Press.
Fitzgerald, F.
1981   "A disciplined charging army." *New Yorker* 57(May 18):53–144.
Fowler, J. W.
1981   *Stages of Faith.* New York: Harper and Row.
Frankl, R.
1985   "The historical antecedent of the electric church." Paper presented to the Society for the Scientific Study of Religion, Savannah.

Freud, S.
1927   *The Future of an Illusion*. Trans. J. Strachey. New York: Norton (1961).
Fromm, E.
1955   *The Sane Society*. New York: Holt, Rinehart and Winston.
Fundamentals, The
1910–1915 Ed. A. C. Dixon. 12 vols. Chicago: Testimony Publishing.
Furniss, N. F.
1954   *The Fundamentalist Controversy, 1918–1931*. New Haven, Conn.: Yale University Press.
Gallup, G. H.
1981   *Public Opinion 1980*. Wilmington, Del.: Scholarly Resources.
1983   *Public Opinion 1982*. Wilmington, Del.: Scholarly Resources.
Garrison, C. E.
1976   "The effect of participation in congregational structures on church attendance." *Review of Religious Research* 18(1):36–43.
Geertz, C.
1966   "Religion as a cultural system." Pp. 1–46 in M. Banton (ed.), *Anthropologial Approaches to the Study of Religion*. New York: Praeger.
1973   *The Interpretation of Cultures*. New York: Basic Books.
Glaser, B. G., and A. L. Strauss
1967   *The Discovery of Grounded Theory: Strategies for Qualitative Research*. Hawthorne, New York: Aldine.
Glock, C. Y., and R. Stark
1965   *Religion and Society in Tension*. Chicago: Rand McNally.
1966   *Christian Beliefs and Anti-Semitism*. New York: Harper and Row.
Gove, W. R.
1978   "Sex differences in mental illness among adult men and women: An evaluation of four questions raised regarding the evidence on the higher rates of women." *Social Science and Medicine* 12B: 187–198.
Gove, W. R., and J. F. Tudor
1973   "Adult sex roles and mental illness." *American Journal of Sociology* 78:812–835.
Graves, J. R., and G. H. Orchard
1855   *A Concise History of Foreign Baptists*. Nashville: Graves, Marks, and Rutland.
Guth, J. L.
1982   "The education of the Christian right: The case of the Southern Baptist clergy." Paper presented to the Society for the Scientific Study of Religion, Providence.

1985   "Political activism among a religious elite: Southern Baptist min-
        isters in the 1984 election." Paper presented to the Society for
        the Scientific Study of Religion, Savannah.
Hadaway, C. K.
1978   "Denomination switching and membership growth." *Sociological
        Analysis* 39:321–337.
Hadden, J. K.
1985   "Religious broadcasting and the mobilization of the New Chris-
        tian Right." Presidential address to the Society for the Scientific
        Study of Religion, Savannah.
Harper, C. L., and K. Leicht
1984   "Explaining the new religious right: Status politics and beyond."
        Pp. 101–112 in D. Bromley and A. Shupe (eds.), *New Christian
        Politics*. Macon, Ga.: Mercer University Press.
Harrison, P. M.
1959   *Authority and Power in the Free Church Tradition*. Princeton, N.J.:
        Princeton University Press.
Herberg, W.
1960   *Protestant Catholic Jew*. New York: Doubleday, Anchor Books.
Hofstadter, R.
1964   *Anti-intellectualism in American Life*. New York: Knopf.
Hoge, D. R.
1976   *Division in the Protestant House*. Philadelphia: Westminster.
Hoge, D. R., and J. W. Carroll
1973   "Religiosity and prejudice in northern and southern churches."
        Journal for the Scientific Study of Religion 12:181–197.
1978   "Determinants of commitment and participation in suburban
        Protestant churches." *Journal for the Scientific Study of Religion*
        17:107–127.
Hoover, J. E.
1957   *Masters of Deceit*. New York: Holt.
Horowitz, I. L.
1982   "The new Fundamentalism." *Society* 20(1):40–47.
Hunter, J. D.
1981   "Operationalizing Evangelicalism: A review, critique and pro-
        posal." *Sociological Analysis* 42:363–372.
1982   "Subjectivization and the new Evangelical theodicy." *Journal for
        the Scientific Study of Religion* 20:39–47.
1983   *American Evangelicalism: Conservative Religion and the Quandary
        of Modernity*. New Brunswick, N.J.: Rutgers University Press.
James, W.
1935   *Varieties of Religious Experience*. New York: Longmans, Green.

Johnson, B.
1960   "Do holiness sects socialize in dominant values?" *Social Forces* 39:309–317.
1962   "Ascetic Protestantism and political preference." *Public Opinion Quarterly* 26:35–46.
1964   "Ascetic Protestantism and political preference in the deep South." *American Journal of Sociology* 69:359–366.
1971   "Max Weber and American Protestantism." *The Sociological Quarterly* 12:473–485.
Johnson, B., and M. Shibley
1985   "How new is the New Christian Right? A study of three presidential elections." Paper presented to the Society for the Scientific Study of Religion, Savannah.
Johnson, S. D., and J. B. Tamney
1982   "The Christian right and the 1980 presidential election." *Journal for the Scientific Study of Religion* 21:123–131.
1985   "Mobilizing support for the Moral Majority." *Psychological Reports* 56:987–994.
Jorstad, E.
1970   *The Politics of Doomsday*. Nashville: Abingdon.
Kanter, R. M.
1972   *Commitment and Community*. Cambridge, Mass.: Harvard University Press.
1977   *Men and Women of the Corporation*. New York: Basic Books.
Kellstedt, L.
1985   "The Falwell platform: An analysis of its causes and consequences." Paper presented to the Society for the Scientific Study of Religion, Savannah.
Kluegel, J. R.
1980   "Denominational mobility: Current patterns and recent trends." *Journal for the Scientific Study of Religion* 19:26–39.
Lang, K., and G. Lang
1960   "Decisions for Christ." Pp. 415–427 in M. R. Stein, A. Vidich, and D. White (eds.), *Identity and Anxiety*. Glencoe, Ill.: Free Press.
Latus, M. A.
1984   "Mobilizing Christians for political action: Campaigning with God on your side." Pp. 251–268 in D. Bromley and A. Shupe (eds.), *New Christian Politics*. Macon, Ga.: Mercer University Press.
Lechner, F.
1985   "Fundamentalism and sociocultural revitalization in America: A sciological interpretation." *Sociological Analysis* 46:243–260.

Leighton, D., and C. Kluckhohn
1947   *Children of the People.* Cambridge, Mass.: Harvard University Press.
Lenski, G.
1953   "Social correlates of religious interest." *American Sociological Review* 18:533–544.
Liebman, R. C.
1983   "Mobilizing the Moral Majority." Pp. 50–72 in R. C. Liebman and R. Wuthnow (eds.), *The New Christian Right.* Hawthorne, New York: Aldine.
Lienesch, M.
1982   "Right-wing religion: Political conservatism as a political movement." *Political Science Quarterly* 97:403–425.
Lindsey, H. (with C. C. Carlson)
1970   *The Late Great Planet Earth.* Grand Rapids, Mich.: Zondervan.
Lipset, S. M., and E. Raab
1970   *The Politics of Unreason.* New York: Harper and Row.
1981   "The election and the Evangelicals." *Commentary* 71(3):25–31.
Lofland, J., and N. Skonovd
1981   "Conversion motifs." *Journal for the Scientific Study of Religion* 20:373–385.
Lofland, J., and R. Stark
1965   "Becoming a world-saver: A theory of conversion to a deviant perspective." *American Sociological Review* 30:862–875.
Lorentzen, L. J.
1980   "Evangelical life-style concerns expressed in political action." *Sociological Analysis* 41:144–154.
Loye, D.
1977   *The Leadership Passion.* San Francisco: Jossey-Bass.
Luckmann, T.
1967   *The Invisible Religion.* New York: Macmillan.
McGuire, M. B.
1977   "Testimony as a commitment mechanism in Catholic Pentecostal prayer groups." *Journal for the Scientific Study of Religion* 16:165–168.
McNamara, P. H.
1985   "The New Christian Right's views of the family and its social science critics: A study in differing presuppositions." *Journal of Marriage and the Family* 47:449–458.
Maranell, G. M.
1974   *Responses to Religion.* Lawrence: University Press of Kansas.
Marsden, G. M.
1971   "Defining Fundamentalism." *Christian Scholar's Review* 1:141–151.

1980   *Fundamentalism and American Culture*. New York: Oxford University Press.
1983   "Preachers of paradox: The religious new right in historical perspective." Pp. 150–168 in M. Douglas and S. Tipton (eds.), *Religion and America*. Boston: Beacon Press.

Martin, D.
1962   "The denomination." *British Journal of Sociology* 13:1–14.
1969   *The Religious and the Secular*. New York: Schocken.

Marty, M. E.
1969   *The Modern Schism*. New York: Harper and Row.
1976   *A Nation of Behavers*. Chicago: University of Chicago Press.
1982   "Fundamentalism as a social phenomenon." *Review and Expositor* 79(1):19–29.

Marx, G. T.
1967   "Religion, opiate or inspiration of civil rights militancy among Negroes?" *American Sociological Review* 32:64–72.

Marx, K.
1844   "Contribution to the critique of Hegel's philosophy of right." Pp. 43–59 in T. B. Bottomore (ed. and trans.), *Karl Marx: Early Writings*. New York: McGraw-Hill (1964).

May, R.
1972   *Power and Innocence*. New York: Norton.

Mead, G. H.
1934   *Mind, Self and Society*. Chicago: University of Chicago Press.

Milgram, S.
1974   *Obedience to Authority*. New York: Harper.

Moberg, D. O.
1962   *The Church as a Social Institution*. Englewood Cliffs, N.J.: Prentice-Hall.
1972   *The Great Reversal*. Philadelphia: Lippincott.

Monaghan, R. R.
1967   "Three faces of the true believer." *Journal for the Scientific Study of Religion* 6:236–245.

Moore, H. A., and H. P. Whitt
1985   "The new religious right: A test of the value dislocation hypothesis." Paper presented to the Association for the Sociology of Religion, Washington, D.C.

Nash, D.
1968   "A little child shall lead them." *Journal for the Scientific Study of Religion* 7:238–240.

Neitz, M. J.
1981   "Family, state and God: Ideologies of the Right to Life movement." *Sociological Analysis* 42:265–276.

236 / Bibliography

Niebuhr, H. R.
1929   *The Social Sources of Denominationalism.* New York: Harper.
Niebuhr, H. R. (with D. D. Williams and J. M. Gustafson)
1956   *The Purpose of the Church and Its Ministry.* New York: Harper.
Nordin, V. D., and W. L. Turner
1980   "More than segregationist academies: The growing Protestant Fundamentalist schools." *Phi Delta Kappan,* February, pp. 391–394.
O'Dea, T. F.
1957   *The Mormons.* Chicago: University of Chicago Press.
Orum, A. M.
1970   "Religion and the rise of the radical white: The case of southern Wallace support in 1968." *Social Science Quarterly* 51:674–688.
Parenti, M.
1967   "Political values and religious cultures: Jews, Catholics, and Protestants." *Journal for the Scientific Study of Religion* 6:259–269.
Parsons, T.
1963   "Christianity and modern industrial society." Pp. 13–70 in E. Tiryakian (ed.), *Sociological Theory, Values, and Sociocultural Change.* New York: Free Press.
Peek, C. W., H. P. Chalfant, and E. V. Milton
1979   "Sinners in the hands of an angry God: Fundamentalist fears about drunken driving." *Journal for the Scientific Study of Religion* 18:29–39.
Pentecost, J. D.
1958   *Things to Come.* Grand Rapids, Mich.: Dunham.
Perin, C.
1977   *Everything in Its Place.* Princeton, N.J.: Princeton University Press.
Pierard, R. V.
1970   *The Unequal Yoke.* Philadelphia: Lippincott.
Pierard, R. V., and J. L. Wright
1984   "No Hoosier hospitality for humanism: The Moral Majority in Indiana." Pp. 195–212 in D. Bromley and A. Shupe (eds.), *New Christian Politics.* Macon, Ga.: Mercer University Press.
Piers, G., and M. B. Singer
1971   *Shame and Guilt.* New York: Norton.
Primer, B.
1979   *Protestants and American Business Methods.* Ann Arbor, Mich.: UMI Press.
1980   "The failure of southern Fundamentalism." Paper presented to the Southwestern Historical Association, Houston.

Quebedeaux, R.
1974   *The Young Evangelicals.* New York: Harper and Row.
Quinney, R.
1964   "Political conservatism, alienation and fatalism." *Sociometry* 27: 372–381.
Richardson, J. T.
1975   "New forms of deviancy in a Fundamentalist church." *Review of Religious Research* 16:134–141.
Richardson, J. T., M. W. Stewart, and R. B. Simmonds
1978   "Conversion to Fundamentalism." *Society* 15(4):46–52.
1979   *Organized Miracles: A Study of a Contemporary, Youth, Communal, Fundamentalist Organization.* New Brunswick, N.J.: Transaction Books.
Robbins, T., D. Anthony, and T. E. Curtis
1973   "The limits of symbolic realism: Problems of empathetic field observation in a sectarian context." *Journal for the Scientific Study of Religion* 12:259–272.
Rohter, I. S.
1967   "The righteous rightists." *Transaction* 4(6):27–35.
Rokeach, M.
1960   *The Open and Closed Mind.* New York: Basic Books.
1970   "Faith, hope and bigotry." *Psychology Today* 3(11):33–37.
Rokeach, M., and L. Mezei
1966   "Race and shared belief as factors in social choice." *Science* 151:167–172.
Roof, W. C.
1974   "Religious orthodoxy and minority prejudice: Causal relationship or reflection of localistic world view?" *American Journal of Sociology* 80:643–664.
1978   *Community and Commitment.* New York: Pilgrim.
Roof, W. C., and C. K. Hadaway
1977   "Shifts in religious preference in the mid-seventies." *Journal for the Scientific Study of Religion* 16:409–412.
Rose, S.
1985   "Women warriors: Power and prayer in family relations." Paper presented to the Association for the Sociology of Religion, Washington, D.C.
Sandeen, E. R.
1970   *The Roots of Fundamentalism.* Chicago: University of Chicago Press.
Schwartz, G.
1970   *Sect Ideologies and Social Status.* Chicago: University of Chicago Press.

Sennett, R.
1980   *Authority*. New York: Knopf.
Shupe, A., and W. Stacey
1983   "The Moral Majority constituency." Pp. 104–117 in R. Liebman and R. Wuthnow (eds.), *The New Christian Right*. Hawthorne, New York: Aldine.
Simmel, G.
1950   *The Sociology of Georg Simmel*. Ed. K. Wolfe. Glencoe, Ill.: Free Press.
Simpson, J.
1983   "Moral issues and status politics." Pp. 188–207 in R. Liebman and R. Wuthnow (eds.), *The New Christian Right*. Hawthorne, New York: Aldine.
1985   "Socio-moral issues and recent presidential elections." *Review of Religious Research* 27:115–123.
Skerry, P.
1982   "The Fundamentalists." *Commentary* 73(5):98–104.
Smidt, C.
1983   "Evangelicals v. Fundamentalists: An analysis of the political characteristics and importance of two major religious movements within American politics." Paper presented to the Midwest Political Science Association, Chicago.
Smith, T. L.
1957   *Revivalism and Social Reform*. New York: Abingdon.
Stark, R., and W. Bainbridge
1980   "Networks of faith: Interpersonal bonds and recruitment to cults and sects." *American Journal of Sociology* 85:1376–1395.
1985   *The Future of Religion*. Berkeley: University of California Press.
Stark, R., and C. Y. Glock
1968   *American Piety*. Berkeley: University of California Press.
Stark, R., and L. Roberts
1982   "The arithmetic of social movements: Theoretical implications." *Sociological Analysis* 43:53–68.
Stellway, R. J.
1973   "The correspondence between religious orientation and socio-political liberalism and conservatism." *Sociological Quarterly* 14: 430–439.
Strickland, B. R., and S. C. Weddell
1972   "Religious orientation, racial prejudice and dogmatism: A study of Baptists and Unitarians." *Journal for the Scientific Study of Religion* 11:395–399.
Sutherland, E. H., and D. R. Cressey
1978   *Criminology*. 10th ed. Philadelphia: Lippincott.

Swidler, A.
1986   "Culture in action: Symbols and strategies." *American Sociological Review* 51:273–286.

Takayama, K. P.
1975   "Formal polity and change of structure: Denominational assemblies." *Sociological Analysis* 36:17–28.

Tipton, S. M.
1982   *Getting Saved from the Sixties.* Berkeley: University of California Press.

Travisano, R. V.
1970   "Alternation and conversion as qualitatively different transformations." Pp. 237–248 in G. P. Stone and H. A. Farberman (eds.), *Social Psychology Through Symbolic Interaction.* New York: Wiley.

Troeltsch, E.
1931   *The Social Teachings of the Christian Churches.* Trans. O. Wyon. New York: Macmillan.

Truzzi, M., ed.
1974   *Verstehen: Subjective Understanding in the Social Sciences.* Reading, Mass.: Addison-Wesley.

U.S. Department of Commerce, Bureau of the Census
1982a   *1980 Census of Population and Housing, Advance Estimates of Social, Economic, and Housing Characteristics.* Washington, D.C.: U.S. Government Printing Office.

1982b   *1980 Census of Population and Housing, Summary Characteristics for Governmental Units and Standard Metropolitan Statistical Areas.* Washington, D.C.: U.S. Government Printing Office.

Warner, R. S.
1979   "Theoretical barriers to the understanding of Evangelical Christianity." *Sociological Analysis* 40:1–9.

Weber, M.
1905   *The Protestant Ethic and the Spirit of Capitalism.* Trans. T. Parsons. New York: Scribners (1958).

1922   *The Sociology of Religion.* Trans. E. Fischoff. Boston: Beacon Press (1964).

1968   *Economy and Society.* Trans. E. Fischoff, H. Gerth, A. M. Henderson, F. Kolegar, C. W. Mills, T. Parsons, M. Rheinstein, G. Roth, E. Shils, and C. Wittich; eds. G. Roth and C. Wittich, New York: Bedminster.

Weissman, M. M., and J. K. Myers
1978   "Rates and risks of depressive symptoms in a United States urban community." *Acta Psychiatrica Scandinavica* 57:219–231.

White, O. K., Jr.
1986   "Is there a Morman new right coalition? Another assessment." *Review of Religious Research* 28(2).
Wilcox, C.
1986   "Evangelicals and Fundamentalists in the New Christian Right: Religious differences in the Ohio Moral Majority." *Journal for the Scientific Study of Religion* 25:355–363.
Wood, M., and M. Hughes
1984   "The moral basis of moral reform: Status discontent vs. culture and socialization as explanations of anti-pornography social movement adherence." *American Sociological Review* 49:86–99.
Woodward, K. L., J. Barnes, and L. Lisle
1976   "Born again! The year of the Evangelical." *Newsweek* 88(17): 68–78.
Wuthnow, R.
1983   "The political rebirth of American Evangelicalism." Pp. 167–185 in R. Liebman and R. Wuthnow (eds.), *The New Christian Right*. Hawthorne, New York: Aldine.
Yinger, J. M., and S. J. Cutler
1984   "The Moral Majority viewed sociologically." Pp. 69–90 in D. Bromley and A. Shupe (eds.), *New Christian Politics*. Macon, Ga.: Mercer University Press.
Zwier, R.
1984   "The New Christian Right and the 1980 elections." Pp. 173–194 in D. Bromley and A. Shupe (eds.), *New Christian Politics*. Macon, Ga.: Mercer University Press.

Index